D0058635

ADVANCE PRAISE FOR
THE ARCHIPELAGO OF HOPE

"When Indigenous Peoples meet one another for the first time it's as if we've always known each other. Gleb's powerful and knowledgeable book captures that essence and the intimate ties we have to our Mother Earth. This book is like reading my own ancestry. We say that 'all things are connected' and these stories show us how related we all are."

—Patricia Cochrane, Inupiat Eskimo,
Executive Director Alaska Native Science Commission

"Indigenous people around the world are the only ones with a track record of living in relative balance with their surroundings for thousands of years. There was never a more important time in human history for their perspective and wisdom. *The Archipelago of Hope* is extremely timely and informative as we confront the reality that the growth imperative of the technologically-driven global economy must be abandoned as we embrace the health of Mother Nature as the source of our survival and health."

—David Suzuki, winner of the UNESCO Kalinga Prize for Science
and the United Nations Environmental Medal

"There could be no more accurate or prescient way to see our climatic future than through the eyes of Indigenous people, whose survival depends on the intimacy with which they interact with living systems. In *Archipelago*, longtime inhabitants of earth give us their eyes and ears, and we, who can be dumb-founded by an overwhelming onslaught of information, find a precious wisdom that is bestowed to those who patiently abide in the life of the world."

—Paul Hawken, *New York Times*
bestselling author of *Blessed Unrest*

"Exciting and hugely important. Raygorodetsky listens to the voices of those who are so often unheard and overlooked: the world's indigenous peoples. These people are also in possession of deep knowledge that will be needed for us to heal ourselves and the planet. *Archipelago of Hope* will be an important resource in the tumultuous years ahead."

—Scott Wallace, *New York Times* bestselling author of
The Unconquered: In Search of the Amazon's Last Uncontacted Tribes,
National Geographic contributor

"*Archipelago of Hope* is at once a clarion call for action and an inspirational compendium of steps that indigenous peoples around the world are taking to address the world's changing climate. We have much to learn from the peoples whom Gleb Raygorodetsky has met and his elegant, evocative writing will immerse the reader in the places and experiences of those peoples."
—Eleanor Sterling, American Museum of Natural History

"*The Archipelago of Hope* shares important stories and sophisticated biocultural strategies. I highly recommend this inspiring book, with warm, loving photographs and many other resources, to lead us to a better appreciation of the rich biocultural diversity of our shared world, and a more inclusive and humble approach to stewarding it through these times and into the future."
—Dr. Rajindra K. Puri, University of Kent

"This finite blue-green planet creaks under growing pressure. Solutions must come from within: we will all need to find ways of living with a light touch on the planet, and yet at the same time, bring well-being and contentment. This fine book develops a much-needed narrative of hope. We should listen and learn."
—Dr. Jules Pretty, OBE, University of Essex

"Although scattered throughout the world in oceans of change and conventional development, indigenous cultures are indeed islands of hope—for their historical roots, for their intimate connection with the land, for their wisdom, and for their resilience. It is precisely this resilience which should be cause for reflection, learning, empathy, and solidarity."
—Gonzalo Oveido, Senior Advisor,
International Union for the Conservation of Nature

"Few writers, anywhere in the world, know and understand the complex relationship indigenous people have with climate as well and deeply as Gleb Raygorodetsky. I am so gratified, and they should be as well, that he has finally put his knowledge and wisdom in one concise and ever-so-readable document."
—Mark Dowie, Massachusetts Institute of Technology,
author of *Conservation Refugees*

"There is no better time then now for the world to learn from this important work by Gleb Raygorodetsky as he respectfully allows the Indigenous voices, those most impacted by climate change, to shine through in his writing."
—Sheila Watt Cloutier, Nobel Peace Prize nominee,
author of *The Right to Be Cold*

THE
ARCHIPELAGO
of HOPE

WISDOM AND RESILIENCE
FROM THE EDGE OF CLIMATE CHANGE

GLEB RAYGORODETSKY

PEGASUS BOOKS
NEW YORK LONDON

THE ARCHIPELAGO OF HOPE

Pegasus Books Ltd.
148 W 37th Street, 13th Floor
New York, NY 10018

Copyright © 2017 by Gleb Raygorodetsky

All images © Gleb Raygorodetsky

First Pegasus Books edition November 2017

Interior design by Maria Fernandez

All rights reserved. No part of this book may be reproduced in whole or in part without written permission from the publisher, except by reviewers who may quote brief excerpts in connection with a review in a newspaper, magazine, or electronic publication; nor may any part of this book be reproduced, stored in a retrieval system, or transmitted in any form or by any means electronic, mechanical, photocopying, recording, or other, without written permission from the publisher.

Library of Congress Cataloging-in-Publication Data is available.

ISBN: 978-1-68177-532-6

10 9 8 7 6 5 4 3 2 1

Printed in the United States of America
Distributed by W. W. Norton & Company, Inc.
www.pegasusbooks.us

To Kobeta and Rai—for giving me a chance;

To Onca—for making me a better human;

To Aidan—for teaching me the right perspective;

To the Indigenous custodians of biocultural heritage—for inspiring hope; and

To the readers—for being willing to listen.

CONTENTS

FOREWORD

———

I ndigenous peoples' traditional knowledge is increasingly gaining recognition, most significantly in national, regional, and global processes
that are seeking solutions to the ecological crises of climate change and
biodiversity erosion. Indigenous or traditional knowledge is the wisdom
and know-how accumulated from the past to the present, which guide
a wide array of human societies in their interaction with their environment. Until recently, the domination of Western modern science meant
that traditional knowledge was labeled as primitive, superstition, and
unscientific, and many traditional knowledge holders were despised and
oppressed.

Fortunately, many Indigenous peoples who live and work with the
environment around them persisted in using and developing their
knowledge on and relationships with the ecosystem and the resources
found therein. Their worldviews, values, cultures, and spirituality are

intricately linked with the ways they relate to the environment, and with their past, present, and future, the living and the nonliving, and the seen and the unseen. The Indigenous peoples' rituals ensure that they respectfully engage with all of these elements. In this context, it is not difficult to understand what Indigenous and traditional knowledge mean and why they value the past in order to sustain and enhance well-being. This centuries-old body of knowledge seeks to guarantee a good life for future generations.

The Convention on Biological Diversity's Article 8(j) urges governments to respect, preserve, and maintain knowledge, innovations, and practices of Indigenous peoples and local communities. A working group on Article 8(j) and related provisions has been established as a mechanism to guide its implementation. Indigenous peoples are actively engaged with this body, and this is where they share their views on how traditional knowledge can be used and how their rights to their traditional knowledge can be protected.

Indigenous peoples live in all regions of the world, inhabiting 22 percent of the world's global land area where 80 percent of the world's biological diversity is found. These significant numbers show that Indigenous peoples are crucial players in preventing biodiversity erosion. Even with this evidence, however, there is still a long way to go before governments and the dominant society will effectively implement their obligations under the Convention on Biological Diversity.

The United Nations Framework Convention on Climate Change (UNFCCC) has been a latecomer in recognizing the contributions of traditional knowledge and how it can provide solutions to climate change. In its twenty-first Conference of Parties (COP), held in 2016, the decision was made to strengthen knowledge, technologies, practices, and efforts of local communities and Indigenous peoples related to addressing and responding to climate change. It called for the establishment of a platform for the exchange of experiences and sharing of best practices on climate change mitigation and adaptation in a holistic and integrated manner among the greater global community.

These global decisions were the results of conscious and systematic advocacy by Indigenous peoples and their supporters in order to get sovereign states to recognize, respect, and protect their rights. The end result of this long-term work was enshrined in the United Nations Declaration on the Rights of Indigenous Peoples (UNDRIP) and in the implementation of these conventions. Part of the rights contained in this UNDRIP is their right to maintain, control, protect, and develop their cultural heritage, traditional knowledge, and traditional cultural expressions, and their right to protect and develop their intellectual property over these (Article 31).

In performing my mandate as the UN special rapporteur on the rights of Indigenous peoples, I am always in constant search of documents and books that provide evidence not only of how Indigenous peoples' rights are violated but, more important, those which tell what Indigenous peoples are doing to survive and solve the problems they face. Before I was appointed to this mandate, my colleagues and I at the institution Tebtebba (Indigenous Peoples' International Centre for Policy Research and Education), had engaged with the negotiations in the Convention on Biological Diversity and the UNFCCC. Our aim continues to be to ensure that the respect and protection of the rights of Indigenous peoples will be considered in the decisions and programs made by these conventions. I was directly involved in the drafting and negotiations of the UN Declaration on the Rights of Indigenous Peoples since 1985 until its adoption in 2007. Article 31, which pertained to traditional knowledge and traditional cultural expressions, was of utmost importance.

Gleb Raygorodetsky's *The Archipelago of Hope* supports the arguments I have been using to convince the United Nations and the countries within it that it is in their self-interest to respect and protect traditional knowledge of Indigenous peoples as this will contribute to solving problems of climate change, biodiversity erosion, and the gross mismanagement of the gift that the earth provides to everybody. *The Archipelago of Hope* provides real-life stories of how Indigenous peoples develop and use their traditional knowledge and operationalize the values of reciprocity, solidarity, and collectivity as a way to live life. *Archipelago* shows the realities Indigenous peoples face as they further develop and use their knowledge to increase their communities' resilience to climate change and enhance the biocultural diversity in the land around them. Amid the jargon and abstraction emanating from academic circles and in the negotiations and decision-making processes within the Convention of Biological Diversity and the UN Framework on Climate Change, Raygorodetsky's book provides a very refreshing and authentic insight into the contributions Indigenous peoples provide and the challenges they face as they assert their right to maintain, control, and develop their traditional knowledge—and live their way of life.

I worked with Gleb when he was a program officer of the Christensen Fund, which supports efforts to enhance biocultural diversity. We collaborated on organizing the Indigenous Peoples' Global Summit on Climate Change in Anchorage, Alaska, in 2009. I was impressed with his extensive knowledge on biocultural diversity and his enthusiastic support for Indigenous peoples who are on the front lines of biodiversity conservation and sustainable use. I heard some of the same stories documented on the pages of this book. When he told me that he was writing this book I was thrilled by the news. I believe that *The Archipelago of Hope* makes an important contribution toward convincing the skeptics—of which there are still many in government, research, and activist communities—that Indigenous peoples provide solutions to many of the world's environmental and social problems.

It is with great pleasure that I welcome the publication of this book, and I thank Gleb for his devotion and enthusiasm in writing it and sharing these stories and wisdom with the world. For those who have not yet learned of, or come to understand, Indigenous knowledge and its contributions to our earth, I urge you to read this book. For those who are familiar with the issue and are already supporters, please use this book as a model to share your own experiences and stories on traditional knowledge.

Victoria Tauli-Corpuz
UN Special Rapporteur on the Rights of Indigenous Peoples
Executive Director, Tebtebba
Baguio City, Philippines

THOUSANDS OF STORIES

—∞—

"We, the Maasai," says Mr. Olood Saitaga, a respected community elder, "are completely dependent on our cattle. When the cattle die, we die too." Even Mr. Saitaga's skin, the color of dark-roast coffee, seems to offer little protection from the scorching heat of the Kenyan sun. He tucks the traditional crimson-blue shúkà robe between his legs and, folding his lanky, angular frame, squats in the mottled shade of a small acacia tree. From the welcome coolness, he looks out toward the distant mountains—a shimmering blue band suspended between the vast expanse of hazy sky and scorched savannah streaked with the rippling plumes of acacia trees. Mr. Saitaga delicately positions his wide-brimmed leather hat on his right knee. With the palm of his *large sinewy hand, he brushes his close-cropped hair, the color of the large, silver hoops stretching his earlobes.*

"We used to know when it would rain," he says softly. "Now it is hard to predict whether it will rain or not. We haven't had long or short rains for years and are suffering in the extreme."

Mr. Saitaga's metal bracelets clink as, clearing his throat, he wipes his parched lips with the back of his hand. "Animals, women, children, and men—all have suffered greatly. Most of our animals have died," he says, gesturing toward the mummified carcass of a cow a few yards away, its teeth protruding through sun-withered lips in a ghostly snarl. The flies buzz incessantly over the cow's carcass, as the unyielding sun continues to roast the savannah, vaporizing Mr. Saitaga's quiet lament.

Less than two generations ago, local stories about the impacts of—and responses to—climate change would have been unheard of anywhere in the world. Today, there are thousands stories that are similar to the one Mr. Saitaga shared on video with the Conversations with the Earth project co-founded and facilitated by the participatory video nonprofit InsightShare. Super Typhoon Haima in the Philippines, Hurricane Matthew in Florida, record flooding in the Canadian Rockies and California, Australia's mega fires, Peru's deadly deluge—not a month passes without mainstream and social media buzzing with the news of yet another record-breaking weather-related calamity. While arguments about global warming rage on among politicians and lobbyists, there is no denying that the overall trajectory is toward extreme weather events becoming more frequent and intense—which is exactly what climate science foresees to be the future of our planet—as the concentration of carbon dioxide in the atmosphere and temperatures continue to rise. Climate change, in other words, is no longer something that is likely to happen in a distant future—it is already here.

Nobody knows this better than Indigenous communities who, having developed an intimate relationship with landscapes and ecosystems over generations, have been observing climate change for decades and increasingly bearing the disproportionate burden of its impacts. Skolt Sámi reindeer herder and salmon fisherman Mr. Jouko Moshnikoff knows firsthand that winters are becoming warmer in his part of the world, and the outbreaks of parasitic autumn moth are becoming more frequent and widespread. The moths are threatening to wipe out birch forests—an important source of spring food for his people's reindeer. For the Indigenous communities like Moshnikoff's, climate change is not a theory, a political spin, or a fund-raising strategy—it is an inescapable reality of daily life.

These communities—islands of biological and cultural diversity in the ever-rising deluge of development and urbanization—are humankind's "Archipelago of Hope," for here lies our best chance to remember—or learn—how to care for Earth in a way that keeps it healthy for our descendants.

Within these pages, we will encounter diverse Indigenous peoples around the globe reaching deep into the well of their traditions and innovating to come up with creative responses to the many challenges of climate change. Though culturally and ecologically fitting to their specific circumstances, their approaches are ultimately relevant to all of us.

The Archipelago of Hope is based on over two decades of my work with Indigenous peoples around the world. Drawing on this deep experience, I have sought to explore how climate change fits within the multitude of other challenges—whether ecological or economic—affecting Indigenous communities, and what it takes for them to find ways to deal with the added pressures. We visit local peoples on different continents where climate change is a fact of life—the Skolt Sámi in Finland, the Nenets and the Altai in Russia, the Sápara in Ecuador, the Karen in Thailand, and the Tla-o-qui-aht Nuu-chah-nulth in Canada. Intimate portraits of local men and women, youth and elders, spiritual leaders, and craftsmen emerge against the backdrop of their traditional livelihoods, helping readers understand what it is like to live on the front lines of climate change. What these people recount is sometimes brutal—corruption that disempowers, pollution that sickens, education that rips children away from their families, and even development that kills—but this is balanced with the positive, the adaptive, the compelling, and often the spiritual.

While I draw on the most up-to-date climate science, my aim is not to write a treatise of facts and predictions but to help those of us living a step or two removed from the natural world engage with these rich cultures, and to understand our collective biocultural heritage that is intertwined with traditional practices. We might learn how to carve a halibut hook, listen to spirits, plant a medicinal garden, or catch a reindeer.

An important disclaimer—though there is no single definition of "Indigenous," there are a number of common characteristics that the United Nations uses to describe Indigenous peoples. They must:

- possess a distinct, often a minority, population relative to the dominant postcolonial culture of their country;

- have a distinct language, culture, and traditions influenced by living relationships with the ancestral homeland; and

- demonstrate a resolve to maintain and reproduce their ancestral environments and systems as distinctive peoples and communities.

To my knowledge, none of these apply to my own ancestors. The Archipelago therefore is in no way my attempt to speak *on behalf of* the Indigenous peoples. Rather, I hope it is a way to respectfully share with readers what I have learned over the years of being an ally to the Indigenous peoples working on climate change, conservation, land-use management, and many other critical issues of our time.

We have the knowledge that can contribute to finding solutions to the crisis of climate change. But if you are not prepared to listen, how can we communicate this to you?

—Marcos Terena (Xané leader,
Inter-Tribal Committee of Brazil)

CHAPTER ONE

INTO THE WIND

UNEASY STROLL

We were following a gravel footpath on Addison's Walk. The setting was idyllic, the previous days' labor had been fruitful, but something was bothering me and I could not quite put my finger on it. The path wound its way around a triangular water meadow by the River Cherwell at the southeastern end of Oxford University, less than a mile upstream from where it meets the River Thames. Ahead of us, I could see the Great Tower of Magdalen College through the opening in the crowns of the beech trees that flanked the walk. The fallow deer—a regular feature of the meadow during the winter months—were not around, having been moved off the pasture to allow for the spring bloom of snake's-head, a delicate dapple-purple flower that in the old days would blanket ancient meadows throughout England every spring. With the meadows all but gone, the water meadow on the grounds of Magdalen College is one of the flower's few remaining refugia. The blooming snake's-head turned the meadow into a vibrant tapestry of thick jade and amethyst threads. Some of this rich color seemed to rub off on the gray underbelly of the British sky, turning it mauve in fading daylight.

As we walked, our local guide expounded on the great Ionians of the past—C. S. Lewis and J. R. R. Tolkien had kicked up the gravel along this same path, conjuring up the realms of Narnia and Middle-earth in their minds. The names of other Oxford alumni and scholars rolled off the guide's tongue in a who's who of the worlds of art, science, politics, and faith over the past few centuries—everybody from Oscar Wilde to Rachel Maddow, Michael Palin to Margaret Thatcher, Stephen Hawking to Kate Beckinsale. The air was heavy with scholarship, distinction, and prestige. It was hard to find a more apt setting for an international scientific conference.

Why then did I feel so uneasy? After all, I had just spent two days listening to presentations by some of the brightest minds working on an issue I cared about deeply, both personally and professionally—climate change. Though our conference was not held in the Great Hall of Christ Church, an inspiration for Harry Potter's Hogwarts, the setting at the Oxford University's Centre for the Environment was by no means any less impressive. Moreover, the theme of our gathering—Indigenous peoples and climate change—was precisely the topic I had been researching as part of my job at the time. I had been developing a global grant-making strategy for the Christensen Fund—a private foundation in California working on "backing the stewards of cultural and biological diversity"— to support the efforts of Indigenous peoples worldwide to look after their ancestral territories. Scholars from such respected research institutions as the Missouri Botanical Garden, Tyndall Centre for Climate Change Research, Diversity International, International Union for the Protection of Nature (IUCN), and others had gathered at Oxford University in April 2007 to reflect on the progress in climate change research, policy, and action.

The experts who were gathered there were steeped in the most up-to-date information coming out of the latest UN climate change report. This wasn't a conference to contemplate whether climate change was real or when it might occur. Despite the spin by the climate change deniers, the report's conclusions were unequivocal. First, climate change is real. Second, if humankind doesn't do something drastic about reducing greenhouse gas emissions soon, many parts of the world may become unsuitable for human habitation due to sea level rise, permafrost melt, droughts, floods, fires, and other calamities. The Oxford conference participants' own field research carried out around the world had also taught them that the impacts of climate change are real and dramatic, as the concentration of greenhouse gases in the atmosphere, and subsequently temperature, continued to rise.

This group of experts had come to Oxford because of their growing apprehension that the Indigenous peoples and local communities who bear the brunt of the climate crisis, yet have contributed the least to it, continue to have virtually no voice in the global discourse on the issue. Despite their low-emissions traditional lifestyles, which, after all, embody the best aspirations of the modern society striving to wean itself off fossil fuels, the Indigenous knowledge of the land, waters, weather, and seasons continued to be largely ignored. The conference participants contended that excluding Indigenous peoples and local communities from the global discourse on climate change was not merely unjust. Ignoring local and Indigenous peoples and their knowledge—such as growing and using traditional foods as a source of adaptation to warmer weather, relying on non-mechanized, traditional transportation to reduce reliance on fossil fuels, and protecting rain forests on their traditional territories to absorb atmospheric carbon—limited humankind's collective ability to address the multiple challenges of climate change that lie ahead.

Presenters at the Oxford conference stressed that though they made up a mere 4 percent of the world's population, Indigenous peoples are caretakers of more than a fifth of the earth's surface, with close to 80 percent of the planet's remaining biodiversity found on their traditional territories. For ages, such communities have maintained an intimate and vibrant relationship with their environment, guided by their traditional knowledge. Passed on from generation to generation through oral teachings and sustained through daily practice, their knowledge is based on an intimate understanding of landscapes and seascapes born out of the firsthand, tactile, and sensual relationships only possible when a people so deeply inhabits a place. It is a know-how as well as a worldview, an intuition as well as a vast "database" of observations and experiences. It is intimately tied to local languages and is never held in its entirety by an individual but always by a collective—a family, a community, a tribe, a territory, or a nation. This knowledge is a foundation upon which day-to-day activities are organized and local rules of conduct among community members, their territory, and other living beings—be they neighbors, animals, or spirits—are based.

Pharmaceutical companies, hippies, and ethnobotanists figured out long ago that traditional knowledge could lead to newer, better, and more effective medicines. They certainly used this knowledge to their considerable advantage, all too often with little regard for the rights and well-being of the original knowledge holders. Still, because it is traditionally passed on from elders to youth and shared among the community members through storytelling rather than as a written record, by and large traditional knowledge continues to be considered, by many scientists at least, as hearsay, a mere collection of folktales and anecdotes, not fact. Nothing could be further from the truth, however. Undoubtedly, there are certain differences between what the modern societies consider "real science" and traditional knowledge. But these differences, as the experts gathered in Oxford emphasized, should not lead to a wholesale rejection of the positive contributions that each knowledge system makes to humankind's collective ability to aptly respond to climate change.

Traditional knowledge is based on deep wisdom arising from long-term observations over a relatively small area, embracing the sacred as part of the world we live in and interact with. Science, on the other hand, derives its predictions based on short-term collection of data, suppressing the spiritual. Still, many experts have come to view traditional knowledge as no less rigorous than, and complementary to, conventional science, because both are based on detailed direct observations of natural phenomena, though they draw their final conclusions from their respective underlying worldviews. There are several research fields where traditional knowledge has been recognized as important in providing ecological insights based on the long-term observations of the natural world. These observations lead to developing local methods of environmental management—like traditional savannah burning in northern Australia that enhances local biodiversity and actually helps avoid devastating large-scale fires, or community-managed marine protected areas in the Pacific that conserve marine animals, fish, and reefs. There is also a growing consensus that local knowledge of Indigenous peoples is the solid foundation for local climate change adaptation and mitigation strategies.

"It is a bit disconcerting, don't you think?" Dr. Nancy Turner asked me at the end of Addison's Walk. We were waiting for all the participants to assemble before proceeding to celebrate the conference's success at the Head of the River pub, a local haunt right next to the Folly Bridge. An eminent ethnobotanist from the University of Victoria, British Columbia, Canada, Dr. Turner is admired by her peers and respected by the Indigenous communities she has devoted her life to, documenting their traditional knowledge and wisdom.

"What is?" I asked, uncertainly raising my eyebrows. Dr. Turner's round face broke into a cautious smile and she looked down, as if searching for something she had lost. "Well, here we are," she responded with a sigh and looked up, "going on about such important issues like Indigenous peoples' knowledge and how it is vital to our understanding of climate change—but there are no Indigenous people at the conference! Don't you think that's a problem?"

Of course I did! It finally dawned on me that this was exactly what had been bothering me during the meetings. Caught up in the excitement of the setting and all the rhetoric, I failed to recognize that our group of well-informed and well-meaning Indigenous allies had fallen victim to the same exclusionary thinking they all were trying to overcome in others. They spoke on behalf of the subjects of their research—Indigenous people—instead of letting them take center stage to share their own views and experiences. The organizers had forgotten that any initiative seeking to address ecological or societal challenges either locally or globally must be based first and foremost on respectful, fair, equitable, and transparent relationships between researchers and local communities.

That Oxford gathering was a personal wake-up call for me, plainly showing just how far we still have to go in our work to achieve meaningful and lasting results at the local level, the only place where it ultimately matters.

———

KNOWING THE PLACE

T hrough the fog of time, it is often hard to recognize the precise moment when the first stirring of an idea, a feeling, or a belief takes root in your heart and mind, gradually growing stronger to the point of changing the way you see the world around you. Was it happenstance? A chance encounter with a stranger at a public talk that makes you question your most basic of assumptions? Maybe a film that your friends suggested you watch, because it revealed things about the human condition you were only then beginning to contemplate? Or, perhaps, a book you devoured in one sitting because the author's ideas captivated you so?

My own path to developing a deep respect for the knowledge of local people about their environment goes all the way back to my childhood, when I was still building castles out of the black volcanic sand on the shores of a small village in Kamchatka, a peninsula on the eastern fringes of then Soviet Russia.

In my mind's eye, I am marching down a muddy street, heading home from school, past the gap-toothed grins of wooden fences leaning drunkenly into the street. "Oh, yeah?" I raise my voice. "You just got here, and we've been here forever!" My patched-up black rubber boots slide in the slick muck, and I know that I must slow down or I will get a thrashing if I get dirt splattered all over the navy-blue school uniform my mother just washed and ironed for me over the weekend. I slow down to a more deliberate pace and continue to quarrel with Grib, my schoolmate, a year my junior, over who knows the coolest places around the village—the finer points of local knowledge.

"I bet you've never even been to the lighthouse at Kirpichiki!" I declare. "That's the best place around. You can find some really cool stuff there, if you know where to look. Romka even found a Chinese coin there once. Have you seen Vitka's stone arrowhead? Yeah? Well, that's from that lighthouse too!" Grib quickly concedes that he has yet to explore that part of our village. It would be awesome, he says, if I could show him the lighthouse. I am happy to be his guide. We immediately begin plotting our weekend expedition to Kirpichiki as we trudge home.

My father, Roman Isaakovich Raygorodetsky—a gifted young journalist and writer—first came to Kamchatka in the early 1960s on assignment for the Moscow-based magazine *Yunost*, or *Youth*. After hopping over nine time zones from Moscow in several airplanes, he landed in Petropavlovsk-Kamchatsky, the peninsula's administrative center. He staggered stepping off the airplane ramp, overwhelmed by the site of the majestic sugarloaf of Avacha Volcano towering over him. There and then he decided to make Kamchatka his home. After completing his short assignment for *Yunost*, he gave up his return ticket to Moscow and offered his services to a radio and TV station in Kamchatka. He went to work for them the very next day. Soon thereafter, he met my mother, at the time a waitress at Vostok, a local hotel and restaurant. A couple of years later they welcomed me into their world. Soon after, my father decided that a city was no place to raise his son. He got the job of a special correspondent for the Koryak autonomous region, based in Tilichiki, on the northeastern coast of Kamchatka Peninsula. And, when I was five, we moved.

Tilichiki in the 1970s was a small coastal village of fewer than two thousand people—mostly fishermen, border guards, geologists, various laborers, and Communist Party bureaucrats. One-story, single-family houses crowded the old part of the village, while two-story, wooden apartment buildings lined up along the shoreline in the newer part, at the base of the low hills sheltering Tilichiki from strong northerly winds. A sandspit opposite Tilichiki created the expansive yet well-secluded Bukhta Skrytaya, or Hidden Lagoon, that protected the village from the tempests coming off the Bering Sea. On the spit, the small hamlet of Korf clung to an airstrip large enough for small jets to land after a two-hour flight from Petropavlovsk.

My father, a Ukrainian Jew born in Kharkov and raised in Kiev, spent most of his life trying to stay as far away from the Communist reach as possible. Moving to Tilichiki, he would say, was his escape from the Soviet Union without actually leaving the country. He would point eastward from a window of our second-story apartment facing the lagoon, and say that he could almost see the Iron Curtain—the invisible, yet impenetrable, barrier of secrecy separating the Soviet and American superpowers. With Alaska less than nine hundred miles on the opposite side of the Bering Sea, it really felt like the Iron Curtain had almost a physical presence in Kamchatka. Thankfully, like most Soviet products, the Iron Curtain must have had a few chinks, because our evenings were filled with the crackle of an old Grundig radio reeling in the Voice of America out of the North Pacific.

When I had bragged to Grib about living in Tilichiki forever, I didn't feel I was exaggerating. Not a bit. Time flows perhaps more slowly through a child's mind, and some moments stretch into years. I truly felt like I had lived in the village all my life, though in reality it had been only five years. When I met Grib, my schoolmates and I, who had lived in the village at least as long as I had, all looked down on the city boys who'd just arrived in Tilichiki from *materik*, or the mainland. We were convinced that just like their parents—sent to Tilichiki to work by the Soviet state—these kids had no clue about local life. It never even entered our minds that most of us were also strangers in this land.

I did have some vague recollections of our family's earlier life in the city, but those had faded, eclipsed by the exploits I'd had since arriving in Tilichiki. Picking berries on the hills above the village, fishing off the coal pier, crossing the Bay of Korf in my dad's boat to go hunting, skiing on the frozen lagoon in the winter—every day in our tiny village at the edge of the world was fraught with adventure. Back then, I never paid any attention to the discomforts of village life I would certainly notice today—no running water, public outhouses, half-empty shelves in the local grocery store, open garbage dumps scattered around the village, stray dogs roaming the muddy or snowed-in streets, long and cold winters, and summers full of mosquitoes. These were all interrelated parts of my world, and I couldn't imagine anything better.

I still don't know how my father, an urbanite himself, managed to adapt to and embrace the village life. Maybe it was because he was a reporter and a writer fascinated by the human condition, or maybe because he could hold his drink as well as any of the locals, or maybe it reminded him of his teenage years during World War II, when his family had been evacuated from Kiev to a village in eastern Siberia, or maybe because there, at the eastern edge of the USSR, right next to the Iron Curtain, he finally found some semblance of freedom. Whatever the reasons, soon after our arrival, he became part of a tightly knit group of local men he called *muzhiki*, the real men. They were truck drivers, laborers, mechanics, and electricians—ordinary men with ordinary jobs, but with an extraordinary breadth of knowledge about the backcountry, because they spent most of their lives in the village. Their unassuming demeanor was in stark contrast with the arrogance and the pompous airs of the intelligentsia—the social class in Soviet Russia—often found in writing and artistic circles—that viewed itself as intellectually superior to common laborers. It was obvious, however, to anybody who cared to check, that the intelligence of the intelligentsia was surface-deep and no match for the *muzhiki*, who had intimate knowledge of life and nature— of animals and birds, of weather and seasons, of navigating the waters and traversing the land. All these skills were vital for life in our village. Maybe this is why my father eventually quit his radio job and signed up as a guard at the grocery store's refrigeration unit—to have more time to hang out with *muzhiki* and write about them.

The best fishermen and hunters of our village, these *muzhiki* would steer their tiny aluminum boats, motors revving, across the wide expanse of the Bay of Korf in any weather or time of day; going through the countless rapids of the Kultushino River, all the way up to its source, without losing a single blade from the propellers. They could read the winds and currents, and find the best hideouts for hunting ducks and geese, they knew all the best fishing spots and, of course, would never return home empty-handed. Undeniably, their skills and knowledge of the land exerted a strong pull on my father's imagination, perhaps another reason he sought their companionship and guidance. After apprenticing for a year on a friend's boat, he bought a used one himself to be part of the group. When I turned seven, he began taking me along on the weekend hunting and fishing forays.

Those days were a whirlwind of boats, dogs, tents, and mosquitoes; of staring into the fire and roasting potatoes in the glowing embers; of listening to the stories of fishing and hunting exploits laced with pro-fanities I was warned not to imitate at the cost of my life; of cuddling up inside a vast and warm reindeer-skin sleeping bag and watching the long shadows, cast by the dying fire dance on the tent's tilted walls. Weariness would eventually overtake me, and I would drift off to sleep. In my mind, the *muzhiki* were the coolest men in the village. They were of the land, and having my father being part of the group made me feel like I belonged to this land too.

During the first evening of each trip, the men would guzzle down most of the liquor they brought with them, to "avoid later temptation," they would say. Otherwise nothing good would come out of this hunting or fishing. Often, sitting by a smoldering fire at dawn or dusk, we'd hear the distant whine of an outboard motor, somewhere downstream from our camp. The monotonous drone of the motor pushing the boat up the river would surge and wane like a hefty bumblebee traversing a meadow from blossom to blossom. And, with uncanny regularity, the drone would cut off sharply with a loud shriek, followed by a deafening silence. The *muzhiki* around the fire would chuckle, shake their heads, and raise their vodka-filled enameled mugs to toast yet another novice adventurer making an acquaintance of one of many sandbars on the Kultushino River. The motor's propeller was most definitely broken and now, with no knowledge of these waters, the misadventurers would be blindly paddling the boat through a maze of channels and tributaries in search of a landing spot where they could fix it. I would also snigger, nod all-knowingly, and sip my hot tea laced with condensed milk. I was delighted to be sitting snug by the fire with my father and his knowledgeable friends, our motors intact, instead of being part of the crew on the ill-fated boat, paddling to shore in the chilly dusk.

These were my early lessons in valuing local knowledge and the first taste of an intimate relationship that develops between the people and the place over time. In retrospect, these initial learnings were more like *Local Knowledge for Dummies*, given the history of the place I came to discover only much later. Our village's past was similar to many such settlements throughout the Soviet Far East. Tilichiki was built by the Soviets on the traditional territory of the Indigenous Koryak people, who had herded reindeer, fished for salmon, and hunted seals for millennia before the Russians arrived. The village was built to subjugate this traditional culture and bring the Koryak "primitive" society into the fold of Communism. This, of course, simply meant eradication of their traditional way of life, customs, and language. The Koryak generations-deep local knowledge and their relationship with the land had been undoubtedly far superior to anything the *muzhiki* could ever learn.

I remained ignorant of this history until much later, when more truthful accounts of the Communist past began to emerge during the breakup of the Soviet Union. As a kid, all I knew of the Koryak people was based on the distorted images of their "primitive" culture I saw around our village. There were neglected, poorly dressed Koryak kids from the *Internat*, a residential school for native children who were brought to our village for the duration of a school year from small Indigenous settlements or reindeer camps around the region. Some of these kids I knew, and a couple of them were my good friends. There were also local Koryaks drinking themselves into a stupor, passing out behind the tiny village liquor store. I didn't know any of them but saw one or two every other day. I suspected, however, that there was more to the Koryaks than these grotesque caricatures of a *culture undone*. I saw glimpses of it in what my father would bring back from his trips to reindeer herding or fishing camps to produce radio and newspaper reportages—photos of herders in their traditional clothes, or some objects of their traditional culture he wished to use himself, like a Parenski hunting knife or a *kukul'*, a sleeping bag made of reindeer skin.

Though obviously very naive, my early encounters with local knowledge were powerful enough to shape my worldview. Soon after we moved, I developed severe eczema on my legs and hands. The itchy, often bleeding sores must have looked ghastly, but I wasn't troubled by them too much. I even learned to use an occasional flare-up on my hands to great personal advantage—a legitimate excuse not to practice piano. My parents obviously tried everything to heal, or at least ease, my condition, but none of the conventional creams or ointments prescribed by local doctors did me any good. I was about twelve, when, during one of our regular summer visits to my father's relatives in Kiev, Ukraine, ten time zones west of Kamchatka, my uncle suggested that we should visit a *travnik*, or an herbalist, to see if any folk remedies could help me. I suspect that, by this time, my father was ready to try anything. We took a cab to one of the new Kiev developments to find the herbalist. After driving in circles around dozens of absolutely identical concrete apartment towers, we finally found the one with the *travnik*'s flat.

A hobbit-like figure opened the door of a tiny first-story apartment. The diminutive herbalist was wearing a faded long-sleeve shirt buttoned up tight around his neck and tucked into his trousers, which were pulled up almost to his chest. He ushered us into the main room, dimly lit with the gray afternoon light filtering through old flowery curtains draped across the solitary window. It was as if we had climbed inside a hobbit's burrow. The pungent aroma of herbs, drying in bundles on the walls and ceiling, filled the air. After a few preliminaries, the herbalist examined me quickly and then questioned my father about my condition. After a few minutes, the hobbit declared that it was the bad spirit in my father that was responsible for my affliction and that to heal me, he would need to purge my dad a bit. He pointed to a small chair for me to sit on and tapped a spot on the spring bed next to himself for my father. I was relieved that I would not have to consume any herbal concoctions, undoubtedly obnoxious, and happily sat down to witness the ordeal. While my father's philosophical musings ranged from dark matter to spiritual, from evolution to creation, specific religious practices were never part of our life. "Things I do for you," I read on his face, as my father—his eyes rolling to the ceiling—surrendered to the hobbit.

There were no cauldrons bubbling with witch's brew, nor magicians drawing pentacles on the floor to summon spirits. The hobbit simply pulled a small box of matches from of his deep pants pocket, counted some out, and lined them up next to himself on the bed. Then he closed his eyes, put his left hand on my father's forehead, and began to pray. He muttered for a bit, moved a single matchstick aside, and repeated the prayer. For a few minutes nothing happened—just another murmured prayer and another matchstick added to the growing pile. It all looked quite amusing, but I tried to keep a straight face. My father stoically played his part in this theater of the absurd, but it was clear that he was rapidly losing his patience. Then he belched. The herbalist raised an eyebrow. My father apologized. The herbalist nodded, saying that it was a good sign and continued with his prayers. Another burp. More murmurings. Then another belch. Within five minutes, my father had his shirt unbuttoned down to his chest and his handkerchief soaked with the sweat he had to continuously wipe off from his forehead. His incessant belching resembled a lion's roar thundering over an African savannah. He no longer apologized. The little man continued his prayers unfazed, as if he were reading a Sunday paper. I was sinking deep into my seat, not knowing what to think.

My father's torment continued for about an hour. When the herbalist finally stopped his prayers, the belching stopped. My father was visibly exhausted but tried to keep a brave face for my sake. Of course he would have lots of bad spirit in him, he said, given the tough life he had led. The healer agreed—my father still had quite a bit of bad spirit in him and would have to come back for a few more sessions. In the meantime, the healer gave me some herbs and instructed when and how to use them.

My father never went back to see the hobbit. My eczema cleared up after a couple more years, most likely, my parents were told, because we left the northern village and moved to warmer climes. To this day, my scientific training fails me in explaining our encounter with the herbalist. But ever since, I have had a deep awareness of how our logical mind can be blind to the mysterious and subtle powers of the universe that is unseen, intuitive, and of spirit.

As I got older and looked for ways to deepen that sense of intimacy with the world I first developed in Tilichiki, my learnings multiplied. During my academic training, both in Russia and later, after immigrating to the United States, in Alaska and New York, I realized that in wildlife or conservation biology, the scientific lens of statistical models, maximum sustained yields, predator control, and conservation "offsets," provided me with a very skewed view of the natural world—a black-and-white snapshot of nature as a collection of resources to be managed to satiate human appetite. Such a soulless egocentric view of the world was definitely not what I was searching for. When Cheryl, my wife, whom

I met in Alaska during my studies, got a job as a biologist working with the Gwich'in people, a group of Athabascan-speaking Canadian First Nations, we moved to Inuvik, a town above the Arctic Circle at the end of the Dempster Highway in Canada's Northwest Territories. There, I was fortunate to get a chance to help the Gwich'in people develop a project that nurtured my evolving understanding of the value of local knowledge. The Gwich'in Traditional Ecological Knowledge Project tapped the deep well of collective local knowledge of Gwich'in elders, hunters, trappers, and fishermen about their traditional territory and local biodiversity important for their culture. I finally felt that my work was getting me closer to gaining insights into the true nature of human relationship with the land.

Wherever my life and work have taken me since, I longed for that deep connection with the landscape, approaching it with the respect and reverence I often saw reflected in the eyes of local people—men and women, elders and children, hunters and herders, farmers and fishermen, headmen and healers. Whether these local people were Evèn reindeer herders of Kamchatka or Caboclo fishermen of the Brazilian Amazon, Aleut fur seal hunters of the Pribilof Islands in the United States or Kuku Nyungkal rain forest guardians of Australia—I have treasured every chance I got to learn from them, always trying to understand the subtleties of their intimate relationship with their ancestral territory.

Today, as a research affiliate at the University of Victoria's POLIS Project on Ecological Governance—a center for transdisciplinary research that investigates and promotes sustainability—I continue to work on finding ways to strengthen local voices and respect for local and Indigenous knowledge at all levels of decision making, whether it is a UN agency developing a climate change assessment agenda or a First Nation community concerned about the future impacts of a proposed mine on its freshwater supply.

As the negative ecological and societal consequences of our actions become increasingly apparent, there is a growing recognition that we must move away from the ways of thinking and acting based on the dominant worldview that sees people as separate from nature, which got us into our current predicament in the first place. In recent years, a number of integrative disciplines—systems science, resilience science, ecosystem health, ethnoecology, deep ecology, Gaia Theory, and others—have sought ways to advance our understanding of the complex, nonlinear, and multidimensional relationships between people and nature, incorporating insights from both the biological and social sciences as well as Indigenous knowledge. Various organizations working on biodiversity conservation, cultural preservation, and sustainable development are increasingly relying on such holistic approaches in their work.

Out of all these emerging approaches, one way of looking at the world, and our relationship with it, has particularly resonated with me. *Biocultural diversity* is a product of millennia of coevolutionary relationships between humans and their surroundings, when people rely on their environment for survival while adapting to and modifying it. Biocultural diversity reflects a tremendous variety of biological and cultural relationships around the globe. As Dr. Luisa Maffi, one of the pioneers in this field, documents in her book *Biocultural Diversity Conservation: A Global Sourcebook* many of these systems continue to endure today worldwide. Most of the examples in the book—from relying on taboos to maintain traditional conservation sites in the Marshall Islands to using traditional knowledge to coexist with endangered crocodiles in the Philippines—come from Indigenous peoples who continue to maintain biocultural systems by practicing their time-tested ways of looking after their traditional territories. The very reason biocultural systems have persisted to this day is that they are very resilient, which simply means that, when facing change, they are capable of learning and adapting by self-organizing to maintain their essential functions. Tight feedback between social and ecological parts of a biocultural system ensures that it responds to changes in timely and appropriate ways, often detecting approaching shifts long before they are capable of flipping the system into a new state. Indigenous knowledge of the environment is one such feedback mechanism that enables communities to monitor the state of the system and detect change before it is too late.

⸺ ∞ ⸺

NEW WINDS

F irst off," said Tero Mustonen in a slight Finnish accent, his elongated vowels and softened consonants reminding me of syncopated beats of a yodel, "I want to tell you that when Alestine Andre heard that I was coming here, she wanted me to give you her regards. She asked me to tell you that the Gwich'in project is still going good." It is a small world. Alestine, a Gwich'in herself, was at the Gwich'in Social and Cultural Institute when I was working on the Gwich'in Traditional Environmental Knowledge Project back in Inuvik. I was pleasantly surprised to discover that Tero knew her and happy to learn that the project I had helped launch and steer almost a decade before had endured and continued to benefit local people.

We had just stepped out of the Kaufmann Theater, a small auditorium next to the Hall of Northwest Coast Indians, the oldest hall at the American Museum of Natural History in New York City. We had been there for the past three days at an international symposium, "Sustaining Cultural and Biological Diversity in a Rapidly Changing World: Lessons for Global Policy." The symposium brought together leading conservation scientists and development practitioners, representatives of nongovernmental organizations, research and educational institutions, and, unlike the Oxford gathering the previous year, members of local and Indigenous communities. We all gathered to help articulate a shared vision for conserving biological and cultural diversity worldwide as a way of addressing the multitude of environmental and social problems besetting us and the planet, including climate change.

Tero and his colleague Vyacheslav Shadrin, the head of the elders council for the Yukaghir people from the Kolyma region in northern Russia, presented at the session on Indigenous peoples and climate change. Both men represented the Snowchange Cooperative, a global nonprofit organization Tero cofounded over a decade earlier to advance the role of traditional knowledge in environmental policy and practice. Headquartered in the village of Selkie, Finland—where Tero is a headman and a traditional-seine-net master—Snowchange is a respected international community-based network of Indigenous and non-Indigenous members developing locally appropriate solutions to the challenges of climate change. Their work has been very important in advancing the global recognition of Indigenous knowledge in climate change adaptation and mitigation efforts. Their ultimate goal, as Tero puts it: "To see our cultures come back—a complete rebirth on the land!"

What brought us out of the auditorium was Tero's concluding remarks at the end of the climate change session. After spending an entire day in the confines of the stuffy auditorium, his words jolted me into wakefulness.

"Our elders gave me permission to share this information with you," said Tero to emphasize to the audience that though what he was about to share was not his own knowledge, he had been given permission to share by the original knowledge holders. "They want you to know that new winds are blowing across the land now. They do not know these winds but still try to greet them." He paused, lowering his microphone, either trying to let us take in what he had just said or looking for the right words to properly convey his message. "To really understand what climate change means," he continued, "you need to spend time with us on our land."

Tero's words cut through the tangle of PowerPoint presentations and endless soliloquies with the precision of a fisherman's blade, revealing the very essence of the challenges faced by local communities. I wanted to learn more from Tero, and so we eventually found a moment to sit down and talk about his work at Snowchange.

"You should come for a visit," he said at the end of our conversation before we headed back inside the auditorium. "Our partners in northern Finland are Skolt Sámi from Sevettijärvi near the Näätämö River. They are doing some good work to rebirth their culture and we are helping them to take care of their land and adapt to climate change." He paused and smiled. "For you it will be like going back to the Gwich'in, only instead of the wild caribou, it's domestic reindeer!"

A hefty Finn, Tero looked small, perched on the edge of a long and wide bench in the dark hall. Imposing totem poles, house posts, sculptures, and ceremonial masks carved out of ancient western red cedars loomed over our heads. They looked out of place, jostling for a spot against the walls and partitions of alcoves packed with artifacts of cultures almost forgotten. The old dyes faded from their carved ancient faces and their cedar skin had turned the color of cured tobacco. Since arriving at the museum from research expeditions long ago, their mother-of-pearl eyes have peered past one another, through the walls and display cabinets, as if searching for the horizons and clouds, seas and mountains of their homelands, from which they were plundered in the name of science—the coastal villages of Kwakwaka'wakw, Haida, Tlingit, and other peoples of the Pacific Northwest. They longed for an escape from this stale hall of preserved cultures and a return to the fresh air of living communities.

"Sounds like a great idea, Tero," I responded eagerly, ready to greet the new winds traveling across the land and sea. And so my new journey began. Over the next several years I sought to bring Indigenous voices on climate change to the global audience. In 2009, as a program officer of the Christensen Fund, I helped arrange an Indigenous Peoples' Global Summit on Climate Change in Alaska, a global gathering of the Indigenous peoples where they formulated key messages to bring with them to the global climate change meetings. With non-profits InsighShare, Land is Life, Project World, and Conversation du Monde—led by Nicolas Villaume, an award-winning photographer, I helped cofound a project called Conversations with the Earth (CWE)— an Indigenous-led multimedia initiative that amplifies Indigenous voices in the global discourse on ecological and cultural challenges facing the planet, including climate change. More than a million visitors saw CWE exhibits at the National Museum of Denmark, in Copenhagen; the Smithsonian's National Museum of the American Indian, in Washington, DC; and the United Nations Headquarters in New York. I also helped develop the Indigenous Peoples Climate Change Assessment—a global partnership of Indigenous communities developing culturally appropriate ways of addressing climate change. More important, however, I was privileged to spend time in several Indigenous communities around the world, learning about their lives and the challenges of climate change they have been facing. The challenges that all of us, however reluctant and frightened we might be to acknowledge it, will face for generations to come.

CHAPTER TWO

CHANGING
WITH THE LAND

———⦿———

BACKBONE

The pale smoke and the pungent aroma of kippered fish escape a
stainless steel box perched on top of a small fire, as Tero Mustonen
quickly lifts the lid. On the top rack of the smoker, a dozen *muikku*, or
vendace, a European cisco, cure above the smoldering alder chips.

"Almost ready," Tero announces, closing the lid.

"Smells delicious," I remark wistfully, inhaling the mouthwatering
aroma. The scent reminds me of the smoked herring my father would
bring home from his fishermen friends, the *muzhiki*, back in Tilichiki, the
coastal village where I grew up. The Pacific herring used to be abundant
along the eastern coast of Kamchatka Peninsula until industrial fishing
fleets wiped out most of the stock in the middle of the 20th century. By
the time we moved to Tilichiki in 1970, the herring was gone—no milt
turning the coastal waters chalky, like a glacial-fed stream; no strands
of seagrass turgid with sticky roe; no herring scales washing up on the
shore. And so it remained until, one windless early-summer day in the
mid-1970s, as if stirred by gusts of wind, the surface of our small lagoon
frothed with schools of herring, coming in to spawn on the seagrass beds.
Everybody grabbed anything resembling fishing gear—a fishing rod, a
hand net, or just a bucket—and, crowding on the shoreline, scooped up
the frenzied fish by the hundreds. Over the following weeks, families
around the village salted and sun-dried their catch, and hot and cold-
kippered herring was on our menu for the rest of that summer.

Sharing my recollections with Tero, my lips smacking in anticipation
of our meal, I ask him if smoked vendace tastes like kippered herring.

After all, I say, there must be a reason why its North American relative, cisco, is also called "lake herring."

"I wouldn't know. I don't eat fish," Tero replies nonchalantly. He takes the smoker off the fire and puts it on an old log to cool off. Stirring and spreading the coals with a birch branch to let the fire burn out, he explains, somewhat reluctantly, that ever since his childhood he's been allergic to fish. I ask him why, then, is he Selkie's respected seine master, proudly carrying his people's fishing tradition of seining vendace and other fish in the area's lakes.

"The universe self-organizes in many unexpected ways," Tero muses philosophically as we walk back to his house—a 250-year-old log building he and his wife, Kaisu, bought several years ago.

"In our community, we must rely on each other. Like, my neighbor and friend doesn't fish himself, so he gets his fish from me," Tero explains. "But he is a great houndsman and hunter, who depends on the forest for grouse, capercaillie, moose, and hare. I never hunt, but Marko shares with us what he gets from the forest. Neither does he travel to meetings like I do, to stand up and make speeches about why our forest is so important to us. So, there must be a reason why I'm a seine master who cannot eat the fish." He pauses and then guffaws, "More's left for my community."

After we first met at the symposium at the American Museum of Natural History in New York, it took me some time to take Tero up on his invitation to visit him. But, eventually, I found a way across the Atlantic to Finland, to learn what climate change means to local communities that are members of the Snowchange Cooperative.

Driving a large burgundy cargo van he uses to deliver fish from his seine around the village and to various customers, from a wholesaler and to a local restaurateur, Tero picked me up at the municipal airport Joensuu, where I flew in from Helsinki, and brought me to Selkie. The village houses are scattered along the top of a low ridge overlooking forested foothills and dozens of lakes, many still brimming with fish. The ridge gives the community its name—Selkä, or backbone, in Finnish. This old Finnish-Karelian settlement of fewer than three hundred souls is located in southeastern Finland, about thirty miles from the Russian border. Because of Selkie's proximity to the major historic hunting and trading route from Lake Ladoga to the White Sea and Northern Baltic, the first written records about Selkie come from Russia. The documents reveal that the region has been home to, first, the Sámi and, from the 15th century, to the Eastern Finns who spoke Karelian, a language distinct from Finnish. This is the last place in Europe where hunting and fishing traditions remained the principal occupations until the 1800s.

As Tero carries the smoker toward the house, he describes our upcoming trip. We will drive more than six hundred miles northward, across the Arctic Circle, to the small Skolt Sámi community of Sevettijärvi, a member of the Snowchange network, to meet Vladimir Feodoroff, a retired Skolt working on a climate change adaptation project with Snowchange. We will also spend time with his daughter, Pauliina, Tero's good friend, who coordinates the project, as well as several community members who are partnering with Tero and Snowchange on the project.

Tero has been working with Indigenous communities on climate change for a long time. Before getting a PhD in human geography, he earned his master's degree in political science at the University of Tampere, where he explored the relationship between the fluid concepts of boundaries in nomadic Indigenous cultures, like the Sámi, and the rigid borders imposed on them by the conquering agrarian societies, be they Swedish, Russian, or Finnish. While wrapping up his thesis, Tero landed a part-time job teaching environmental policy and Arctic issues at Tampere Polytechnic that helped him develop relationships with Indigenous communities around the Arctic. Their collaboration on documenting traditional ecological knowledge, land-use practices, and approaches to climate change gave birth to a community-based network that Tero and his partners called Snowchange Cooperative to emphasize what bound their diverse communities and cultures together. For Tero, however, it is the other meaning of the Finnish word for snow, *lumi*, that captures the true nature of Snowchange—"a call to arms."

"We are not doing our work for some abstract noble cause," explains Tero. "On the contrary, we have a very selfish motivation—to see our villages thrive, as our forests are restored to prime condition, our fisheries are strong, and our hunting areas are healthy. Those of us who appreciate the full meaning of this want to see our Finnish-Karelian culture come back—complete rebirth on the land. What we've been doing with Snowchange is very exciting, not just because of what we've been able to accomplish but because it's also a bit of 'punk rock'—we get to play with the 'big boys,' but we have our own unique way of doing things." Snowchange has made significant contributions in the field of traditional knowledge research to such global efforts as the Arctic Council's Arctic Climate Impact Assessment, the Arctic Biodiversity Assessment, the UN's Intergovernmental Panel on Climate Change (IPPC) Assessment Reports, and others.

"Snowchange is guided by the laws and traditions of the land," reflects Tero with satisfaction. "Because of this, we work on the issues that are important to our communities, even when nobody else would consider it. As a true community-based network, we are not driven by the need for funding, careers, or mission statements created to fit the funders' needs. Snowchange is all about grassroots—the communities that still have a connection with the land, like Selkie. Ultimately, this is the only thing that works. Other things—like science, national debates, or media—aren't irrelevant, but are not as meaningful for us. When I speak on behalf of the diverse Snowchange communities at various meetings," reflects Tero, "I don't take this mandate for granted. I have to earn it daily. To stay grounded, I spend a lot of time on the lakes and in the bush with our elders." Two Finnish elders, members of the network's steering committee, who have lived on the land all their lives, guide Tero and

Snowchange's work. "That's where I get the nourishment for my body and my soul.

"We work a lot with the Sámi, but the first thing I say after greeting the audience, just to make sure that there are no misunderstandings," Tero continues, "is that I am a Karelian Finn, not a Sámi. Our people have a lot in common. The remnants, shards, pieces of Finnish land-based traditions—like our seining—are still in place, despite the many changes we've experienced. We are dealing with the similar problems many Indigenous communities are facing the world over—alcoholism, drugs, and physical and psychological abuse. We are also in the same exact predicament as the Sámi regarding the impacts of forestry, mining, and climate change on our community."

After a few years of running the network out of Tampere, Tero and his wife, Kaisu, bought several acres of hayfields, old-growth forest, and buildings in Selkie from a local elder. Upon learning about Tero's work, he offered Tero the opportunity to buy his homestead, Havukkavaara, confident that the ancient dwellings and the land, with the old-growth forest, will be looked after for years to come.

Havukkavaara means Hill of Eagles, or Birds of Prey, in Finnish. In the old days, when the forest was three hundred to four hundred years old, golden eagles might have nested here, says Tero, as hawks still do. Early written documents describe an outpost built by the state to claim control over two thousand hectares—roughly half the area of the modern-day Selkie—for hunting and fishing. The cabins were originally built for a forest ranger, a warden of the Swedish Crown who ruled over the region on and off, until, after the Finnish War of 1809, the area became the Grand Duchy of Finland within the Russian Empire.

Soon after moving to the community, Tero was elected a village's headman and has worked hard to protect the old-growth forests near the village slated for clear-cutting by the state forestry company, Metsähallitus, and to reclaim the wetland that had been drained for peat production by another state company. Though as busy as ever, in his second term now, Tero continues to make time to practice traditional summer and winter seining.

We take off our muddy boots in the spacious Arctic entrance to the old house and enter the vast room that is a kitchen, dining room, and bedroom all wrapped into one around a massive old Russian stove. The whitewashed plastered brick structure takes up a good quarter of the room, its mantel and cooking surfaces cluttered with sooted pots and pans of various shapes and sizes.

Inside, woven linen rugs line the broad painted floorboards. A long dining table and benches, made of similar boards, all mementos of the region's ancient forests, sit along the farthest wall. Tero sets the smoker down on a woven table runner, slices up some dark rye bread, and uncorks a bottle of local blueberry wine. Out of the oven comes a crock of boiled potatoes and a vegetable casserole Kaisu baked for dinner. I slide on the bench along the wall closer to the smoker and we dig in. The delicate texture and kippered flavor of vendace is not as strong as I remember the herring to be, but just as mouthwatering.

After dinner, Tero walks with me to the sauna—a recently built cabin where I am to spend the night in the attached guest room. Outside, the weather-beaten logs of the old buildings silhouetted against the pale streaks of bare alder and birch trees melt into the asphalt gray and misty October evening. The dark soil is soft and moist, still to be hardened by the autumn frost. Tero tells me that the cold is, yet again, late in arriving this fall—one of many signs of the warming climate in Finland. Last spring, their storage shed was flooded during the extreme snowmelt, something that has not been recorded in all the two and a half centuries of Havukkavaara history.

Summer and winter seining has always been an important subsistence activity for Selkie villagers, but now climate change is making it more difficult to practice. Ice leads on the local lakes no longer appear in regular places, making winter travel more treacherous for the locals. According to the old Selkie residents, the winter of 1986 was the last real winter, when the lakes and rivers froze by mid-November. These days, the ice doesn't form until January, when the temperature finally dips below −4 degrees Fahrenheit for several nights in a row. The spring breakup, on the other hand, starts earlier, shortening the ice fishing and travel season. As summers become warmer—the hottest day on record in Finland was 99 degrees Fahrenheit, recorded in 2010, not far from Selkie—the fish seek cooler waters at the bottom of the lakes, making seining less successful.

According to climate models, the average annual temperature in Finland is expected to rise at least three degrees Fahrenheit by 2040, and up to twelve degrees Fahrenheit by 2100. Though the models predict more precipitation in Finland, most of the increase is coming from less frequent but more intense rain- and snowfall—a trend observed in other parts of the Arctic as well. In the summer, downpours and warmer temperatures will get more common, while cold snaps will become a thing of the past. The snow season will continue to grow shorter, and the days with freezing "rain-on-snow," when the deep freeze following such a drizzle encases the pastures in a hard crust of ice, will become more common.

But even more troubling, says Tero, are the changes already under way in northern Lapland, above the Arctic Circle, where we are heading tomorrow at dawn. Compared to the rest of the country, climate change has been unfolding at a much faster rate there, and has already had an impact on the life of the Sámi reindeer herders and fishermen. Over the last decade and a half, the ice and snow conditions in Lapland have changed dramatically. The freeze-up used to take place in November, but now it comes in December or even January, and sometimes rivers do not freeze at all. When the lakes and rivers do freeze, the ice is no longer as thick and as strong as it was in the past, making the herders uneasy about traveling along their customary winter trails over frozen water. Bogs and marshes also freeze late, which makes reindeer travel more challenging and forces Sámi to change their travel routes and adjust their annual herding calendar. Because the snow season now starts later, the soft blanket of snow normally protecting lichen—the main winter food of reindeer—is much thinner and doesn't last as long, leaving the reindeer food more vulnerable to the cold and overgrazing. In the winter, spells of warm weather are becoming more common, leading to "rain-on-snow" events, which makes it almost impossible for reindeer to dig up their lichen. The herders then have to buy supplemental fodder, like hay and food pellets, if they do not want their animals to starve, which puts a greater financial strain on their enterprise.

Now, however, is the time to get some rest, says Tero, wishing me good night. We will have plenty of time to talk about it on our long drive to the Skolt homeland tomorrow.

⁂

PEACEMAKING

E arly in the morning, under low leaden skies, we head out to Sevettijärvi, the center of the Skolt Sámi Settlement Area. Tero expertly pilots our small rental Ford northward—a red dot streaking through the drab autumn landscape of denuded forest stands scattered over hills and valleys, surrounded by the lakes, wetlands, and streams of northern Karelia. We stop for lunch at the roadside town of Kuusamo, just south of the Arctic Circle and halfway to our destination. Tero fills up the tank, and I wander through the gas station's minimart hoping to spot a sign of the approaching Land of Reindeer. I am rewarded in the meat section, where I find *poro* (Finnish for reindeer)—row upon hanging row of sliced smoked sausage, and the freezer full of reindeer meat cuts and bones, among a few packs of frozen wild cloudberries and lingonberries. It is pork and pasta for lunch at the gas station cafeteria, but Tero lifts my spirits with a promise of the best of the Sámi Arctic cuisine we will sample at Porotila Toini Sanila, a small Skolt Sámi family-run hotel just outside of Sevettijärvi, where we will stay.

Tero's relationship with the Arctic and the Skolts goes back to his childhood fishing trips in Lapland. He remembers falling asleep in the tent, as his dad talked to the Skolts visiting their fishing camp late into the white Arctic summer nights. Tero grew up knowing that the Skolts were a very special people, because his father always spoke highly of the Skolts as very knowledgeable and skilled fishermen and reindeer herders. When he got older, he learned the history of the Skolts and, eventually, found a way to develop a long-term working relationship with them as part of the Snowchange's work.

The Skolt Sámi are a small but culturally and linguistically distinct group of the Eastern Sámi. Historically, the Skolts' traditional homeland spanned hundreds of miles over the vast area, from the shores of Lake Inari in the west to the Kola Bay in the east, and the present-day location of the Russian city of Murmansk. Of the seven hundred Skolt Sámi living in Finland today, two-thirds live in Sevettijärvi, located about three hundred miles above the Arctic Circle, where the two months of continuous summer sunlight follow the eight sunless weeks of winter. Though the village is located a mere forty miles away from the frigid Arctic Ocean, the warm North Atlantic Drift branch of the Gulf Stream makes it one of the warmest areas of Northern Europe.

Skolts are considered to be the most traditional Sámi reindeer herding and fishermen group because they retain their native language and continue to rely on a centuries-old customary governance system, a community council called *Sääbbar* in Skolt that makes decisions about land use, fishing, and herding. Fishing used to be the Skolts' main traditional livelihood, supplemented by hunting of wild animals, including wild reindeer. Small reindeer herds were kept for transportation, milk, and as decoys to lure wild reindeer to hunt. As wild reindeer stocks declined in the 19th century, Sámi began to gradually switch to reindeer herding but kept their fishing practice strong.

In the old days, Skolt family groups would arrive at their autumn lake sites at the end of August to fish and gather reindeer. After the winter frost in October, families would move to their early winter sites along the rivers to go ice fishing, hunt game birds, and trap for fur. By late December to early January, everybody would gather at their winter villages to spend the coldest time of the year socializing and getting ready for the next fishing season. Skolts would spend the reindeer calving period, between April and May, looking after their herds, before setting them free until the fall. Summers were spent on family lakes fishing for salmon. And the annual cycle would be repeated. Despite multiple social and environmental changes, says Tero, many elements of this perennial ritual continue to be practiced by the Skolts.

"Adapting to change is nothing new to the Skolts," Tero explains. "They've gone through dramatic shifts many times in their history." The Skolt Sámi story is one of resilience and adaptation, as they have maintained the core of their traditional relationship with the land in the face of social and political upheavals.

For centuries, the Skolts' homeland has been in the middle of a power struggle between Russia, Denmark-Norway, and Finland. As national boundaries drifted east to west and back again, Skolts found their national allegiance shift from one nation to another, sometimes overnight. After Russia's victory in the 1808–1809 Finnish War over Sweden, the Skolt traditional territory became part of Russia's Duchy of Finland. A century later, after the Great October Revolution of 1917 dethroned the Russian Tsar, Finland became a sovereign state for the first time. As part of the Treaty of Tartu, signed between the Soviet Union and Finland in 1922, Russia ceded to Finland the region of Petsamo, including a portion of the Skolt traditional territory that gave Finland access to the Arctic Ocean.

A mere two decades later, in 1939, the Soviet Union invaded Finland, with no provocation, during what became known as the Winter War—the prelude to World War II. When WWII ended in 1945, Finland was forced to surrender the entire territory of Petsamo, including the Skolt Sámi territory, back to the USSR. The Skolts were given a choice between staying on their traditional territory and becoming part of the Soviet Union, or leaving their homes for Finland. The Skolt families in the western part of the Skolt traditional territory went to Finland, which turned out to be a prudent choice, because few Skolts who stayed in the now-Soviet-controlled area survived collectivization, persecution, and gulags.

Most of the Skolt refugees in Finland spent the first winter living near Lake Inari, in abandoned military barracks and cabins that were left after the war along the new border with the USSR. The Finnish government designated this area as the Skolt Sámi Settlement Area, to enable the refugees to continue their land-based traditions of reindeer herding and fishing. In the past, this area was home to the Näätämö Skolts who became fully assimilated into the mainstream society in the late 1800s. By 1949, the Skolts moved into neat, red-painted, two-room cabins built by the Finnish government along the lakes and streams stretching from the northern shore of Lake Inari to the Norwegian border. A school, a health center, and a Russian Orthodox Church were built, forming the nucleus of the village of Sevettijärvi, named after the nearby lake. With the eventual enactment of the Skolt Settlement Act, the Finnish government allowed Skolts to herd their reindeer, gather hay and lichen for them, collect firewood, cut timber for buildings, and build fishing cabins.

"Way before the Skolts relocated here after World War Two," says Tero, "the Sevettijärvi region was already somewhat known to the Skolts. They had stories about Sevettijärvi from the old days. They moved through here for hundreds of years during reindeer migrations, and on hunting and fishing trips."

Though there are some similarities between the Skolt Sámi Settlement Area and their traditional homeland, there are also significant differences. The former is situated in the transition zone between the forest and treeless tundra, while the latter is located largely in the forested boreal zone. To survive here, the Skolts had to develop a new intimacy with the land, which was not easy. It took years for the Skolts to settle in the new ways, and to feel like the land accepted them, and that they had adjusted to a new way of living. "This history," says Tero, "helps the Skolts today navigate the challenges of climate change," as once again they must develop a new relationship with a changing land.

In the summer of 2007, Snowchange received a call from its partners in Murmansk that two large Canadian mining companies—Barrick Gold and Puma Exploration—were gearing up to begin mining on the Skolt Sámi land in Russia. Immediately, Tero wrote to the International Sámi Council—a governing body representing Sámi of all four Nordic countries (Finland, Sweden, Norway, and Russia)—asking for help. Ms. Pauliina Feodoroff—the newly elected president of the Sámi Council at the time, and a Skolt Sámi herself—immediately responded. Soon, they were working together on a land-use study to demonstrate that the area where the mining operations were planned was not vacant but was, in fact, the traditional territory of the Skolt Sámi, who have lived there for centuries. With a little bit of the funds they managed to raise, Tero and Pauliina started cross-border exchanges between the Finnish Skolts and their distant Russian relatives, as part of the land-use documentation and mapping work based out of Sevettijärvi.

"Snowchange's work with the Skolts and other Sámi is very straightforward," explains Tero. "It's a peacemaking plan. We are trying to address the painful legacy of centuries of encroachment and assimilation by southern Finns on traditional Sámi territories. All the work that we are doing with Sámi is about this, be it a land-use mapping or climate change adaptation project. It is all about reconciliation," he says. "If we can create and maintain a respectful relationship with the Sámi and return to them the land and rights they ought to have, we are also healing ourselves as a nation," he concludes.

This work led to the development and publication of the *Eastern Sámi Atlas* which, through photographs and maps, shows how and when different groups of Eastern Sámi, including the Skolts, used to live on their traditional territory. The volume was a communal effort at making the Skolts' unseen histories visible. For their work on this project and the publication of the atlas, the Snowchange Cooperative—a Finnish organization—was recognized by the Skolt Sámi with the "Skolt of the Year Award" in 2011.

The highway winds through the southern part of the region, where a mix of thin pine and birch forests carpets the rocky landscape. Farther north, pine trees are replaced by the stunted Arctic vegetation. The road snakes around lakes and streams—some fringed with dwarf birches and willows, others ringed only with mossy boulders. Five hours after crossing the Arctic Circle, we reach Lake Inari. This 400-square-mile body of water is large enough to support fifty commercial fishermen hauling in over three hundred tons of whitefish every year. The road takes us along the lake's northern shore, at the southern edge of the Skolt Sámi Settlement Area, for about ten miles and continues northeast for another thirty miles until we reach the smaller Lake Sevettijärvi. We pass by the village's center—the school, church, and Skolt administration offices cluster on a small promontory jutting out into the lake—and continue for another twenty minutes northeast, toward the Norwegian border. Finally, a small blue road sign with plain white lettering—POROTILA TOINI SANILA—directs us from the main highway toward our home away from home for the next few days.

A small family guesthouse and a reindeer farm run by the Sanila family, the hotel sits on an isthmus separating Lakes Sevettijärvi and Kirakkajärvi. We pull up to a large unremarkable one-story building housing the office, kitchen, dining hall, a sauna, and several guest rooms. Greeting us at the door, Ms. Toini Sanila is glad to see Tero, who is her regular tenant during his visits to the community. A retired school principal, now in her sixties, Ms. Sanila still seems to hold on to her pedagogic habits, and, after giving him a hearty hug, jokingly chastises Tero, like a mischievous student, for being late. The frozen ground crunching under her boots, Ms. Sanila—a portly, yet spry, diminutive woman—immediately marches us off to our cabin. It is a brick-colored *kota*—a hexagonal traditional Sámi log cabin—one of several such guest huts scattered around the main hotel building, all surrounded by groves of stunted pine trees, water, and mossy boulders.

As we unpack and get ready for the promised dinner, Tero tells me that since her retirement a few years ago, Ms. Sanila has been running the Porotila hotel with her grown daughters. Business has been reasonably good, with quite a few tourists coming here throughout the year to fish the area's lakes and rivers and watch the northern lights in the winter.

Our dinner is as delicious as Tero promised—a simple collection of hearty traditional dishes, including sliced cold-smoked salmon, dark rye bread, creamy salmon soup, and a reindeer stew with mashed potatoes and fried mushrooms, followed by a cloudberry cake. After we finish off the seconds, Ms. Sanila joins us for tea and a chat. A Finn herself, she married a Skolt reindeer herder and moved to Sevettijärvi in her youth. Now a respected Skolt elder, she has definitely lived through a few changes around Sevettijärvi.

"The main difference," she observes, "is that now there is less snow than before." She recalls that when she had just moved here in her teens, there was at least three feet of snow every winter. Now everything is in flux—some winters have very little snow, and others have too much. Mid-winter temperatures are not as consistent as before, shifting from cold to warm and back again.

Her family keeps some reindeer, so Ms. Sanila knows firsthand that predictable weather is a must for successful reindeer herding. Timely freeze-ups in early winter are essential for a herder to be able to travel over lakes and small rivers to gather his animals. But, when the freeze-up comes late, traveling on skidoos along traditional reindeer migration routes becomes unsafe and reindeer roundups have to be postponed until later in the winter. By then, however, a lot of the fat the reindeer put on over the summer and early fall melts away and the quality of meat diminishes.

As a hotel owner, Ms. Sanila has also noticed that, with the fall freeze-up coming later, and the spring thaw arriving earlier, the winter tourist season is getting shorter. When a couple of years ago there was an unusually warm spring, they lost about a third of their tourist income. "Why would anybody want to come here if they can't ski or ride a skidoo?" she asks sardonically.

The summer weather has also been changing. It is a lot warmer now, compared to when she was young, she remarks. In the past, June and July weather was warm and wet and reindeer moved to higher windswept areas to escape mosquito swarms. Trying to hide from the bloodsucking menace, the animals would bunch up into herds, making it easier for the Skolt herders to round them up and push them to a corral for branding or vaccination. When the summer weather is hot and dry, like recently, mosquitoes are not as abundant, and gathering the reindeer into herds becomes more challenging. At the same time, mushrooms—an important seasonal reindeer food—do not grow in the dry soil, forcing the herders to once again look for extra feed for their animals.

Despite all these seemingly insurmountable challenges, Ms. Sanila feels confident that the Skolt will find a way to adapt their livelihoods, culture, and even language to the changing circumstances, be they climate change or whatever else life throws at them, just as they've done for hundreds of years.

SAUNA

Perched on the top shelf of a small Finnish sauna, Tero and his Skolt companions, Vladimir Feodoroff and his brother Teijo Feodoroff, are all sweating profusely. We left Sevettijärvi this morning on foot and, after a few hours of hiking and canoeing across a couple of lakes, made it to an all-season fishing camp. A cabin, a sauna, a couple of storage sheds, and a smokehouse—the camp sits on a riverbank within the middle reaches of the Näätämö River, one of the four remaining free-flowing rivers in Finland that still supports wild populations of Atlantic salmon. The river meanders for fifty miles from Lake Inari northward to the Skoltefossen falls at the Norwegian border and, ten miles farther, flows into the Barents Sea.

Vladimir ladles up cold water from a bucket and splashes it on the almost incandescent rocks. A sharp pop follows, as the water, bypassing the steam stage, explodes into a wave of scorching heat that bounces off the ceiling over our heads, scalding my scalp. After a few minutes, I excuse myself, and, scrambling down to the floor, step outside into the sauna's Arctic entrance, ignoring the jeers from Vladimir, Tero, and Teijo, who are just getting warmed up. As I sit on the bench to cool off, steam enveloping my lobster-red flesh, I remember why I never really enjoyed subjecting myself to these fiery adventures.

In Tilichiki, the village of my childhood, almost none of the houses had running water, and to take a bath or a shower, we would go to a public bathhouse, *bania* in Russian. The men's wash-up area had a couple of long tiled benches where, after filling up a shallow aluminum pail with water, we'd soap up before jumping in the shower. It wouldn't take me long to get washed, but I always had to wait for my father, who would spend at least an hour in the small *parilka*, or steam room, adjacent to the washing area. He worshipped the heat, as all real *muzhiki* should, he would say. If, by the end of our visit, the skin wasn't peeling off his nose and ears, then it wasn't a good session. I am certain that my heat intolerance was a source of disappointment to him, as I never quite acquired a taste for the fine art of self-scalding, and could not endure more than a minute or two of the ordeal. I would shoot out of the steam room, through the washing area, all the way into the changing room and wait for my father.

Back inside the Finnish sauna, I share this childhood memory with my new Skolt friends. Vladimir puts the ladle aside and, wiping his sweaty brow, turns to me with a smile and a nod. "Skolts and Russians have a lot in common," he says. "Saunas, food, clothing—all because we've lived side by side for such a long time."

"That's right," chimes in Teijo, who is getting a bit agitated, as the spirit from a few shots of vodka he had before the sauna is starting to catch up with him. "We used to rule this land!" he almost shouts, slapping his bare knee. "From here and all the way to Murmansk, it was all ours! Then all that mess with the Soviets broke out and now we just have a sliver of our traditional territory left." He shakes his head in frustration. "Our elders always talked about the great fishing our people had back there. Now we are just hoping we can keep the Näätämö River fishery going. It's the only salmon fishery we have left."

With all the talk, nobody is splashing water on the rocks and the sauna is finally starting to cool off. We dress and head back to the main cabin, where two other Skolt companions, Jouko Moshnikoff and Illep Jefremoff, are preparing our dinner.

The fishing camp is situated near a large deep eddy—a good spot to catch salmon. After the war, when the Skolts settled around Sevettijärvi, their traditional annual pattern of movement on the land had to be abandoned in favor of living in permanent villages, because there simply was not much room to roam. The Skolts were allowed to fish anywhere within the settlement area and to build fishing cabins at their seasonal fishing sites. A number of Skolts, like Jouko's grandfather and father, built their cabins along the Näätämö River and use them regularly throughout the year.

As Jouko throws a birch log into the fireplace, I recall the few dried-up birch stumps we passed on the way here. I ask about what happened there and Vladimir describes how in 1966, there was an outbreak of a birch pest, the autumnal moth, that denuded the trees. The pest does not normally survive cold winters, which used to be the norm here, but that particular winter, the thermometer didn't dip below −31 degrees Fahrenheit, and, as a result, the moth numbers exploded the following summer.

"I remember going fishing with my mother and it was like walking through a heavy snowfall in the middle of the summer," Illep recalls. A key contributor to Snowchange's land-use documentation and mapping work for the *Eastern Sámi Atlas*, Illep has deep knowledge of Skolt traditional activities along the Näätämö watershed. He describes how fish feasted on the moths that fell into the streams like snowflakes. Soon after, the birch trees withered and died. The few birch stumps we saw are all that remain of the once lush birch forest, which used to be a good place to hunt ptarmigan and hare. Budding birch leaves are also an important spring fodder for reindeer craving fresh nutrients after a long winter diet of lichen. During the last decade, two new outbreaks of autumnal moth infestation were reported just across the border in Norway. The Skolts worry, says Illep, that as the climate warms, the moth outbreaks will become more frequent and widespread, wiping out remaining birch groves and destroying an important food source for reindeer.

Dinner is finally ready and we all sit at the table overflowing with food. Like the generations of Skolts welcoming guests to their camps before him, Jouko passes around reindeer stew and cold-smoked salmon—both key parts of the Skolts' subsistence and cultural heritage. The fine-fibered and lean reindeer meat helps Skolts maintain their food security in a changing landscape and climate. It is also a source of income, though it comes at a cost.

After Finland became an EU member, in 1995, the Skolt Sámi have had to follow burdensome EU regulations and standards for meat processing to be able to sell reindeer meat on the EU market. To comply with the new rules, the Finnish Reindeer Herders' Association replaced two hundred field slaughterhouses with ten new EU regulation-compliant abattoirs staffed with managers and veterinarians who oversee the annual processing of fifteen thousand tons of reindeer meat destined for the EU market.

Vladimir says that having to comply with the EU standards has made looking after reindeer more expensive for the Skolts, because they had to build their slaughterhouses on their own dime, and had to change when and where they can gather their herds. Many traditional practices—such as leaving some spilled blood and *rapamaha*, or reindeer stomach contents, on the ground to help fertilize and renew the trampled soil inside the corral—became forbidden and are no longer part of the reindeer-herding cycle. Moreover, the traditional method of killing and butchering reindeer inside a corral was pollution-free, but now chemicals must be used daily to disinfect EU-certified abattoirs.

But being part of the global economy also brings certain benefits, concedes Jouko. These days, his table does not just have the traditional gifts of the Skolt land but also displays some store-bought offerings from faraway places, also part of the EU market—apples from Spain, vodka from Estonia, coffee from Italy. As a Japanese Honda generator chugs outside the cabin to give us some light while we relish the meal, I ask the group about this blend of local and global in their daily life. They certainly enjoy the benefits and conveniences of the global economy, they tell me, but they know that it doesn't come for free. They suspect that the changing climate they are experiencing is the price we are all paying for the fossil fuel–infused food production and transportation system that, while delivering goods to their homeland, makes their traditional livelihoods, like salmon fishing, increasingly difficult to maintain.

SOUL OF SALMON

S kolts still consider themselves to be fishermen more than herders. Though they catch a variety of fish—whitefish, grayling, perch, burbot, pike, and brown trout—it is the Atlantic salmon that has historically been their main source of sustenance. The most productive Skolt Sámi salmon fishing area remaining is the Näätämö River watershed, where many fishing camps, including Jouko's, are located. In the old days, salmon was used as a tribute payment to the Russian czar, and old taxation records show that Skolt Sámi have been harvesting salmon on the Näätämö River since the 16th century. These ancient scrolls, carefully preserved by generations of Skolts, are now part of the Memory of the World program of the United Nations Educational, Scientific and Cultural Organization (UNESCO). They are recognized as "a unique expression of how documented decisions of the government were understood already centuries ago as safeguarding the fundamental rights of the [Skolt Sámi] community." Cash economy, refrigerators, and grocery stores have all diminished the need for salmon but not its value, whether as a source of sustenance or cultural identity. For the Skolts of Sevettijärvi, the Atlantic salmon fishery continues to be an important part of their everyday diet.

Regrettably, the name Atlantic salmon no longer conjures up the vision of a strong silver bullet of a fish—the wild relative of Pacific salmon—surging up the frothing rapids of untamed rivers. The image that has replaced it is the motionless rows of flabby, pink-colored flesh of its farmed doppelgänger in countless fish aisles throughout grocery stores. But wild Atlantic salmon, dubbed the King of Fishes, persists in a few watersheds on both sides of the North Atlantic. People can still witness this amazing fish navigate from the ocean to its birthplace, after years and thousands of miles spent away from home, vigorously surging upstream against the punishing current.

We sample Jouko's cold-smoked salmon as Vladimir reminisces about his childhood spent on the river. Born in 1950, he grew up fishing for salmon, mostly with his grandmother, in the streams and lakes of the Näätämö watershed, as well as herding reindeer across its taiga and tundra landscapes. He started rowing a fishing boat as soon as he was strong enough to hold an oar. "There was no other food in the summer but salmon and other fish," he says wistfully. All his grandparents did was fish, and Vladimir relished rowing the boat for them.

"My grandfather Vasko knew the soul of salmon," says Vladimir, pausing for emphasis. "He was one of those rare Skolts who understood the watershed from its estuary to the headwaters. He showed me many secret things about the land and water—the source of our knowledge and our way of life. Like, he had this deep understanding of the relationship between salmon and freshwater mussels. He always knew where to collect the best freshwater pearls."

Released into a stream, a mussel egg latches on to the gills of a salmon and travels with the fish as a parasite for about a year. When it finally leaves the salmon, it attaches to the gravel at the bottom of a stream and begins to grow into an adult mollusk. Because they need good natural conditions, freshwater mussels are used as an indicator of river health. Presently, they are endangered in northern Finland, because not all the elements required for their survival are present— salmon are not as abundant, water quality is not great, and gravel beds at many old salmon spawning sites are covered with organic sediment because of pollution.

"I treasure those early memories," says Vladimir. "I can remember the first few times checking salmon nets from the rowboat and thinking that this fish was very special. For me, I guess, this is where the spark for our salmon work came from."

As Snowchange's work with the Skolts evolved, the impacts of climate change on local livelihoods became more and more evident. Through community discussions, a local consensus emerged that, while significant, the climate change challenges for reindeer herding could be managed. The herders felt that they already had some tools at their disposal to make sure that their herds had a future—they could move animals to better pastures, or, if the pastures failed, buy some extra feed for the animals. Their salmon fishery, on the other hand, was of much greater concern to them, because of growing pressures of habitat destruction, pollution, overfishing, fish farming, and, now, climate change.

Salmon are anadromous fish, spending their lives in both fresh and salt water. In cold northern rivers, like Näätämö, it takes fish longer to grow than in warmer streams, and juvenile salmon can spend between two to eight years in freshwater before they become sufficiently large to migrate to the ocean. For the next one to four years, the open seas are their home until they mature enough to return back to spawn in the river of their birth. Unlike their Pacific relatives, which die after spawning, Atlantic salmon become kelts, or post-spawners, that travel back to the estuary or the ocean to feed, before returning to spawn the following year.

Historically abundant throughout the North Atlantic, wild Atlantic salmon populations currently teeter on the brink of extinction in the United States and parts of southern Canada. They have completely disappeared in Switzerland, the Netherlands, Belgium, the Czech Republic, and Slovakia. In Finland, before World War II, there were thirty to forty wild salmon rivers. Today, because of development pressures, there are only four watersheds that still have salmon, and Näätämö River is one of them. The river's salmon fishery remains an important source of livelihood for the Skolts. The Näätämö watershed supports an annual catch of about a dozen tons of salmon, which is just a tenth of what is still caught annually in the Tana River, the largest of the four remaining wild salmon watersheds in Finland.

According to Dr. Eero Niemelä, an Atlantic salmon expert from the Natural Resources Institute of Finland, salmon has the capacity to adapt to small incremental changes in the environment. But if the changes unfold too fast, as is happening now, it is unclear how the fish will respond. The timing of spawning depends on the air and water temperatures. If the river water becomes warmer than normal, juvenile salmon could grow quicker and become ready for their ocean voyage ahead of their schedule. Similarly, as the coastal waters warm up, there may also be a lot of food for juvenile salmon, which would choose to remain feeding near the coast, instead of migrating to the high seas in search of food. In this way, warming temperatures, as a result of climate change, may be beneficial for salmon stocks, according to Dr. Niemelä. At the same time, as the coastal waters warm up, southern predatory fish species, like mackerel, also move northward, feeding on juvenile salmon, which obviously reduces salmon survival.

"Hot and dry summers are new to us," observes Vladimir. "The low water level, like we had last year, causes lots of problems for Näätämö salmon, as do the warm water temperatures." When water level is low at the freeze-up time, he continues, the spawning sites may freeze all the way to the bottom, often destroying salmon eggs. Vladimir and Illep found dead roe in deep pools along the main river channel, a sure sign that the previous year's spawning had failed. The year before that, however, the water level in the river was too high because of the abundant snowmelt, and the strong river current washed out salmon eggs from the gravel bottom, killing them. But high water levels also prevented any fishing or poaching that year, allowing more salmon to reach the spawning grounds at Näätämö headwaters. "Nothing's black and white," remarks Vladimir.

The fact that Atlantic salmon can return to their stream to spawn for several years in a row is good news for the Skolts, because it increases the salmon's resilience to climate change. The first-time spawners mix with the kelts every year, guaranteeing that even if the spawning fails one year, there will be salmon coming back in the future. But as uncertainty about the river conditions increases from year to year, the Skolts feel that their salmon need all the help they can get if they are to remain their cultural touchstone and a source of their sustenance.

Determined to do everything possible to improve the survival of the Näätämö salmon, the Skolts launched the Skolt Sámi Survival in the Middle of Rapid Change project in partnership with the Snowchange Cooperative, as part of the international Indigenous Peoples' Biocultural Climate Change Assessment Initiative, or IPCCA, a global network of Indigenous communities from India, Thailand, the Philippines, Panama, and Finland working on developing culturally appropriate strategies to cope with climate change. The project's goal is to help the Skolts develop a climate change adaptation plan focused on sustaining the Skolts' traditional Atlantic salmon fishery along the Näätämö River. There is little the Skolts can do about the Norwegian Sydvaranger mine—an open-pit iron-ore mine that pollutes the fjord connected to the estuary of Näätämö River. Neither can they prevent an increase in diseases and genetic contamination because of the farmed Atlantic salmon escaping from fish farms along the Barents Sea coast of Norway. But they are confident they can help salmon on the Finnish side of the border. After monitoring spawning sites and holding several community-based workshops and discussions, the Skolt-Snowchange partnership drafted the Näätämö River Collaborative Management Plan proposing a set of specific recommendations that, the Skolts hope, gives them a better say in how the salmon fishery and the river are managed.

Even small changes made by humans on the Näätämö River, Vladimir explains, can undermine the salmon's ability to adapt to climate change. When something even seemingly as trivial as moving rocks in the stream takes place—like when tourists make a river crossing—it impacts salmon traveling up the river to spawn. However subtle and small the changes may appear to an ignorant eye, Vladimir explains, they have big consequences for the salmon. One of Näätämö's tributaries, the Vainosjoki River, for example, can no longer support salmon runs because it was largely destroyed in the 1960s, when the government dredged the central channel to create a river route for small boats. Today, long braids of algae cover the rocks of the Vainosjoki stream, a sure sign of a nutrient imbalance in the water from increased erosion and eutrophication. Warming water temperatures make it easier for the algae to thrive, competing with the river's fish for oxygen and light. Part of the collaborative plan is to restore the Vainosjoki River, to see salmon return.

The project partners feel that the existing state salmon fisheries management arrangement—based on transboundary bilateral agreements between the governments of Finland and Norway that date back to 1873—is too top-down and rigid. They hope that the Skolt collaborative plan will help create a space for equitable participation of all the groups who want their own relationship with the Näätämö River and the salmon to be healthy for generations. This includes restoring traditional salmon-spawning grounds and reducing populations of predatory species, like pike and burbot, that pray on juvenile salmon. Skolts set nets under the ice to catch these predators.

THE COLOR OF
NORTHERN LIGHTS

I sail through the frosty crisp air in a steep arc. One moment, as if riding a bucking bronco, I am holding on for dear life to the sliver of a seat behind Teijo Feodoroff, who is weaving his snowmobile through the willow shrubs along a tussocky winter trail. The next instance—as Teijo swerves the machine sharply down a short precipitous bank toward a frozen lake—my rear end parts with the seat. After a brief and ungraceful pirouette, I land spread-eagle in a snowbank flanking the trail.

I am back in Sevettijärvi, toward the end of the Lapland winter, to witness the Näätämö salmon collaborative project in action and watch the Skolts setting nets under the ice to catch pike and burbot. This time I am staying at the Peuralammen Camp—a set of cozy brick-colored cabins that Teijo and his partner have been running on the outskirts of Sevettijärvi. Teijo's English is only a few words, better than my nonexisting Finnish, but we manage quite well, mostly with grunts and hand gestures. I actually enjoy the succinct nature of our laconic communication—it means I have fewer distractions from observing Teijo's work.

As we reach a straight section of the snowmobile trail, Teijo hits the full throttle, and I must duck behind his helmet from the biting wind. Over his shoulder, I glance the vibrating speedometer needle hovering around the fifty-mile mark. A bit too fast for my liking, especially since I still have nothing to hold on to. It is hard to imagine that half a century ago, the only way to get around this winter land was on skis and reindeer sleds. Though not as dramatic as the post-World War II relocation to Finland, the "snowmobile revolution" was another social transformation that played havoc with the Skolts.

According to Dr. Pertti J. Pelto, an anthropologist who worked with the Skolts in the 1960s, the first snowmobile, a Bombardier Ski-Doo from Canada, was purchased by a schoolteacher from Partake, a cluster of log houses near Sevettijärvi, in 1961. His sole intention was to use the machine to haul wood and supplies. A few years later, the full-scale snowmobile revolution, in the words of Dr. Pelto, was under way.

Before the snowmobiles arrived, the Skolts would spend most of the year with their reindeer. Each family relied on the animals to haul water from nearby streams, fish and meat from distant lakes and herding areas, firewood and building supplies from the forest. In the winter, the herders would make frequent trips from their village to the herds, chasing away predators and getting fresh meat. Most families made a couple of long annual trips to Norwegian trading posts to fetch supplies. Each trip usually required four sleds pulled by four draft reindeer, with a couple more animals following each sled as a backup. Such traditional herding practices meant that animals and herders were in constant contact, which made reindeer more tame and easier to manage. The Skolts' transportation system was more reliable and ecologically friendly than even that of other Arctic Indigenous groups, such as dog teams of the Inuit, who had to hunt and fish to feed their draft animals. Reindeer sleds provided a self-sufficient system that was independent of outside sources of energy—whether meat, fish, or fuel—because they could find food pretty much anywhere. But the arrival of snowmobiles changed this system and lifestyle forever.

Soon after the first snowmobile was brought to Sevettijärvi, Skolts began to buy the machines for reindeer herding. A trip to fetch supplies on the Norwegian side of the border that in the past lasted three days by reindeer now took only five hours by snowmobile. The winter of 1962 was the first time the Skolt reindeer heard the din of a snow machine engine. In just five years, all the reindeer work was done on snowmobiles. As new, safer, and faster snowmobile models—more suited for driving on rough terrain—proliferated, the change became irreversible. The few herders who tried to keep their draft reindeer felt that because of their slow pace they were falling behind the others in the herding business. The last reindeer race in Sevettijärvi was held in 1967. By 1971, a mere ten years after the first snowmobile was introduced, each of the seventy-two households in the village had at least one snow machine.

Everything, however, comes at a price. The snowmobile revolution pushed the Skolts into a regime of cash dependency, debt, and unemployment, disrupting their traditional egalitarian society. To purchase a snowmobile, gasoline, spare parts, and repairs, Skolts needed a significant amount of cash—a new machine would set them back US $1,000, with gas and repairs adding up to another $400 per year. Yet these expenses were now considered a household necessity, as herding reindeer with snowmobiles became an accepted sign of progress.

More troubling was the rapid deterioration of the intimate relationship between the Skolts and their reindeer, because the racket and stench of the machinery drove reindeer away. The animals were no longer led on foot or skis into the roundup area, but, to save time and money, were pushed as quickly as possible toward the corral with the machines. These intensive roundups had such a negative impact on the health of the animals that their average weight dropped compared to the presnowmobile days. As a result, herders had to sell more animals in order to earn enough cash to cover the cost of snowmobiles and their maintenance.

Moreover, stressed-out and frightened by the noise and chase, reindeer cows had fewer calves. Reindeer learned to avoid snowmobiles at all costs and to hide in the most inaccessible parts of the forest. The average number of reindeer in Sevettijärvi dropped from fifty-two to about twelve per household in 1971, a mere decade after snowmobile introduction. Almost two-thirds of the Skolt households abandoned reindeer herding and became unemployed, because it was hard to find any paid work.

These changes led to a rapid shift toward a more settled way of life. Many skills that were important for maintaining the Skolt herders' status and prestige—managing draft reindeer, training herding dogs, the physical stamina required for keeping up with the herd on skis over a long distance, survival skills in the forest and tundra—were all replaced with new qualities related to mechanical proficiency and fiscal savvy. Still, despite all these challenges accompanied by the dramatic and rapid societal shifts, reindeer herding has remained at the heart of the Skolt Sámi culture and way of life.

We cruise along the frozen lakes and streams, threading our way through the northern boreal landscape that the mid-March sun is slowly pulling up from under the thick blanket of winter snow. We cross trails cut through the deep snow by reindeer, and a couple of wolverine tracks. Just as I start to loose the feeling in my frozen toes, Jouko guides his skidoo off the main trail in a large loop and stops in the middle of what looks like an expansive frozen lake. Teijo pulls up next to him. I jump off my perch and trudge around the snow machines, stomping my feet, trying to warm up. Teijo pulls out a pouch of tobacco and hand-rolls a couple of cigarettes for himself and Jouko. They lean against the snowmobiles and talk in Skolt. By the way they gesticulate, I know that they are discussing how to proceed with the task at hand—setting up a fishing net under the ice.

Puffs of crystalline breath mix with the pearly smoke wafting from his cigarette as Jouko unfastens ice-fishing gear from his sled. From the images I saw a couple of days ago at SIIDA—the national museum of the Finnish Sámi, in Inari, a seat of Finnish Sámi Parliament, just a ninety-minute drive from Sevettijärvi—I recognize one of the tools as a traditional Sámi *tuura*, or an ice spud. A three-foot-long wooden shaft with a heavy iron spearhead, this giant icepick is used to chisel out an opening in the thick ice. Jouko unties an ice saw for cutting out big chunks of ice by hand. The large spiral of a hand auger that Teijo sticks into the snow takes me back to my childhood ice fishing days and the smell of fresh cucumbers at the end of a long winter.

Back in Tilichiki, in early spring, I would drag my aluminum sled, stacked with a couple of ice rods, an auger, and a cloth rucksack, onto the ice of Hidden Lagoon near the village. After drilling a couple of holes, I would sit on the sled and jig for smelt—a delicious slender silver fish we called *ogurechnik*—from *oguretz*, Russian for "cucumber"—that schooled above the seagrass under the ice. I always hoped for a good catch but never did manage to snag anything close to the mounds of frozen fish piled up next to the more seasoned fishermen. Once in a while, though, I would get lucky and, returning home after a long day out on the ice, I would proudly declare that we were having *ogurechnik* for dinner. And what a joy it was to have my mother happily fuss over me—the family provider, she would call me with a proud smile. As a dozen or so little fish thawed out in the sink, our tiny kitchen would be awash in the aroma of fresh cucumbers, which is forever etched into my mind as the smell of departing winter.

Several smoke breaks later, Jouko and Teijo cut two large holes in the ice to set a stretched fishing net under it. They cover the openings with a piece of cardboard and snow to keep it from freezing overnight, and mark the spot with a couple of willow twigs so they will be able to find it after a snowfall. Over the next few days, they will return to the nets to pull out several large pikes and burbots—salmon predators that the Skolts are after, as part of implementing the collaborative plan, to give salmon young a fighting chance of surviving,

The sun is already dipping below the horizon when we head back to the cabins. Our ride through the dusk seems a lot faster than our ride out to the fishing spot, but it is probably because I am just too numb from all the bouncing and the cold to be able to accurately judge the passage of time. When we get back to the Peuralammen Camp, I rush to the sauna to thaw out my frozen limbs, appreciating the lure of the scalding heat a bit more. The giant curtains of stellar light rippling in the sky beneath the stars halt me in my tracks when, nice and warm, I head back to the cabin. The northern lights are green, but the flashes of red along the edges of the aurora borealis give me pause. According to the Skolts' traditional beliefs, northern lights are the souls of the people who died a violent death and are now in the land of the dead. If the Skolts' relationship with the land and other people is balanced, these souls are peaceful, and the northern lights are green and blue. When this relationship is in trouble—the northern lights turn red, warning the Skolts of the imbalance.

The color of the aurora overhead seems like an apt reflection of the difficulties that the Skolts are facing as they try to convince the Finnish authorities to officially acknowledge the value of recommendations in the Näätämö River Collaborative Management Plan. Even when there is some action on the plan's recommendations by the government, like reducing pressure on salmon from non-Skolt fishermen, it is done without recognizing the contributions made by the Skolts toward salmon management. This is nothing new to the project's participants, who see this attitude as a manifestation of the government's ongoing disregard of Skolts' traditions, rights, and, more fundamentally, their humanity.

THE MAGIC

A ll my life, I've been taught to think of myself and my people as damaged," says Pauliina Feodoroff, Vladimir's daughter and the Skolt salmon collaborative plan coordinator. She leans forward from the wooden bench toward the stone fireplace in the corner of a log cabin and puts a split birch log on top of the glowing coals. Strips of paper bark shrivel up, crackle, and burst into flames, setting her tired face aglow. As I listen to Pauliina, I can't help but feel that the source of her glow is not the dancing flames of the burning logs but the fire within. Her story, like the one of her people, is a tale of resilience against formidable odds.

In the late 1970s, Pauliina's mother, a Finn from central Finland, got a job as a nurse up north, where she met Vladimir. Tragically, both of them carried a recessive gene for a very rare genetic disease, nonketotic hypoglycemia, which leaves children of the carriers severely handicapped.

The three children they had before Pauliina died when they were very young. Pauliina's brother, born a few years after her, was very ill and died when he was seven. Growing up surrounded by death, Pauliina was convinced that she was, in her own words, "deeply damaged and should never pass her own genes on to future generations." But when, a couple of years ago, she became very ill, Pauliina had to undergo a series of very rigorous tests to help determine the cause, including a genetic screening test.

"My doctor told me that I did not carry the gene for hypoglycemia, and my genes were healthy and strong," says Pauliina, still with a chuckle of surprised amazement. "All my life I believed what I was told by the officials. Doctors told me that I was a damaged person. My government told me that my people's culture and language were dying. I felt like I've had 'extinction' tattooed on my forehead. Yet, I'm still alive and well, and so are my people. In spite of everything."

Two narratives about Pauliina's people, perpetuated by the government, shaped her childhood. The first one was a story of the Indigenous peoples, like the Skolts, being less intelligent than non-Indigenous persons. "We were told that we were genetically weaker and had less nerve cells in our brains than the Finns," Pauliina recalls with a frown. The second storyline was that because of where the Skolt Sámi were on the cultural evolutionary ladder, they were simply doomed to extinction and their days were numbered. "As children, we were taught to count our 'blood percentage' to show that we had as little 'native' blood in us as possible," recalls Pauliina. "Pity those poor bastards who are one percent Sámi! Who is half Sámi? Who is a quarter?" she jeers mockingly.

As a Skolt, Pauliina explains, her father's time in the residential school was filled with psychological and physical abuse. Because of the way the Skolts and other Sámi were treated in Finland, he felt that it was better for him to drop out of reindeer herding and for his children not to speak their native language. After getting some vocational training, he got a job with a national telecommunication company that was laying the first optical cable in Finland. He managed to continue salmon fishing at his cabin on the Näätämö River. When he was sacked in his early fifties, he decided to return to reindeer herding. Pauliina had just turned eighteen then and had begun studying theater in Helsinki, quite far away from her father's return journey to his people's traditions. Yet, when she learned about it, she pursued every opportunity to follow him on the land.

"I'd hear about a reindeer roundup, and fly home," she recalls. "He'd get very angry with me, telling me to go back to school. He didn't want me there, but I blamed him for keeping me away from my language, my people, and my community. It was a very difficult period for us—full of conflict. It's taken a long time to heal. Still, I don't blame him now for what he did." Pauliina sighs. "Everybody wants the best for their children. Nobody wants them to suffer."

While taking breaks from her college studies to spend time on the land with her father, Pauliina worked hard to learn more about her culture and her people's plight. In recognition of this, her community put her name forward to represent them on the new government committee set up to resolve Sámi land- and water-rights issues. This was the beginning of her life in Sámi politics. Later, she became a member of the International Sámi Council and, soon thereafter, she was elected to be the president of the council, where she worked for four years to protect Sámi old-growth boreal forests from logging and mining.

"In 2008, when my wife and I had the first of our two daughters," recalls Pauliina, "I was told in no uncertain terms by the Sámi politicians that, since I am a lesbian, it would be best for me to disappear from the Sámi political scene." So she resigned from the council and moved back to Helsinki with her wife, to run a theater company, while working on different projects in her community through a local nonprofit, Sámi Nue'tt, she'd cofounded with several friends. She has continued to work on the climate change adaptation project with Snowchange and a Skolt language nest in Sevettijärvi.

"I've had a passive understanding of the Skolt Sámi language, since I've heard it all my life," explains Pauliina. "But I never got to practice it, because my father would not speak it to us. For the last few years now, I've been learning how to read and write in Skolt. Obviously it's not my strongest language—in addition to Finnish, I am also fluent in Swedish, English, and North Sámi—but at the same time it's not my weakest language either. My two little girls are learning Skolt too, as our cultural roots grow deeper." Pauliina's daughters are five and three, and already they speak Finnish, Swedish, and Skolt. It doesn't faze them that their grandfather herds reindeer and their mother sings traditional Skolt songs and directs a Finnish theater company. Whether they are at a Skolt fishing camp or their Helsinki apartment—they feel they belong everywhere. Pauliina wants them to keep their connection with the Skolt territory strong, as the land changes.

The interdependencies of the sun, water, air, forest, fire, wildlife, fish, and people that have emerged and coevolved since the glaciers retreated northward in this part of Europe more than nine thousand years ago are changing rapidly. As the climate shifts, the weather pendulum starts to swing erratically, making it hard for the Skolts to rely on traditional weather- and season-forecasting signs. In the old days, the transition from season to season was gradual and predictable. Ant behavior was one of the Skolts' traditional ways of forecasting the weather. If there were no ants on the surface of an anthill, they expected rain in the next two to three hours. If the weather was foul, but the ants were coming up to the surface, then the sun would be out in a few hours. The herders used clouds to predict changes in wind, and animal behavior and the appearance of the moon and stars to foresee rain and snow conditions. The northern lights were also used to predict the arrival of snowstorms, while the alignment of certain stars was used to decide on berry picking and other land-based activities. If the northern lights were low in the sky, a snowstorm was coming; if they were high, it was going to get very cold.

Today, these indicators are not as reliable as they used to be. The weather has become a hodgepodge of things, making it much harder to predict. To anticipate weather today, Skolt Sámi rely on a mixture of modern tools and traditional knowledge. Weather reports on the local radio are as closely tracked as the behavior of birds, animals, and even dogs.

"The thing with climate change," says Tero, "is that you might have one weather pattern here in the foothills, but it would be completely different in the valley. It could be hailing in one place, dumping snow in another, and the trees could be budding somewhere else."

The future of the Skolts and their land during this time of climatic upheaval depends on their ability to find ways of maintaining the balance in their relationships with the land and water, forest and tundra, reindeer and salmon. Skolts feel that this could be achieved only through respectful collaboration with others who have a stake in the future of the region and its biocultural systems, be they government officials, Norwegian fishermen, or a Finnish nongovernment organization (NGO). "It is the time to say goodbye to some things we'll never see again," says Tero. "But it is also time to build new knowledge. And this knowledge could only emerge through keeping strong connections with the traditional territory."

"Nobody chooses where they are born," Pauliina continues. "I was born to be part of a people who just happened to be living on the land that had resources somebody else wanted. When the mining boom came to the Skolts' lands, the smelters literally melted the land with acid rain. There were also nuclear tests on the Soviet Kola Peninsula, with the radioactive fallout drifting in our direction. It damaged not just the land and the forest but also my people, because for us, everything is connected and everybody is related.

"This realization almost crushes you mentally." Pauliina pauses, gathering her thoughts. "But there is also a glimmer of hope—if the land can heal, even if it takes a long time, it means that we can also heal together with the land. When I am on the land, I get the knowledge from it directly through my body. Nobody holds power over me when I am here. Nobody says that their knowledge is superior to mine and if I don't do exactly what I'm being told, bad things would happen to me. There is no need to desire more of something, to want some magic from somewhere else. The magic is already here, all around us. If we stay with the land and take care of it, it will give us everything we need."

CHAPTER THREE

THE EDGE
OF THE WORLD

A thousand miles east of the Skolt Sámi territory lies the "Edge of the World," or Yamal, in the language of local Indigenous reindeer herders, the Nenets. Just like the Skolts, they are facing climate change, as well as the reality of, in Pauliina Feodoroff's words, "living on the land that had resources somebody else want[s]." Over the last two decades, the Yamal has become a hotspot of natural gas and oil development in the Russian Arctic. As I find out during my visits to Yamal, the Nenets have a pragmatic long-term view of their own predicament. They are certain that, if given a chance to continue their timeless migration, they will outlast any oil and gas boom on their territory and find ways to adapt to climate change.

TUNDRA SEA

B uoyed by roaring rotors, the large aluminum gondola of our Mi-8 helicopter surges and plunges on the thermals above the emerald swells of the Arctic tundra rolling toward the horizon. Patches of snow on the eastward-facing riverbanks, and occasional white specks of swans on muddy lakes, are like whitecaps on the choppy water below. The coffee-colored lakes drift beneath us like lion's mane jellyfish—rimmed with coronas of rivulets and streams draining into them. Conical shapes surface on a distant rise, like navigation buoys on an ocean wave, guiding us toward a sheltered harbor in the ever-changing tundra sea. Our destination is a *stoybishe*—a summer encampment of reindeer herders. The helicopter blades whip up a sandstorm as we land at the edge of the encampment a few minutes later. When the dust settles, a group of herders, their wives, and kids of all ages emerges from the conical *chums*, or tepee-like tents, and stroll up to greet us. We have arrived at the Edge of the World.

The Yamal Peninsula is an ancient glacial outwash, a slab of frozen alluvial sands peeled off from the Siberian mainland by the mighty Ob River that brings snowmelt and rainwater from the Altai Mountains on Russia's southern border with China, Mongolia, and Kazakhstan, and carries it for more than 2,000 miles north to the Arctic Ocean. The 400-mile-long and 150-mile-wide thumb-shaped peninsula is bound by the shallow waters of the Gulf of Ob to the east, the Baydaratskaya Bay to the west, and the vast Arctic Ocean to the north. This rugged terrain, located two times zones, or approximately 1,200 miles, northeast from Moscow, remains snowbound for two-thirds of the year, with three of those nine months ruled by blowing blizzards. It is a fragile environment where, if damaged, the land takes decades or even centuries to recover, and the loss of a single species upsets the ebb and flow of the entire ecosystem.

I first came to Yamal in the winter of 2014, on assignment for *National Geographic* magazine, to help research an article about the rush for oil and gas development in the Arctic, including the Bovanenkovo gas field, the largest deposit of natural gas in Yamal. I arrived in the dead of winter, on Christmas Eve, and, after a few days in Moscow meeting several environmental and oil and gas industry experts, I flew to Salekhard, Yamal's regional center. Through the airplane window, I peered into the dark void. It felt like we were voyaging "where no man has gone before," among the flickering clusters of stars, reflected in rare constellations of urban lights below. But not a single electric light flickered in the all-enveloping

Arctic darkness, as, the following day, I looked out the window of a train chugging north along Yamal's 350-mile-long railroad, the northernmost railway in the world. Only the green ribbons of the aurora borealis shimmered above, illuminating the snowbound landscape, when we crossed the longest railroad bridge in the Arctic over the frozen Yuribei River. Once, I glimpsed a distant conical shape of a *chum*, in the twilight of the Arctic winter afternoon. Though a mere gray shadow in the deep blue dusk, the sight was comforting and reassuring—human beings managed to make a home in this vast, seemingly barren Arctic wilderness, way before the age of electricity.

REAL PEOPLE

Of the 16,400 people living in Yamal, more than 11,500, or 70 percent, belong to the Numerically Small Peoples of the North, the official Russian designation for Indigenous Peoples of the Russian North and Far East that number fewer than 50,000. The Nenets reindeer herders, who have lived in Yamal since time immemorial, make up the majority of the Indigenous population. Russian traders arrived here at the end of the 16th century, on the heels of Yermak—who led a band of Cossacks into the region to begin the conquest of Siberia for the Russian tsar Ivan the Terrible. The Russian name for the Nenets was *Samoyed*, or self-eaters—a "strange" northern tribe who, according to the Russian chronicles of that period, drank human blood, had mouths between their shoulders, and perished every winter. The name, however, most likely has a more prosaic origin. In the language of their western neighbors, the Sámi, *Saam-Edne* means the Land of the People. Though their own name, the Nenets, or Real People, was officially returned to them by the Soviet State after Russia's Great October Revolution of 1917, it came at a price—the tribal leaders, shamans, and their land rights were taken away by the Soviet state, because shamans and tribal leaders were considered a threat to the new regime.

According to Dr. Bruce Forbes, a professor of geography at the University of Lapland's Arctic Center, who has spent more than two decades working with the Yamal Nenets, the Nenets are one of the most resilient Indigenous groups in the Russian Arctic and Circumpolar North. Originally hunters and fishermen who kept just enough tame reindeer for transportation and as decoys for hunting wild reindeer, the Nenets switched to large-scale reindeer herding relatively recently, three to four centuries ago, when several ecological and sociopolitical factors converged. As the Russian Empire expanded into northern Siberia from the late 1500s, the Nenets began spending more and more time away from the mainland on the remote Yamal Peninsula. During the same period, reindeer numbers began to grow, following a number of cool-weather periods that favored reindeer fertility.

Having large reindeer herds guaranteed the Nenets access to a reliable supply of food, clothing, shelter, and transportation, which allowed them to remain on the Yamal Peninsula longer, largely autonomous from the Russian government and Orthodox Church. In the winter, the tundra Nenets would return south, to the forest edge, to get wood for building their *chums* and sleds, and bring their herds to the winter pastures rich in *yagel*—reindeer moss, an important winter food of reindeer. As a result, Nenets remained relatively free of the Russian yoke, almost until the Soviet period. The Nenets have managed to sustain their language, worldview, customs, and governance, as well as their land-use traditions of herding, hunting, and fishing. And the eight-hundred-mile perennial journey of the northern nomads has continued to be one of the longest annual migrations on earth.

According to Forbes, several factors have contributed to the Nenets' resilience—the vast landscape has enabled their long-distance migration; an abundance of fish and game has complemented their reindeer diet; they have found ways to conform to the Soviet production-driven management system without compromising their own cultural and subsistence needs; and, after the collapse of the Soviet state, they managed to shift to smaller, family-owned herds that are better suited to changing land use and climate shifts. As new pressures escalate and converge, however, the future of the Nenets at the Edge of the World looks increasingly precarious.

Over the last two decades, industrial development and climate change have been testing the Nenets' resilience. Russia's quest for new sources of hydrocarbons, to replace declining production in aging oil and gas fields in southern Western Siberia, has reduced the total area of reindeer pastures in Yamal and restricted the movement of the reindeer herds on the peninsula, leading to overgrazing in some areas. Climate change—with increasing permafrost thaw, shifting seasons, unpredictable warm spells in the winter—has further challenged the Nenets' ability to sustain their way of life.

RAIN-ON-SNOW

Inside his spacious *chum*, Yura Khudi—clad in a camouflage hoodie, with the unzipped mosquito netting covering his chest like a large bib—squats on a stumpy stool made of several tattered flats of pink and blue Styrofoam, laced together with a string. His wife, Katya, wearing a flowery cotton dress, hangs a freshly filled sooty kettle over the fire in the middle of the *chum* and, with a dried-up goose wing, sweeps the crumbs off the low-set plywood table. Yura's eighty-year old mother, Nina, reclines on the rolled-up blanket at the opposite side of the tent. With her knobby fingers, she is rummaging in her sewing kit, sorting through spools of thread. Her six-year-old grandson, Alik, is playing on the reindeer skins in front of her.

Yura was born in a spring blizzard, on an island in the middle of the Yuribei River, as his father's herd milled around the *chum*. That was more than thirty years ago. Today, he is the *brigadier*, or the leader of the brigade of reindeer herders. The military-sounding rank is a relic of the Soviet system of *sovkhoz*—state-run collectives that used to provide employment to reindeer herders, hunters, fishermen, and their spouses. I am visiting Brigade #4, one of eighteen groups making up the Yarsalinski *sovkhoz* that survived the collapse of the Soviet Union by transforming into a municipal enterprise. On average, a brigade employs eight herders who look after the reindeer. Each of the brigade's eight *chums* houses one or two families and has an assigned *chumrabotnitza*—literally a woman working in the *chum*—responsible for the upkeep of the dwelling, looking after the herder's clothes, and cooking. The three municipal herding enterprises—Yarsalinski and Panayevskoye in in the south, and Yamalski in the north—account for less than a fifth of the four hundred thousand Yamal reindeer. Most of the animals are privately owned by close to a thousand nomadic Nenets families living on the peninsula. Still, the municipal enterprises are the only land users in Yamal recognized by the government, representing the herders' interests in addressing many challenges they face along their migration routes, including massive industrial development projects, such as the Bovanenkovo gas field.

"It's about fifteen miles from here to Bovany," Yura says, spooning some loose tea and sugar into his enamel mug. "Bovany" is short for Bovanenkovo, which sits directly on their *nederma*, or migration route. "It'll take us three to five days to move the herd—we say *kaslat'*—to get there. A few days past Bovany are our summer pastures by the Kara Sea. We're going to make it all the way to the coast for the first time in over two years," Yura says, holding out his mug for Katya to fill it up with boiling water from the gurgling kettle. "Our herd's only beginning to recover from the big die-off two years ago, when the pastures got covered with ice. The surviving reindeer were just too weak to travel far, the spring breakup came too early, and we got stuck crossing the river. The Brigade Number Eight usually migrates just to the west of us, and they had similar problems. We knew that we wouldn't be able to make it to the summer pastures on the coast and get back for the winter, so we decided to stay further south."

Climate change in the Russian Arctic is more palpable than in many other regions of the world. While the average global temperature has gone up by 1.4 degrees Fahrenheit during the last one hundred years, in the Siberian Arctic it has increased twice as much. In November 2013, a sudden unseasonably warm spell brought rain to southern Yamal. A deep freeze followed, encasing most of the winter pastures in an ice carapace, impenetrable to the hooves of reindeer trying to dig up the life-giving lichen. This "rain-on-snow" extreme weather event—or *salaba' ya* in Nenets—covered a vast area of Yamal lichen pastures, making it impossible for most herders to move their animals to unaffected pastures. As climate warms, such events are becoming more frequent. More than forty thousand reindeer died during that season throughout Yamal. A number of Nenets families with small private herds lost most of their animals and had to switch to fishing while rebuilding their herds.

"With no food, reindeer can last a couple of weeks or so," explains Yura, blowing on his steaming tea and taking a cautious sip. "But they weaken quickly and cannot pull the sleds. Soon enough they just lie down and don't get up." The following year, explains Yura, another early spring breakup prevented their herd from advancing north far enough to make it to the coast. But he assures me that nothing is going to stop them from reaching the summer pastures this year.

The *chum*'s canvas flap entrance is shoved in, as a reindeer pushes inside with its velvet antlers lowered to the ground. It pauses in front of the fire, shakes vigorously, and flops down to meditatively chew its cud.

"This young cow lost its mom in the freeze-up," says Yura, putting his mug down on the table covered with a checkered plastic tablecloth that has seen better days. "We raised her ourselves, inside the *chum*, and she now hides here from mosquitoes." He grins. "Hopefully next year she'll have a calf of her own to help rebuild the herd. We are down to about three thousand reindeer now, half of our herd's normal size, a mix of private reindeer and those owned by the enterprise." Yura grabs a biscuit from a plastic bag on the table, dips it into the hot tea, and, smacking his lips, savors the sweet mush.

"It's not easy for us to rebuild the herd," he continues with a sigh. "The main Yarsalinski enterprise needs to sell reindeer meat every fall if it doesn't want to go bankrupt. We get about eight thousand rubles [US $140] for a large bull, weighing about one hundred and twenty pounds, and less for a cow, because it is three times lighter. We did try to hold some animals back, but our director told us off. Instead of skipping that year's annual cull to let the herd increase quicker, he told us to kill three hundred animals for meat, because we needed money. Obviously, this way it'll take us several years longer to build up the herd to its normal size."

Yura's black-and-white reindeer-herding dog—a shaggy miniature ancestor of the Samoyed breed—is panting on the floor next to the reindeer. Suddenly, it perks up its ears and, coiled tail wagging and tongue lolling, rushes outside the *chum*, toward the approaching low rumble of voices.

"We must get ready to *kaslat'*," says Yura, getting up. "You'll ride with my older brother, Nyadma," he adds before exiting the tent. "He was the brigadier before retiring last year, but he still leads us when we move the camp, so you'll have the front-seat view." He gives me a thumbs-up and, following the dog, steps out of the *chum*. His son, Alik, follows him.

TIME TO *KASLAT'*

Outside, I am swept up into a well-choreographed "circle dance" of herders, their wives, and kids breaking the camp. The canvas tent covers are untied and pulled down from all eight *chums*, the skeletons of the tent poles are dismembered and, together with tent covers, loaded up on *vandako*, large freight sledges. The bedding, provisions, and cooking utensils are also packed up, wrapped in waterproof canvas, and lashed with ropes to regular sleds. To move their camp, each *chum* needs between two to four *argish*—a caravan of six to eight sleds tied one after another and pulled by draft reindeer bulls, up to one hundred animals total.

As soon as the *chums* are down, the herders, their sons in tow, head away from the campsite—coiled *arkans*, or lassos, in their throwing hands or slung over their shoulders. Some *arkans* are in the traditional style, made of braided strips of tanned reindeer skin. Others are modern—plastic ropes coated with yellow or blue plastic for water resistance, brought home from exchange visits with the Finnish Sámi. Alik and the other boys stumble over tussocky tundra as they trail Yura toward a thicket of antlers emerging from behind clumps of dwarf willows. This is a small herd of draft reindeer bulls, around two hundred to three hundred animals strong, which are used to pull the sleds from one campsite to the next.

Some herders form a sparsely spaced line and begin pushing the animals from the rear toward a funnel of old fishnets, stretched between several sleds arranged in a makeshift corral. Other men and boys—swinging their *arkans*, whistling, and barking commands to their dogs—flank the herd as it slowly advances toward the enclosure. Groups of bulls try to break out and sprint back between the herders. Some succeed, but most are turned back, and a few are lassoed by their horns, bodies, or legs. The dogs dart to and fro, barking and snapping at the escaped reindeer, trying to drive them back toward the herd. The captured animals are quickly led away from the corral to their owners' sleds, where they are hitched up. In about half an hour, the bulk of the herd is pushed inside the enclosure and their retreat is cut off with a long rope held at waist level by women clad in traditional *yagushkas*, or reindeer-skin coats. The herders step inside the corral and wade through the churning herd—a chest-deep vortex of fur and antlers parting in front and closing behind them.

To a herder, each reindeer is a distinct blend of colored muzzle, unique splatter of spots, and behavioral quirks that make it stand out in the herd. The herders spot their bulls with no trouble, confidently grabbing them by the horns. To make sure that the other herders do not claim his animals, during the first year of the animal's life, each herder notches the reindeer's ears with a pattern of permanent nicks particular to his family. The caught animals are lashed up either individually, or in groups, and brought out of the corral, where the herders' children and wives lead the reindeer to the sleds. The entire operation, *erkolava* in Nenets, takes about an hour before all the bulls are harnessed into their owners' sleds and the brigade is ready to *kaslat'*.

Everybody takes a tea break before moving out. The ex-brigadier, Nyadma Khudi—now a mentor to his younger brother, Yura, in the fine art of brigadiership—is sitting on the dry tundra next to his tightly packed *argish*. Pairs of reindeer—some standing, others lying down—are tied to all but the lead sled, which has five bulls strung up to it in a fan hitch, similar to the Inuit dog sleds. Pavlik, Nyadma's five-year-old grandson, clad in a small *malitza*—a male bell-shaped coat of reindeer skins—wanders over from the *argish* of his father, Aleksandr, Nyadma's eldest son. Nyadma's wife, Nina, is splashing some steaming tea from a thermos into Nyadma's chipped enameled mug, when the trio of their grown-up sons—Gosha, Ilia, and Semion—walks up from the corral and drop down next to us for a quick snack of dried bread, lightly salted fresh fish, cookies, and condensed milk.

Born during his family's annual migration to Bovanenkovo, Nyadma grew up in the herd. After years of *Internat*, or residential school, and two years of mandatory service in the Soviet Red Army on the border with China, he returned to his homeland to follow in his father's footsteps. He became a herder, and later a brigadier. All of his sons followed in his footsteps and became herders.

Tea finished, Nyadma gets up and, checking his watch, announces that it is nine in the evening and we need to head out. "You'll ride behind me," he says, pointing to a sled and a pair of bulls tied right after his. He quickly strolls around the entire *argish*, making sure that none of the animals are tangled up. Returning to his sled, he gives the lead bull a poke on the rump with a *tyur*—a long, polished wooden pole, with an antler tip, used to encourage the animals to pull the sled. The reindeer begin to pull and we are on our way.

I walk next to my sled for a few hundred yards, following Nyadma's example, to let the reindeer get into the rhythm, before flopping down on my seat of folded reindeer skins. After two summers of disuse, the old trail is overgrown with willow brush and Nyadma often has to drive the *argish* straight through the willows. "You need to have five or six bulls in the lead," explains Nyadma, turning back toward me in his sled. "They trample the shrubs pulling the sled through the willow thickets, and lay down the *nederma* trail for the rest of the *argish* to follow." We descend into a shallow gulch, skirt the edge of a mossy bog, and head up a gentle incline. As we crest the opposite side of the ravine, I turn around to adjust my rucksack tied to the back of my seat. The brigade's caravan of *argishes*— a jumble of regular and racing sleds, high-boarded children sledges, large cargo sleds, and sledges carrying bundles of sacred objects and effigies of spirit protectors—slowly uncoils from the campsite behind us.

Perched on the left side of his sled, his feet firmly planted on a sled runner, Nyadma keeps prodding the back of the lead bull with his *tyur*. As we advance, Pavlik jumps off and back on the sled next to Nyadma, pointing in different directions and pestering his grandfather with incessant chatter in Nenets. Nyadma doesn't say much, just chuckles and, once in a while, gives his grandson a gentle squeeze.

"Uggh-uggh! Uggh!" he grunts softly, from under his mosquito net, urging the animals to pull the sled through shrubs and clouds of mosquitoes. We maneuver for some time from knoll to knoll among the patches of dwarf willows, across streams and bogs, keeping our course into the sun, toward Bovanenkovo.

After about an hour, at the barren top of another ridge, Nyadma pulls up sharply on the *ngeva'inya*, the single rein tied to the head of the leading bull, making the animal turn and stop. "We'll break here for a bit, to let the rest of the group catch up," he declares, fishing out a ringing cell phone from under his *malitza*.

"*Da?*" he answers in Russian and, recognizing the caller, immediately switches to Nenets. We are now within the range of Bovanenkovo's cell phone towers—one of the few perks the brigade gets from having a megadevelopment project in their backyard. Because of the distance, however, the signal is still weak and the best connection is on the hilltops. Other sleds pull up behind us and the soothing harmony of clicking reindeer hooves is drowned out by the cacophony of dial tones and human chatter.

I step away from our *argish* and go on a short walkabout to stretch my legs. It is past midnight, according to my watch. Ahead, the radiant skyline smelters in the flaming kiln of the setting sun, its copper glow splashing over lakes and waterways stretching before us toward the horizon. A distant hum draws my attention. It sounds like a jet's afterburners revving up before takeoff at a remote airfield. The sound, however, doesn't change in pitch, or volume. It provides the background accompaniment for the rest of our journey, and it is coming from the direction of Bovanenkovo, the epicenter of Yamal's energy boom.

YAMAL OR BUST

Historically, Yamal has played an important role in ensuring Russia's prosperity. First, it was a source of "soft gold," or furs, for the Russian Empire that sought to replenish its coffers when its main currency, sable pelts, was depleted in central Russia. In Yamal, as was common throughout the rest of Arctic Russia, the fur traders were after the Arctic fox, or *nokho* in Nenets. Over the last half century, however, the region has become better known for another highly valued commodity—fossil fuels. Yamal's natural gas is the cornerstone of modern Russia's energy strategy, the implementation of which lies in the hands of Gazprom—a Russian state-owned company. Gazprom dominates Russia's domestic natural gas market and has a virtual monopoly on Russian gas exports via pipelines, supplying a quarter of the European Union's natural gas needs. Gazprom's website puts it simply: "There is no alternative to Yamal!"

"As the Soviet-era gas fields become depleted, Russia's natural gas industry must maintain and exceed its current production volume," said Konstantin Simonov, general director of the National Energy Security Fund, whom I met in Moscow, on my way to Yamal. The peninsula's eleven gas fields are estimated to contain over 965 trillion cubic feet of natural gas—a tenth of the proven global gas reserves. Yamal's annual output may reach 12.7 trillion cubic feet of gas by 2030, a volume equivalent to more than 80 percent of the EU's annual natural gas consumption. Today, the peninsula is swarming with dozens of oil and gas companies besides Gazprom, including Gazprom Neft, Rosneft, Lukoil, and Novatek. East of Yamal, just across the Ob Bay, lies the Gyda

Peninsula, also rich with oil and gas deposits, and the likely focus of the next stage of Gazprom's expansion in the Russian Arctic.

"With an explored and estimated gas reserves of 1730 trillion cubic feet, Bovanenkovo is the largest gas field on the Yamal Peninsula," Gazprom's CEO Alexey Miller—looking as stiff and tense as a uniformed pupil delivering a school project to a stern tutor—reported to Russia's president Vladimir Putin during the nationally televised launch of Bovanenkovo's new processing facility in 2014. To get at Bovanenkovo's natural gas deposits, Gazprom constructed a railroad and a seven-hundred-mile pipeline connecting the gas field to the main natural gas supply grid in southern Russia. In addition, Bovanenkovo has its own international airport, with a 1.6-mile runway large enough for commercial jets bringing thousands of workers from cities across southern Russia, who fly in for a monthlong shift before heading back home for four weeks of rest and recuperation. The infrastructure, covering one hundred square miles, is embedded into an expansive web of paved all-weather roads linking processing facilities, power stations, and buildings housing shift workers. At full production capacity, Bovanenkovo is expected to be a temporary home to several thousands of shift workers and contractors.

"I can just about reach it," says Aleksandr, Nyadma's eldest son, stretching upward and, with the tips of his fingers, touching the gray and smooth underbelly of the giant metal serpent—a gas pipeline—snaking over the tundra and across the path of Brigade #4. Walking next to his sled, Aleksandr guides his *argish* under an elevated section of the gathering pipeline that carries natural gas from a wellhead to a compressor station and then to the processing plant. As the rest of the brigade passes under the pipeline—one of several we are to cross over the next three days—kids jump off their parents' sleds and, by themselves, or with Aleksandr's help, clamber on the back of the metal snake for a "ride" and to check out the view from the top. They wave and shout greetings to their mates and families passing below.

According to the Nenets herders and Gazprom managers, the elevated pipeline is an example of a balanced coexistence between the state's development interests and the Nenets' traditional land uses. When development projects began to appear throughout post–Soviet Russian North in the 1990s, threatening to destroy the local environment and culture, the Nenets reindeer herders, prominent Nenets intellectuals, budding environmental nongovernment organizations, and their international partners, rose against it. Local NGOs, such as Yamal, representing the social and economic interests of the Nenets, organized public hearings to secure Gazprom's commitment to minimize the impacts of its operations on the local landscape and people. An elevated pipeline allowing reindeer herds to pass underneath is one of the technological solutions used by Gazprom to help the reindeer and the Nenets continue moving across Yamal unimpeded. Of greater significance, according to Gazprom, is the fact that just in 2016, the Program of Complex Development of Resource Deposits in Yamal and Adjacent Waters transferred more than US $116 million of Gazprom revenue to the regional budget to build housing and schools, construct reindeer-meat processing and storage facilities, and assist the Nenets with helicopter and railroad transportation. Gazprom's attempts to mitigate some of its social and ecological impacts, however, are proving challenging because of climate change.

THAWING EARTH

O ne cannot argue with the data," said Dr. Alexei Osokin, assistant director of engineering at Gazprom Dobycha Nadym, whom I met during my winter visit to Bovanenkovo. "There is no doubt that the climate is warming." Weather and permafrost data for the last twenty-five years from meteorological stations and gas wells around Yamal reveal a clear warming trend, with an average increase in temperature of 1.3 degrees Fahrenheit between 1976 and 2010. Where Osokin and many of his Russian colleagues diverge from the global scientific consensus, however, is in projecting this trend into the future and attributing blame for the observed changes to human agency. "Yes, the temperatures have increased," Osokin conceded, "but, given the history of the earth's cold and warm periods, we can't really be sure that the warming trend will continue. It's just as plausible that it's a product of natural variability, as it is of human activity, and it's quite likely that another cooling period is just around the corner."

Despite his optimistic outlook on the future climate change in Yamal, however, Osokin acknowledged that the current warming trend makes infrastructure construction and maintenance in Yamal challenging. As permafrost thaws in the summer, Gazprom has to invest in building refrigeration units to keep the ground frozen around the wellheads, pilings, and pipelines. On the other hand, Osokin noted, permafrost also plays a very useful role in Bovanenkovo. Despite the documented warming trend, the average temperature of the deep layers of permafrost in Yamal remains below freezing (around 24.8 degrees Fahrenheit). Osokin assured me that based on their models, even under the most extreme scenarios of temperature increases, the deep layers of permafrost will not melt away. This allows Gazprom to reduce surface pollution around Bovanenkovo by freezing the by-products of its drilling operations deep underground. Drill muds and other liquid waste are injected into underground reservoirs steamed out of the permafrost at depths below two hundred feet. At this depth, the waste will eventually freeze, though it may take several decades, Osokin explained. This approach makes the clean up significantly cheaper for Gazprom than shipping the pollutants south by train. Twenty-eight reservoirs have been built and filled to date. They will ultimately hold a total of twelve million cubic feet, the equivalent of 145 Olympic-size swimming pools, of drilling and production waste, which Bovanenkovo is expected to generate during its life span of approximately thirty years.

Osokin acknowledged, however, that the warming climate might manifest itself in unexpected ways. The summer of 2012, for example, was one of the warmest on record. It brought about three weeks of 90-degree Fahrenheit weather to Bovanenkovo. Almost immediately, there was a spike in the rate of permafrost thaw, and a major sinkhole (120 by 400 feet wide, and 20 feet deep) opened up right next to Bovanenkovo's central power line. At the time, the workers were able to backfill the crater, secure the power line, and freeze the ground by installing additional thermal exchange units. But the likelihood of a repeat event is high.

Of potentially much greater concern, however, are such unnatural natural events like the Yamal crater. In the summer of 2014, a 130-foot-wide and 115-foot-deep pit opened up in the middle of the tundra, nineteen miles southeast of Bovanenkovo. Experts believe that it was created as a result of methane gas exploding from the deep layers of permafrost. As the "permanently" frozen earth thaws out, the methane hydrates locked up deep underground transform from a solid to gaseous state and, increasing in volume nearly 160-fold, blasts through the upper layers of soil in an eruption. The eminent Yamal permafrost expert, Dr. Marina Leibman of the Siberian Branch of the Russian Academy of Sciences, visited the site several times. According to her, similar eruptions may occur in Bovanenkovo, causing considerable damage to the infrastructure, including the underground waste disposal sites. More recently, in the summer of 2016, a video made by a group of Russian researchers puncturing a three-foot-wide "bubble" of tundra and lighting up the escaping methane, went viral on social media. And in the summer of 2017, two more crater eruptions were reported in Yamal, one occurring near a herding camp.

After passing under the pipeline, Nyadma chooses an elevated patch of tundra for our camp—a traditional campsite the herders have used for as long as they can remember. The dry and even ground makes it an ideal place to set up the brigade's *chums*. The spot always has some breeze, which keeps the mosquitoes and black flies at bay. Several nearby lakes are reliable sources of freshwater and fish. The thick willow brush at the bottom of the slope, at the edge of the campsite, is a good source of dry twigs for cooking fires, and provides cover and privacy in this relatively flat terrain, when nature calls. The pipeline we just crossed, however, cuts right through this traditional encampment, shrinking in half the space available for the eight *chums*.

Here, the semicircle of the Nenets' *chums*, surrounded with sleds and reindeer, is a symbol of a cyclical world where people are an integral part of nature, not separate from or positioned above it. Their well-being is a product of the timeless coevolution between the people and their land that provides for current and future generations—wood for the sleds, reindeer skins for the *chums*, fish for the table. The straight lines of the dirt road and the pipeline cutting off the *stoybishe* from the rest of the tundra represent the rival worldview. It sees people in general, and Western civilization in particular, as being beyond the natural laws governing life, entitled to take from nature anything it craves, like natural gas. The future of the Nenets depends on which of these worldviews prevails in Yamal.

———

ARCTIC HEAT

In the Land of the Midnight Sun, above the Arctic Circle, summer nights don't come for weeks. Every twenty-four hours, the solar pendulum swings toward the amber horizon, without dipping below.

Sunset! Without a pause, the sun's flaming orb swings back up, toward the zenith. The light quality changes, and the sky turns the color of silky salmonberries. Dawn!

After a week with the herders, I have grown used to their daily routine. Having to move the camp with the herd through a long evening and part of the night, the Nenets go to sleep only around three or four in the morning. Waking up around noon, everyone gets on with their daily chores. Kids fetch water from the lake or collect dry twigs from the nearby willow thickets for the *chum*'s fires. *Chumrabotnizas* walk to the lake to wash clothes and prepare food upon return. Some herders hike to the nearby streams to check the fishnets they set the night before and bring the catch back to the camp to share with everybody. Others hike to the herd to keep an eye on the reindeer and, if they need to catch bulls for the sleds, move the animals toward the camp. If this is the day to *kaslat'*, the real work of breaking the camp begins in the evening so that we are ready to travel when it cools off a little, around 9:00 to 10:00 P.M.

This has been yet another scorching summer in Yamal, the second in the last four years, with the thermometer hitting 94 degrees Fahrenheit near Salekhard. Before the summer is out, a boy and more than 2,300 reindeer in southern Yamal will have died from an outbreak of anthrax—a direct result of thawing permafrost, according to experts, which allowed animal carcasses buried during a previous outbreak in the 1940s to reemerge, still bearing infectious microbes.

It is hard to find shade in the tundra when there are no clouds to provide relief from the constant sun. The hot weather has taxed both the animals and the herders. It is hard for reindeer to pull the sleds over dry grass and moss. The animals have not completely shed their winter coats either, and tire easily in the heat. Even with my experience of working in the tropics, I still find it too hot to sleep inside the *chum*. But Nyadma is visibly much more uncomfortable with the summer heat, or *epdia* in Nenets, and laments the lack of rain. The herders say that the only escape from the heat is on the coastal tundra, and they are eager to get there soon.

Just as for the Skolt Sámi, sorting out whether warmer and drier weather is good or bad for the Nenets is not clear-cut. Mosquitoes, for example, are not as abundant when it is hot and dry, which, I can vouch, definitely makes camp life more comfortable. But because there are no swarms of mosquitoes harassing the reindeer, the animals do not bunch up into large groups—their typical mosquito-avoidance strategy. Instead, they disperse over a wide area, making it hard for the Nenets to bring the herd together again. There is a silver lining to it all, as well, according to Yura, who is walking up to his *chum* after a swim in a nearby lake, where he went with two of his kids, Alla and Alik, to do his laundry.

"The water's nice and warm." He grins, walking slowly and enjoying the crunchy softness of the tundra under his bare feet. "Normally it's too cold to swim in these lakes. You'd only get in and out, and that's it. But the air's so warm now that we splashed around for almost an hour and didn't even shiver." His kids are trailing behind him, drying their wet hair with the same towel and dragging a sack of washed clothes. They are all smiles—it is a blast to be back home.

Every year, Alla returns home for the summer after spending three-quarters of the year at *Internat*—Russian for residential school—hundreds of miles from her parents. Yura and Katya get to see their daughter only for a day or two, as they pass by the village of Yar Sale, where the *Internat* is based, on their way to and from the winter pastures in late fall and early spring.

Walking next to Alla is her younger brother, Alik, who is helping with the laundry bag. He is six and will start residential school in the fall. Together with Alla, he will board a Mi-8 helicopter, which the regional government sends in late August to collect school-age kids from all the reindeer families to fly them to the *Internat* in Yar Sale.

Around the world, residential schools, financed and managed by the government and often run by churches, have been the preferred means of addressing the "Indigenous problem." Whether in former colonies of Britain, like Canada; or Spain, like Ecuador; or in the Nordic countries, like Finland; the residential school system—designed to "kill the Indian in the child"—has existed well into the 20th century. A similar system has existed in Russia since the Great October Revolution, under the banner of "liberating" the oppressed and "elevating" them to the level of fully functional Soviet citizens. Though superficially it seemed to have had different goals from the colonial and postcolonial residential schools, the unacknowledged consequences of these interventions in Russia were no different than in the colonies. Families were broken up, children were ripped from their homes, the deep roots of ancestral knowledge that nurtured future generations were severed, native tongues were forbidden, and traditional customs and beliefs were outlawed.

Unlike the rest of the world, in post-Soviet Yamal and throughout all the Russian Arctic, the *Internat* system has endured. What is more troubling, given the negative global experience with the residential schools, is that the *Internat* system has become deeply entrenched in the psyche of Russia's Indigenous peoples, like the Nenets. Alla and Alik are the third generation of the Khudi family going through it. Yura, just like his older brother, Nyadma, also went through *Internat*, and feels that, despite all the hurt it brings, there is no other way to give his children a proper education.

"It was difficult during the first few months," Yura recalls of his time in *Internat*. "Mainly, it was the pain of being away from home, apart from my family, my mom and dad. Some kids, especially from the camps not far from the *Internat*, would try to leg it, but they were always caught and brought back. The school was too far from our parents' *stoybishe*," Yura explains. "I had nowhere to go to even try to escape. Eventually, as I got older, I got used to it. It became easier."

We stand outside the *chum*, watching Alla spread the washing on top of an upturned sled to dry. "It was like somebody ripped our hearts out when we first sent Alla to school," Yura recalls, shaking his head. "We missed her a lot. It was very tough, but eventually we got used to it. Now she is going into the fifth grade and it's just part of our life," Yura says with a sigh. This year, it is Alik's turn to go to school, and Yura and Katya are resigned to it. They feel that they have given him the foundation of the Nenets way of life and culture, and he will always be able to fall back on it if he chooses to continue in his father's footsteps. But they both believe that for the boy to get an education that would help him get a job outside of reindeer herding in the future, they have no other choice but to send Alik to the *Internat*, away from home, for the best part of the year.

After a while, Yura walks determinedly to the sled closest to the *chum*, pulls off a canvas cover, and lifts a small Yamaha electric generator out of the sled. "Well, we should charge our phones and laptops, or the kids won't be able to watch movies tonight," he says. He checks the fuel level and jerks on the cord to start the generator.

POTEMKIN'S VILLAGE

Two days later, after hours of gingerly picking our way through the industrial maze, while avoiding roads and skirting pipelines, we finally arrive at a predetermined crossing of the main business artery at the heart of Bovanenkovo. Paved with concrete slabs, the road is the gas field's busiest thoroughfare. Large trucks roll by every minute, and getting across the road is potentially treacherous for both the reindeer and the herders.

A day earlier, a Gazprom helicopter flew in from the administrative center, Salekhard, bringing a road-crossing "inspection" team, made up of representatives from Gazprom, the Yarsalinski reindeer herding enterprise, a couple of NGOs, the regional government, and the local media. After getting his *argish* across the road, Nyadma parks the sleds in the willows on the opposite side and climbs back up to chat with the "inspectors," his boss, and Gazprom staff. One of the officials is Galina Mataras, the director of nonprofit Yamal that, according to her, has been helping address many social and economic challenges facing the Nenets living on their ancestral territory.

"We work closely with Gazprom on many things—from organizing helicopter flights and train transportation, which Gazprom provides to our herders free of charge, to skills training, to organizing and coordinating these road crossings in Bovanenkovo," Mataras explains to me, as we stand on the thoroughfare, watching the main herd mill around in the distance and the brigade's *argishes* queuing up before the crossing. "It's taken a lot of time and effort, but now the crossings are expeditious and safe," Mataras says with some pride. She explains that when the brigade approaches the crossing, Gazprom stops all road traffic. A large swath of white geotextile fabric, normally used as an underlay in road construction, is unrolled across the road to speed up the movement of sleds over the concrete slabs. The Gazprom and local government officials in charge of the crossing have asserted as much. Still, the "white-carpet" treatment the brigade is receiving looks a lot like a Potemkin village to me. Before getting here, we had already crossed three paved roads without any geotextile carpets being laid out for us. The crossings went without a hitch and no sleds were damaged.

Ultimately, for Gazprom, the reindeer road crossings present a fabulous public relations opportunity. As the caravan of reindeer sleighs begins to snake across the road, Gazprom and local media are in full force recording the event. Workers in crisp uniforms—blue coveralls, with the silver Gazprom logo branded on their backs—line up on both sides of the white carpet to take pictures and get selfies with the reindeer. The herders cross the road and, after parking their *argishes* in the willows, not far from ours, climb back up to greet and chat with the visitors. They pick up parcels the chopper brought in the day before from the village and talk business with their trusted sources—a couple of Nenets who spend their summers around Bovany, fishing and acting as intermediaries between the reindeer herders migrating through the area and the rotations of Gazprom shift workers and contractors.

"Who's interested in the fresh fish we'll catch tomorrow?" "Who's buying *punty* [the velvet antlers that the herders cut off for sale before they harden in the late summer]?" "What's the going rate?" "Who's got vodka for sale [which is technically illegal in the 'dry zone' of Bovanenkovo] and for how much?" "Where can we get two hundred loaves of bread?" And so on.

While adults are mingling and talking, kids are racing one another on the concrete road slabs or playing soccer with the pebbles they dug out of the gravel shoulder. After about half an hour of meet-and-greet— handshakes, swapping smokes, laughter, and excited banter—the hustle-and-bustle at the crossing dies downs. The white carpet is rolled up, the "inspectors" climb back into their Toyotas, and, with clouds of soot billowing out of the vertical exhaust pipes of large trucks, the regular traffic resumes.

THE ROAD THAT SHOULDN'T BE THERE

This is it!" announces Nyadma to me after we get back to our sleds. "No more roads or pipelines—now it's a clear path to the coast! We don't have to break camp every night, but can stay for a few days in one spot, do some fishing or hunt some *yabto*, geese." He checks his watch. It is past midnight and he wants to press on with our journey so that we can get to the brigade's traditional camping site, just outside the northern boundary of Bovanenkovo, near a decommissioned sandpit that used to provide material for road construction.

"It's a good place," Nyadma explains, describing how the herders can see far in every direction from the elevated *stoybishe*, which makes it easier to look after the herd. There are also good fishing lakes nearby and lots of water for reindeer—all are important considerations in selecting a summer campsite, especially when it is as hot as it is now.

"It wasn't easy, when Gazprom arrived," Nyadma muses when, after an hour, we stop for a break on a high tundra knoll. He recalls how the railway, pipelines, roads, sandpits, and buildings began appearing everywhere when Bovanenkovo construction started. "We lost a lot to development—our camping sites, *nederma* routes, and our sacred sites. We felt trapped, like there was no place for us to go on our ancestral land. But once the main construction stopped, we managed to figure out our way around this mess. It's like we found a 'golden mean,' where everything balanced out." Nyadma pauses, mulling something over in his mind before concluding. "Of course, we understand that Russia needs Yamal's natural gas. And we can cope with it, as long as Gazprom doesn't build any more roads or pipelines. Otherwise, there's no point for us to *kaslat'* here in the summer. We'll just have to stay down south."

Standing by his sled, he pulls out a pair of field glasses to scout the pass ahead. His twentysomething sons, Gosha and Ilia, pull up their *argishes* next to us. After a minute or so of scanning the horizon, Nyadma points at something in the distance and passes the binoculars to the young men. Each of them takes a peek, and they all begin discussing something agitatedly in Nenets. Their migration route should be clear after the "white-carpet" crossing, they explain to me, but rising above the tundra in the distance is a dirt road that shouldn't be there. It is cutting across the herd's migratory pass and was definitely not there the last time they moved through this area two years ago.

To make it easier for the reindeer to climb over the road where it crosses a reindeer migration route, Gazprom is supposed to build gently sloping road shoulders. There is no sign of such a crossing ahead and the new road cuts us off from the old campsite. We spend a good hour digging into the shoulder, trying to level it for the reindeer to cross. When we eventually make it across the road to the campsite, we find a ten-foot tall ridge of dirt running parallel to the road and stretching southeast toward the horizon, splitting the campsite in half. This is a new pipeline that, just like the new road, shouldn't be here. Nobody asked them about these, Nyadma states angrily.

"We fought with Gazprom at the very beginning of Bovanenkovo construction," recalls Nyadma. "They decided to put a sandpit smack in the middle of our migration route. It was the only elevated tundra where we could camp to stay above the boggy areas near the lakes. After a couple of years of back and forth, Gazprom finally closed the pit, and we could return to using our old migration route. It seemed like things got a lot more coordinated between us since then. That's why this new development is just strange," Nyadma says in exasperation, gesturing toward the road that should not be there. Obviously flustered, he immediately calls Aleksandr Serotetto, the director of Yarsalinski, whom we just saw at the "white carpet" and who assured Nyadma that the pass to the coast was clear. Serotetto is as surprised as Nyadma to learn about the new road and the pipeline. He swears to find out more and get back to Nyadma tomorrow. Meanwhile, the herders are deciding whether they can squeeze all of their eight *chums* on what remains of their campsite, or if they must carry on until they get to the next camping place—another three miles, or three to four hours of *kaslat'* from here.

At this point of Arctic night, the sun is a giant firefly, stuck in the viscous amber of the sky, just above the horizon. It's close to 2:00 A.M. now and, having no desire to spend the rest of the night on the road, the herders decide to stay at this camp. Nyadma plants his *tyur* into the old hearth to mark the place for his *chum*, so that the rest of the brigade can arrange their tents accordingly. We unhitch the reindeer, unpack the sleds, and raise our *chum* for the night, or rather day, of rest.

This whole episode makes it painfully obvious that the idea of a "balanced" coexistence between the Nenets reindeer herders and oil and gas development in Yamal—which I have heard about consistently from Gazprom officials, regional government, NGOs, and even the herders themselves—is no more than a catchy slogan that has little to do with the reality on the ground. As Bovanenkovo continues to expand, the Nenets reindeer herders, whose inherent rights to their ancestral territory remain unrecognized by the Russian state, are being squeezed from all sides. A new processing facility, with all the associated roads, pipelines, and buildings, is scheduled to come online in the next couple of years. Two new railroad lines are being constructed to connect Bovanenkovo and Payuta, in the west with the Port Sabetta, and Novyi Port in the east, respectively. This new infrastructure will sever many reindeer migration routes on the peninsula.

But even more troubling for Brigade #4 is the imminent development of the Kruzenshternskoye gas field on the coast of the Kara Sea, where we are heading, which is projected to come online in the early 2020s. This field lies under the exceptionally rich reindeer summer pastures, which the Nenets herders consider to be a northern "oasis" and the ultimate destination of their annual migration. In addition to a higher diversity of plants for animals to graze on, here the reindeer can also get minerals and micronutrients important for their diet. As the growing footprint of Bovanenkovo reduces the available pastures in the area, the Kruzenshternskoye coastal tundra has become more important than ever.

Next day, there is no news from the director of Yarsalinski about the road and the pipeline. After a few phone calls, Nyadma and Yura huddle up to discuss what to do next and decide to stay at this camp for a few more days. Nyadma's daughter just called him to let him know that she arranged a pass on the Gazprom train to Bovanenkovo. She is coming with her young son to spend the rest of the summer with the brigade. It makes perfect sense, reasons Nyadma, to wait for her here, before continuing onward to the Kara Sea coast.

Though unwelcomed, the "road that shouldn't be here" gives the herders an easy access from their campsite to Bovanenkovo to stock up on more supplies, before they head to the coast. It also helps the *punty* buyers get to and from the herd, instead of having to chase the brigade around the tundra in a *Trecol*—a Russian-made, off-road Humvee-size six-wheeler. Nyadma and Yura are planning on staying at the camp for a few extra days to cut the antlers from the bulls and sell them to a buyer they know, if they can agree on the price. There has been a lot of cell phone chatter between the different herders in the area, unhappy with this year's price of five hundred rubles (about US $8) per pound of velvet antlers, which is lower than the last year's price of six hundred rubles.

"It's still twice as much as we used to get for it a couple of years ago," acknowledges Nyadma. The economic sanctions against Russia and the drop in oil prices halved the value of the Russian ruble relative to the US dollar. But the antlers are destined for the Chinese market and so their USD value remains unchanged. For the herders it simply means that the ruble equivalent they get for *punty* has doubled, allowing them to purchase more food and supplies from the local market, which operates in rubles. Nevertheless, Brigade #4 is determined to get at least 750 rubles per pound of velvet antlers and are trying to coordinate their bargaining strategy with other herding families.

The next day, adults continue with the camp chores. Some do laundry at a nearby lake, others go to the Bovanenkovo grocery store and kiosks to get some sweets and fruit, try to find vodka, which can be had at the right price even in dry Bovanenkovo, but more importantly, to buy fresh bread. Toward the evening, vodka from Bovanenkovo—disguised as bottled drinking water—finds its way into Nyadma's *chum*, where his wife, Nina, normally quiet and withdrawn, gets chatty after downing a couple of shots of vodka. She is filleting the freshly caught fish that her youngest son, Semion, brought from their nets set in a nearby lake. In the summer, the Nenets rarely kill reindeer, replacing it with fresh, or lightly salted, fish caught in the lakes and rivers along their migration route.

Sitting on the *chum* floor by the cold fireplace, Nina wipes the fish clean with a handful of grass and proceeds to methodically deconstruct it with a few precise swipes of her sharp knife. The fish is a mix of *muksun*, a type of whitefish widespread in the Siberian Arctic, and *shokur*, or broad whitefish. She sprinkles the fillets with rock salt and sets them to one side—this is for her family to eat. Fish backbones, tails, and heads go into the dogs' bucket.

Recovering after a long hike from the nets with a sackful of fish, Semion pours himself some tea from a thermos, stirs in three spoonfuls of condensed milk, and grabs a piece of bread with a few chunks of salted fish. After a few bites, he sets his open laptop on the Styrofoam stool and plugs it into an extension cord coming in from a small Yamaha generator *put-put*ting outside. It is a movie night. Each *chum* has a laptop and dozens of pirated movies—the most valued present one can bring when visiting the herders.

"I remember, when I was young and just got married to Nyadma, we used to *kaslat'* around here," Nina recalls, glancing up from her work to the laptop screen, waiting for a movie to come on. "It was a good life— harsh, but wholesome. When Gazprom first came here looking for gas, I got really scared, you know. What's going to happen to our land and us? I thought—they'd suck out all the gas right from under us," she says, cleaning the cutting board with a clump of grass and grabbing another fish from a pile by her side. "I got scared. One day, I thought, we'd all fall into this giant hole they're making right under our feet. We'd tumble down all the way to the underworld where only mammoths and spirits live." She glances at me, her wrinkled face breaking into a toothless apologetic grin, and carries on with filleting the fish, occasionally looking up to see what is happening on the laptop screen, and to shoo away the dogs edging closer and closer to the pail of fish scraps. "And now I've heard that last year they found a big hole in the ground, just south of here. They are saying it's because of the gas," she says, referring to the Yamal crater.

A sudden thunderous roar drowns out most of the sounds inside the *chum*. I step outside to take a look. I can no longer hear the clicking of reindeer hooves, yelping of the Nenets dogs, or the chatter of children. The roar is deafening, as if a jumbo jet is taking off from a runway right next to the tents.

A few hundred yards from the campsite, a sooty pipe belches out a blazing crimson ball of fire—a gas flare releasing pressure in the pipeline. Above this fragment of the shattered sun, the boundaries between tundra, water, and sky transform into a pulsating mirage of swirling blues, browns, and greens, as the familiar landscape features melt into a shapeless quivering phantasm. Sometime later, the gas flare is shut off, just as unexpectedly as it was turned on. As the thermals dissipate around the pipe, everything looks as it should—the next generation of Nenets herders is practicing their lassoing skills on sleds, dogs, and each other, while the next generation of Nenets mothers feed their dolls in a makeshift toy *chum*. For a moment, everything seems as it should be on the edge of the world.

Will the timeless flow of the Nenets and their reindeer continue in Yamal when the gas taps are finally turned off on the peninsula for good, I ask Nyadma. "As long as we are on our land, moving freely along our *nedermas*, we'll do just fine," he reassures me. Then, with a flicker of a mischievous smile in his eyes, he chuckles. "If they suck all the gas out and leave, we'll find a good use for all these buildings and roads they'd leave behind. May be we'd open up a resort here."

CHAPTER FOUR

THE MELTING TOMBS OF ALTAI

B ovanenkovo, and other Yamal gas fields, make it possible for Gazprom to deliver on Russia's promises of steady, or growing, natural gas supply to its international clients, such as China. For this to happen, however, a new southward gas pipeline must be constructed to carry Yamal gas to China through Russia's Altai, which means Golden Mountains in Turkic. If built, this pipeline will bisect the Golden Mountains of Altai World Heritage Site, the sacred landscapes that the Altai people have been looking after for generations.

GOAT-PULLING

I first met Danil Mamyev at a goat-tossing game of Kok-boru, as it is known in Altai—the Turkic-speaking region of south-central Russia. All but forgotten for decades, this traditional contest of horse-riding skills, agility, strength, and stamina has been slowly but surely returning to the region, as part of a post-Soviet cultural revival. Two teams of ten horsemen pass around the beheaded and bled-out carcass of a goat—sort of an oversize and hefty rugby ball. Doing their best to keep it away from the opposing team, the riders try to score a goal by throwing the carcass on top of a *kazan*—a round platform made of sod and as tall as a horse.

From my perch at the top of a steep hill I was watching a match in the weeklong Kok-boru tournament on the outskirts of the Altai village of

Elo. Below me, a cloud of dust was slowly rising at the edge of a make-shift arena. A single horseman burst through the haze, galloping hard toward the opposite end of the field. The undulating hills around the stadium erupted with shouts and ululations of spectators who, until that very instant, had watched the match in complete silence. The dust cloud dissolved into hazy wisps as the other riders—with smacks of short whips, blows of their heels, and short guttural cries—urged their horses in hot pursuit. Well ahead of them, the rider rose up in his stirrups approaching the opponents' *kazan*. Still galloping, he heaved his loot from the saddle and tossed it with great effort. The limp carcass of the dead goat hit the top of the earthen platform with a thud, puffs of dust rising above it, just as the rest of the horsemen caught up with the victorious rider.

"Goaaaalll!" The speakers above the officials' platform crackled with the elation of a commentator who even switched from Altai language to Russian. "One—Nil! The Karakol team takes the lead," he shouted into the microphone as the crowd cheered. I clapped and hollered with the rest of the mob and ambled downhill—past the playing kids, gawking grannies, and scratching mongrels—to the spot where my driver was watching the game.

There had been no direct flights from Moscow to Altai, and I had to catch a five-hour flight to Barnaul, a city on the shores of the Ob River that flows from Altai's glaciers to the icy waters of the Arctic Ocean by the Yamal Peninsula, and then drive for four hours to Gorno-Altaisk, the capital of Altai Republic. Around midnight, a rickety bus reeking of diesel fumes had carried me and other sleepy travelers from the airport terminal to the tail end of an old Ilyushin, a Soviet-era passenger jet. The sight of the old airplane didn't instill much confidence that we would ever make it to our destination. Inside, the rural bouquet of pickled cabbage, sweat, and garlic permeated the cabin, spiked with a miasma of cigarette smoke escaping from the bathrooms at the back of the plane, next to the crooked NO SMOKING sign. I had spent the flight in a sleepless stupor, unable to feel my legs under a heavy backpack resting on my lap. After we arrived, the driver picked me up at the Barnaul airport and we drove at full tilt down the freshly paved federal highway along the Chuysky Trakt—a historic trade route connecting Russia with Mongolia that, in the 1930s, was transformed into a paved highway, M52. We had come to the Kok-boru tournament to meet Danil.

"This is the last game Danil [Mamyev] is refereeing today, so we'll get to talk to him soon," the driver said, taking the last pull on a cigarette cupped in his hand and, flicking it to the ground, pointing toward the field. There, a horseman was silhouetted sharply against a whirling melee of Kok-boru riders, slowly engulfed by rising clouds of dust. Sitting tall on his black horse, Danil was fully clad in black, from the tips of his shin-high leather boots to his T-shirt. A light straw hat was pulled down snugly over his gray Conan the Barbarian mane framing his bronzed face. The horses were milling around, their hooves trampling the goat carcass, as the riders leaned down all the way to the ground from their saddles, trying to grab it and, pulling the goat up into their laps, rushing the opponents' *kazan*. Danil was circling the group slowly on his horse, keeping an eye on the players, ready to halt the game if the opponents broke any rules.

"We'll ask Danil if we can spend the night at the Uch-Enmek Nature Park campground," my driver said. "Hopefully he'll have time to talk to you about the park."

Danil did invite us to stay at the park, but had no time to talk. He had to stay in the saddle and referee several more games to replace an injured colleague. My driver and I ended up traveling from Elo to the Uch-Enmek Nature Park campground on our own, where Danil caught up with us the following day. Beginning with that first meeting, Danil has become a good friend and a guide who, among many things, helped me understand the relationship between mountain communities and climate change.

Mountain regions make up more than a quarter of the planet's surface, providing homes for more than a billion people. The mountain regions harvest water from the atmosphere and store it in snowpack, glaciers, and permafrost. Released from the mountains in the spring, water flows to the lowlands, sustaining rich biodiversity and supporting agriculture. Because of their height, slope, and exposure, mountain ecosystems are more sensitive to climate change than valleys and plains at low elevations. As the air warms, mountain ecosystems are changing, with cold-tolerant alpine plants marching up the slope, as the brush and trees, adapted to the warmer climates, move in. This is happening at the same time as mountain glaciers are retreating and permafrost is melting.

Earth's cryosphere—places on our planet where water exists in solid state, such as mountain glaciers, permafrost like in the Yamal, and the Antarctic ice fields in the southern hemisphere—has been diminishing at unprecedented rates. Normally, the glacial ice is maintained through a dynamic equilibrium between snowfall and snowmelt in the mountains. As the temperatures rise, the scale tips more and more toward the thaw, causing the glaciers to disappear faster than they can be replaced by the winter snow. Over the last century, the European Alps have lost up to 40 percent of their ice, New Zealand, 25 percent, and Africa's Mount Kenya and Mount Kilimanjaro as much as 60 percent. According to the latest IPCC assessment report—the most authoritative and influential reference on global trends of climate change published every seven years—the average rate of ice loss from glaciers around the world between 1971 and 2001 was close to 226 gigatons (billion tons) per year. And over the first decade of the new millennium, that rate of ice melt has accelerated by about 15 percent. In weight, this is equivalent to forty-three thousand Great (Ice) Pyramids of Giza thawing every year. Such loss of glaciers increases the likelihood of catastrophic floods and erosion, and foreshadows a rise in sea level, as the increased glacial melt reaches the ocean.

But glaciers are not just isolated slabs of ice in the inaccessible reaches of anonymous mountain ranges. They are an integral part of the local socioecological systems. Through the ages, glacial advances and retreats have not only carved the landscapes but also shaped the evolution of human societies by raising and lowering sea levels, covering and opening areas suitable for human habitation, and providing water for drinking and irrigation in otherwise inhospitable environments. Though invaluable as a source of robust scientific data, the IPCC and other scientific reports are not very helpful in conveying the true nature of climate change impacts at the local, community scale. The only way to develop such an understanding is by learning from local people who have lived with the changing conditions in the mountains for decades. I searched for this understanding among the local people of Russian Altai. But what initially drew me to this mountainous region, however, was not its changing climate but an innovative conservation approach being developed here. As I learned later, both are inextricably linked.

— ∞ —

GOLDEN MOUNTAINS

T wo thousand miles east of Moscow, and just as far south of Yamal, Altai is a mountainous region where Russia, Mongolia, Kazakhstan, and China converge. Historically, it has been both a home and migration route for countless generations of nomadic tribes. Millennia-old petroglyphs etched into rocky outcrops depict horsemen in pursuit of Asian species of elk, mountain sheep, and mountain goats that still graze on the slopes of the Altai Mountains. The kurgans—burial chambers covered with mounds of rocks—are often filled with objects of a once powerful nomadic culture. Both the kurgans and the petroglyphs are a testament to the resilience of the Altai people, who have continued to maintain their close relationship with the land to this day. Altai still thunders with the hooves of galloping horses and echoes with the cries of herdsmen guiding their sheep and cattle to seasonal pastures, just as their ancestors have done since before the time of Alexander the Great.

Toward the end of the 17th century, Altai became a newfound home for the persecuted Russian *starovery*, or Old Believers, who refused to accept religious reforms imposed by the patriarch of the Russian Orthodox Church, Nikon, in 1652. The reforms, supported by the Russian czar, amounted to more than four hundred pages of alterations to the liturgical texts and rites that Nikon decreed unilaterally in an attempt to better align the Russian Orthodoxy with the Greek Orthodox Church. The changes—like the introduction of a three-fingered sign of the cross—were unacceptable to the *starovery*, who, because of their adherence to the old traditions, were persecuted by the patriarch. Seeking refuge along the eastern fringes of the Russian Empire, many *starovery* made Altai their home.

Today, Indigenous and *starovery* cultures remain strong in Altai, despite a seemingly endless string of social and cultural adversities that have plagued the country during the 20th century. The Great October Socialist Revolution of 1917 was followed by purges of *kulaks*, or fists in Russian, as Soviet authorities called well-off landowners and farmers in the 1920s, although it quickly devolved into an all-out war on anyone potentially subversive to the Soviet regime. During Stalin's reign of terror in the 1930s, hundreds of Altai shamans were exterminated. Just a few years later, the entire country plunged into the Second World War. A short spurt of postwar elation gave way to a long period of economic and social stagnation in the 1960s and 1970s. During the 1980s, *perestroika* (reconstruction) and *glasnost* (openness) brought new hope of revival. But it took the total collapse of the Soviet state in the early 1990s for the slow process of social healing and the cultural revitalization to begin in Altai in earnest.

I'd dreamed of coming to Altai ever since I was a little boy, playing on the shores of the Hidden Lagoon at the northern end of Russia's Kamchatka

Peninsula, three thousand miles east of Altai. It was there that I heard my mother's enchanted tales of her Altai childhood. She described the Katun River burbling over rocks as it rushed past the place of her birth, a two-story log house perched on a steep bank in the *starovery* village of Nizhny-Uimon. In my mind's eye, I saw the towering mass of Mount Belukha—a giantess of local legends—keeping watch over her domain from under a furrowed, snowy brow. I watched my mother and her friends scoop up sievefuls of *gal'ians*—small minnows rolling down the waterfalls during the spring run. I envied her summers, spent at an apiary in one of the valleys near the village, where her uncle and aunt kept bees and made honey. I shivered too, as she described nestling with her brothers and sisters on cold winter days atop a massive Russian stove—a tall brick oven used for heating and cooking that occupied most of the main floor of their log house.

When I was about ten, rummaging through my father's library, I came across a well-worn volume of writings and paintings by Nicholas Roerich. A world-renowned artist and philosopher—as well as a respected scientist, author, explorer, and humanitarian—Roerich, in 1926, spent two weeks of his celebrated Altai-Himalaya expedition in Verkhny-Uimon, a village just a few miles away from the hamlet where my mother was born four years later. Roerich's depictions of the Altai landscape pulsated with such luminous pastels that, along with my mother's tales, they left no doubt in my mind that Altai was a magical land of everlasting mystery where everything was richer, brighter, more radiant and effervescent. Since then, like a distant magnet, Altai has subtly but steadily pulled on my imagination—like a half-forgotten memory that could only be reclaimed when I would finally breathe the air of my ancestors.

As I grew older, I began to suspect that the magical images of Altai I carried in my mind were simply too naive. But I had to wait until we were getting ready to immigrate to the United States, in 1988, to learn about my mother's family history in Altai. The history she tried to escape, when she left Altai in her late teens and never returned. I learned then that during the purges of the 1920s, well before my mother was born, my great-grandfather, his eight sons, and a son-in-law—my grandmother's first husband—refused to abandon their *kulak* way of life. They chose not to surrender the family farms they had worked on for generations to the Soviet collective that was being forced upon local people by the new regime. To set an example for the rest of the village, the Red Army soldiers captured and executed my great-grandfather, his eight sons, and his son-in-law. On the shore of the swift Katun, in the shadow of Mount Belukha, in front of their wives and my pregnant grandmother, the soldiers cut them down with their *shashkas*, or cavalry swords. My mother's surviving uncles were accused of treason and sent to Stalin's labor camps in the north. They never returned to Altai.

I had finally come to Altai for the first time in 2005, as part of a *National Geographic Magazine* assignment to write about Russia's protected area system. As I was researching the story, while wrapping up my graduate studies at Columbia University and working for the New York–based Wildlife Conservation Society in Russia, I had heard of Danil's work to establish the Uch-Enmek Nature Park. His approach was rooted in the emerging global understanding, as well as his personal conviction, that supporting local traditions of land use and management, including protection of sacred natural sites, was a better way of sustaining local biological and cultural diversity than the accepted Eurocentric conservation approaches based on saving "wilderness" and wildlife behind the imaginary walls of strictly protected areas, while restricting human access.

The Uch-Enmek Nature Park became the first such protected area in Altai—and in Russia—intended specifically not to keep "wilderness" away from locals behind the park's boundary but to recognize and protect the ancient relationship between the Altai people and their traditional territory. This included sustaining the movement of nomadic Altai tribes and their herds from summer to winter pastures, as well as their reverential care for the ancestral sacred sites of the Karakol Valley.

UCH-ENMEK

We were up at daybreak, as the first sunrays bounced off the golden mountaintops of the Terektinsky Range surrounding the still-shaded campground. We strolled through the dewy grass toward the kitchen housed in an *ail*—a traditional hexagonal Altai log house under a conical roof.

"Welcome to Uch-Enmek Nature Park," Danil said, stepping out of the kitchen *ail* to greet us. The handshake of his callused, bear paw–like hands, chiseled by hard manual work and years of alpinism, felt firm and vigorous, more reassuring than rough. The steady gaze of his dark eyes exuded power, but it was also full of curiosity. Inside, we sat on a long bench hewn out of a single wooden board well polished from frequent use. The matching wooden table in front of us was covered with a flowery plastic tablecloth and set with our breakfast—sweet rice porridge, slabs of Russian sour bread and butter, Altai cheese, and strong black tea. For the more adventurous visitors there was soup-like traditional Altai tea—butter, milk, salt, and *tolkan*, or ground-up roasted barley, cooked with black tea. We rushed through breakfast, as Danil was eager to introduce us to Uch-Enmek and explain the park's history and significance.

The gravel road wound its way up the Karakol Valley, crossing streams, hugging rocky hillsides, and circling solitary, wooded hills before reaching a wide, open plain. We parked and climbed up a steep trail to the top of a knoll overlooking the valley. Danil made a sweeping gesture toward the distant forested mountains, their peaks dusted with snow.

"This is the heart of the Uch-Enmek park," Danil explained, his sturdy figure clad in the camouflage uniform of a park ranger. "In the distance you can see Uch-Enmek Mountain itself. In our language, *Uch* stands for the number three and *Enmek* means a crown." It was easy to see why—the three mountain pinnacles indeed looked like a three-pointed crown.

When, in the 1990s, Russia broke with the Soviet past of collective ownership and state monopoly of the land, it began reinventing private property in all possible guises, including land privatization. Many local people, who had continued to revere sacred sites around Altai through the decades of persecution by the Soviet state, worried that the culturally significant places, like the ancient kurgans and sacred sites, would be overwhelmed in a land grab. They feared that, once the land became privately owned, instead of being collectively shared, landowners could abuse it at their personal fancy.

Activists like Danil wanted to ensure that Altai's ancestral landscapes, like Uch-Enmek Mountain and the Karakol Valley, remained whole, rather than divided up and sold to the highest bidder. More importantly, they wanted to guarantee that the land was accessible to local people on their own terms, defined by their traditional obligations to the land rather than by private property laws imposed by some outside authority. In 2001, after several years of steadfast work, Danil and his local partners created Uch-Enmek Nature Park, to protect Uch-Enmek Mountain and the Karakol Valley from the anticipated land grab while making the new park a cornerstone for cultural revival through ecological and culture-based tourism, traditional craftsmanship, and education.

"Officially, it's registered as a nature park," explained Danil, "but nature for us, the Altai people, has a different meaning than it does for the government. For us, Altai is a living and breathing being with whom we've developed a relationship over generations, well before there were any states or parks. One cannot put nature in a park."

Danil told me once that even advanced fields of "Western" science, like quantum physics, are not superior to the traditional teachings of his ancestors. As I came to know him better, I was able to fill in the gaps in that simple statement. Danil was not a very good student at school. He had poor grades and barely made it through the Soviet education system, convinced that the only thing he amounted to was to be a *chaban*, or a herder. But during his final years of school, there was a geological expedition working near his village, and he visited the campsite with his father. He admired the geologists' vast knowledge of Altai's landscapes and was impressed by how they managed to use that knowledge to make a living. So Danil decided to learn the trade. He studied hard, passed the college entrance exams, and got accepted into the Tashkent Geological College in Soviet Uzbekistan, then a republic within the USSR, some two thousand miles southwest of Altai. After graduation, he was assigned to the Samarkand Geological Expedition in Uzbekistan, where he worked for the next twenty years before deciding to return to Altai during *perestroika*.

"When I came back," Danil recalled, "geologists were not needed here, so I had to look for any job just to make a living. I had a bit of trouble adjusting to life on my ancestral land—got into fights with locals, broke my finger, and even got beaten up by a bunch of drunken policemen. Things weren't going well for me. It made me pause and think hard about what I was doing. I went to a local shaman, a very knowledgeable woman. 'Altai is not recognizing you,' she said, 'the country has forgotten you.' I then remembered what my parents and grandparents taught me, when I was little. When you return home from being away, they said, you need to let Altai 'rub off' on you. So, I did just that—I rolled on the ground in the Karakol Valley. That was my first step on the long road of reconnecting with Altai. From then on, everything else started to fall into place."

It was around that time that Danil began questioning his scientific training. He grew increasingly certain that what he had learned in school and college was not necessarily better than what his ancestors already knew and had passed on to him through traditional teachings.

In school, he was told that Altai traditional knowledge was false and backward. But his elders taught him not to harm nature, which, as he learned later, was exactly what modern conservation science was advocating. Altai ancient traditions had also taught him that everything was connected, something that quantum physics and ecology began to understand relatively recently. Danil became convinced that Altai traditional teachings simply used a language different from accepted scientific conventions to express the same fundamental principles of how the world works.

"I believe now that my people's traditional worldview is, in many ways, more advanced," Danil continued. "For generations it has taught us how to look after our land. Most of the unspoiled nature that is still found in Altai, and its so-called spiritual magnetism, are here because my people have been following our ancient teachings. The juvenile Western science, on the other hand, has done a lot of damage to our environment and culture. I just hope we can survive its adolescence."

Later, Danil took me for a drive. As we passed by the foot of a rocky overhang, he stopped the vehicle and stepped out of the car. Kneeling down by the side of the road, Danil pointed to a slab of rock half buried in the mud. He poured some water from his flask onto the rock's flat surface, washing off the dirt to reveal the faint etching of an ancient petroglyph. I followed his finger, as Danil traced the outline of the glyph, and recognized the silhouette of a large elk throwing its majestic head back in a bugle, the wavy tines of its antlers almost touching its rump.

"This chunk fell down to the ground from all the way up the slope," Danil said, pointing to the dark rock face above us. I could make out a lighter patch from where the slab must have broken off. "Lately, we've been seeing more cases like this," explained Danil. "These ancient petroglyphs have been with us for generations, but now they crack and break off in many places. It's because the weather's changing. We never used to have rains in winter, or tornadoes and torrential downpours in the summer. But lately these things happen more often, eroding the rocks much faster and destroying our heritage."

On the way back to the car, we talked about organizing a trip around Altai to learn about the local experiences of climate change. Danil suggested that we should travel to the Ukok Plateau, a remote upland on the border with Mongolia. Ukok was part of the 6,200-square-mile Golden Mountains of Altai World Heritage Site announced in 1998 by UNESCO, which, among other tasks, is responsible for the selection, designation, and monitoring of the conservation status of the World Heritage Sites—places recognized for their universal cultural or natural values. As part of UNESCO's Frozen Tombs of Altai project, aimed at protecting the World Heritage Site of the Golden Mountains of Altai, a team of Russian and international experts was working in Ukok to assess the impacts of changing climate on the World Heritage Site. Meeting people and visiting places on the way to Ukok, Danil said, would help me better understand what climate change meant for Altai and its people.

Danil checked his watch. "We should head back to the campground now. We have an outreach program for the park's visitors, like you. Tonight, there is an evening session with Arzhan Kezerekov—a local *kam*, an earth doctor, or a shaman, in our tradition. You shouldn't miss it." As we headed for the campground, Danil explained, "When in Uch-Enmek, you must see Arzhan, to listen to his advice." A strong *kam*, Arzhan was attuned to the ebb and flow of Altai's energy, Danil said. If he sensed any obstacles in my way, he would warn me and try to clear them out of the way, to make my journey safe. But when we made it to the camp, Arzhan was not there, he'd had to rush to another village on an errand. I did not get to see him until a couple of years later, when I returned to Altai to travel with Danil to Ukok.

EARTH DOCTOR

W e arrive at the campground in the gathering dark. The wind is pulling tattered curtains of rain over the tar-papered roof of the *ail*, where Arzhan is holding his session. We jump over swelling frothed-up puddles, and, ducking under the low lintel, enter the dwelling. In the middle of the earthen floor, bright flames are licking the underbellies of charred logs. Along the wall, benches with several visitors fade into darkness. In the flickering light, I see a man crouching by the fire pit. Arzhan Kezerekov is clad in a pair of camouflage pants and a loose, faded T-shirt, which in the dark makes him appear a lot bulkier than he really is.

"Privet!" Arzhan greets me in Russian, and, enclosing my hand in his large fleshy palm, gives it a soft handshake. Motioning toward short tree stumps placed upright around the fire, he invites us to sit down and join the other visitors. A camp cook brings in a tray of mugs with a pot of Altai tea and pours it for us. We sip the steaming, nourishing brew, while Danil briefly talks to Arzhan in the Altai language.

Arzhan's unkempt mop of long stringy hair, clipped short at his temples, shakes with every nod as he listens to Danil. He puts his unfinished mug of tea back on the tray, rubs his hands together, and, picking up a small milk jug and a wooden spoon, kneels by the smoldering logs. Tilting his head to one side, as if listening to the fire, he throws a few spoonfuls of milk into the flames to feed them—an offering for the spirits of the place to ask them to protect the household and provide the family with sustenance. The words of an ancient Altai prayer roll off his tongue like smooth round pebbles carried downstream by the swift Katun.

After the short ceremony, Arzhan reaches in behind his seat and pulls out a goatskin *topshur*, a traditional two-string lute. He passes the instrument over the fire a couple of times to tighten the skin and begins plucking at the horsehair strings, while fiddling with the small stallion-shaped wooden pegs, tuning the lute. Finally satisfied, he closes his eyes and begins to strum the lute purposefully, as if pacing himself before setting off on a long journey. In response to the *topshur*'s call, a guttural twang wells up from deep inside Arzhan's chest, flooding the *ail* with the traditional *kai* melody.

Kai is an ancient style of chanting when a traditional practitioner produces more than one pitch with his vocal cords simultaneously. For Altai people, such songs are a way of connecting and communicating with the earth's physical, ancestral, and spiritual realms. Some Altai singers, like Arzhan, rely on the guidance of their *topshur* as they journey through the sacred landscapes, seeking answers to the questions posed to them directly by, or on behalf of, the people in need. I am mesmerized by Arzhan's *kai* song—the hauntingly beautiful and stirring acoustic blend of all the Altai's elements. In it, I hear the deepest rumblings of the shifting layers of the earth, the crackling of fire in the hearth, the neighing of a horse on a steppe, the bugling of elk in the forest, the tapping of raindrops on parched soil, and the high-pitched swish of air through the feathers of a bird swooping overhead.

After what seems like an hour, Arzhan stops and gently leans the *topshur* against the wall. Shaking his head he chuckles, "Hee-hee-hee! Got carried away there a bit! Had to pull myself back." He rubs his hands again and reaches out for more Altai tea. A few sips later, he chats to the visitors through an interpreter. A South African gentleman, he says, has to carry a snake's skin. The man replies that he already has one on him. That's why he saw it in his vision, Arzhan smirks. Mixing his Altai and Russian words, he then addresses a Russian woman and asks her whether she is expecting or wanting to have a child. Giggling uncomfortably, she denies it, but something in her laugh says otherwise. After finishing his tea, Arzhan extends his hand to me in a farewell handshake. "You'll have a good trip to Ukok," he says. "What you seek will take longer to find than you think, but you must persevere. You are here because Altai and your ancestors called you and you answered their call.

"I don't know why"—Arzhan changes the subject at the end of our brief conversation—"But I can't stop thinking about snow. It fills my head." With a chuckle, Danil asks Arzhan not to invite the snow into the valley just yet. Arzhan shrugs uncertainly and then says something to Danil in the Altai language.

"Yes, of course," Danil replies, nodding. "We'll see Maria." Turning toward me, he explains, "Maria Amanchina is Arzhan's friend. She is one of the few remaining healers still fulfilling their traditional responsibilities and carrying out the rituals to keep Altai healthy and balanced. Arzhan says that we should spend some time with her. She would have a few things to share." We are going to pick up Maria on our way to Ukok, Danil explains. Our first stop on the trip, however, says Danil, is the Aktru glacier, to see the impacts of climate change, for, over the last decades, it has been retreating upslope at a steady pace of several feet a year.

GLACIAL RETREAT

The Kurai steppe lies between the snow-capped mountain peaks of the Altai Mountains to the south and the rolling plains of Mongolia to the east. A five-mile-long, bumpy road leads from the tiny village of Kurai—a few dozen wooden houses clustered at the foothills— to the Aktru glacier, fifty miles from Russia's border with Mongolia. The roofs of the Kurai houses and the cones of traditional *ails* peaking out from behind the high wooden fences are as faded as the treeless steppe surrounding the village.

Danil and I stop for the night at Oleg Boltokov's *zelenyi dom*, Russian for "green house," as locals call this type of hostel—the only place for weary travelers to spend the night and grab a bite on their way to Aktru glacier. Our dinner is served outside, on a long communal table next to the kitchen *ail*. Oleg has just returned from taking a group of tourists to the glacier and, over dinner, we talk about climate change.

Born and raised in Kurai, Oleg is in his early forties and still remembers how, when he was little, there used to be one massive Aktru glacier. As the ice melted, the glacier split into two separate tongues, now almost half a mile apart. As I learn later, the number of Altai glaciers has increased by 25 percent since the 1970s, because the massive ice shield of old split into smaller segments as the ice melted. At the same time, the amount of ice locked in these glaciers decreased by about a quarter over the same period.

"Certainly climate is changing," Oleg says with the same conviction of an eyewitness I heard from the Skolt Sámi and Nenets. "In the past, everybody knew when winter was coming and what to expect during the spring. We could predict what the weather would be like and plan when and where to move our cattle and sheep. That's getting much harder to do now." Oleg describes how last winter came early, but it was mild and with little snow. As a result, the spring pastures remained dry, which made it hard for locals to keep their cattle healthy. Strong winds used to be uncommon, but over the last few years they have been getting stronger, more frequent, and less predictable. In many places, the strong winds hardened the snow, making it difficult for the cattle to move around and find grass.

"The rains are now short, but they come down very hard," Oleg continues, comparing the recent downpours to the prolonged drizzles common in the past. "Still, for the last three years it was very dry, the grass burned, and there was nothing for the cattle to eat. We kept our sheep to eat, but had to sell all of the cattle." Maybe it is because there is less ice in the mountains now, muses Oleg, though different people have different opinions about this. Some even blame it on the rockets being launched into space from the Baikonur in neighboring Kazakhstan. But most locals, especially elders, talk about the poor attitude that people now have toward nature as the root cause of all our environmental troubles.

The Aktru glacier is the most accessible glacier in southern Siberia, Oleg explains, and, in July, tourists can easily walk up to it. Many come from different parts of Russia, drawn by the "untouched wilderness" and a bit of local culture. Oleg himself hosted more than three hundred people last year. But the 13,200-foot-tall Aktru Mountain, which gives birth to the Aktru glacier, is a sacred site for the local people, and the tourists coming here do not behave in a respectful way, Oleg grumbles. They booze, climb all over the place, and make a racket, showing little regard for local people and their traditions. More troublesome is their lack of respect for the spirits, or "bosses," of these sacred places, says Oleg. In addition to the physical impact, the visitors' insolence leaves a heavy spiritual imprint on the land. When they leave, it is the local people who must deal with the consequences of their actions. This includes local shamans carrying out traditional ceremonies to restore the balance between local people, the glaciers, the mountains, and Altai. Ultimately, Oleg concludes, climate change is a symptom of people's ignorant actions upsetting the natural balance of life on Earth.

In the Altai traditional worldview, all natural things—whether plants or planets, bees or boulders, spiders or spirits—are recognized as conscious living beings, endowed with all the functions, feelings, and follies of a person. For Oleg and his kin, Altai is a breathing and sensuous living entity, with which they must keep their relationship in balance if they want to have a good life. If nature is not treated with reverence, reciprocity, respect, and restraint, the relationship becomes compromised, leading to environmental imbalance, such as climate change. Altai people support this relationship through cultural practices and ceremonies that restore and maintain their bonds with local animals and plants, sacred mountains and springs, wind and water. Traditional rituals have always been conducted throughout Altai, even during the repressive Soviet epoch. Each village has an ancient altar that has been used for such ceremonies for generations. To this day, ancestral Altai clans preserve and pass on the lore of their intimate relationships with totem animals and plants, sacred mountains and lakes, their ancestors and spirits.

Indigenous peoples, whether they are the Altai or Skolt, as well as scientists, recognize, however, that Earth's self-regulation is not limitless. If certain conditions within the system change too significantly, or rapidly, the system can pass a tipping point and flip into a new, potentially irreversible, state a lot less supportive of human well-being. According to these insights, climate change is an indicator of the Earth's affliction, a warning that our planet's life-sustaining prowess is being compromised.

The next morning, we leave Oleg's place and head for Aktru. The road snakes along the fields and pastures, past some ancient kurgans. Hugging the undulating foothills, it gains in elevation and turns rougher as we climb. Every tree root and boulder along the way threatens to break our axle in half or throw us from the vehicle. Eventually, we enter the pine forest, which quickly transitions into alpine meadows. Finally, we are crossing moraines—ridges of gravel and rocks deposited by melting glaciers—furrowed by glacial streams. At the mountaineering camp near the Aktru glacier, we meet Oleg's friend Alexander Dibesov, a warden and my guide for the day. From the camp, we follow a narrow foot pass snaking among giant boulders to the crest of a gully carved out by glaciers over millennia. At the cusp of the ridge, Alexander stops and pulls out a pair of binoculars to scan the slopes above us for signs of Argali mountain sheep. In the azure-blue sky, the sparkling arc of a rainbow hangs over a small waterfall. The mist drifting toward us from the cascading water feels refreshing.

"Every summer when I was a kid," recalls Alexander, turning toward me, his closely cropped salt-and-pepper hair sparkling in the sun, "my family would travel on horseback from Kurai up here to Aktru, so that we could sled down the glacier." There is a tinge of nostalgia in his voice and a shadow of a frown on his brow. "The ice used to come all the way down here," he says, pointing to a spot directly below us. "Look where it is now," he continues, moving his arm in a wide arc to point at a soiled tongue of ice, barely visible at the head of the valley, more than a mile away.

"My kids will never sled down Aktru." He sighs. His gaze is unfocused, as if he is trying to recall the sight of the glacier in all its former glory. With a grunt, he gets up from the ground and heads downslope. In my mind, his lament for Aktru glacier is echoing throughout mountain valleys the world over. Like other Indigenous peoples in mountain regions around the world, the Altai people are intimately familiar with the water cycle in all its incarnations—blizzards and icy glaciers, replenishing rains and permafrost. Over the last decades, they have seen it beginning to shift. Extreme weather events rarely experienced in the past—precipitous floods, summer hailstorms, and even tornadoes—are now a regular occurrence. Summer rains have become more intense, the glaciers are shrinking, it rains in winter, and on the Ukok Plateau, where we are heading next, the permafrost is disappearing, threatening Altai's cultural heritage and, indeed, their very survival.

MELTING TOMBS

The Ukok Plateau lies fifty miles south of the Aktru glacier, and more than one hundred miles southeast from Uch-Enmek, where our journey began several days ago. Pinched between the borders of Mongolia to the east, China to the south, and Kazakhstan to the west, almost one thousand square miles of highlands rise eight thousand feet above sea level. The area is home to rare and endangered animals, including Argali mountain sheep, the wild *manul* cat, and the roving snow leopard. And dozens of medicinal and endemic plants grow among the dozens of ancient kurgans.

There is little wind, and the trills of grasshoppers wax and wane in hazy heat above the grassy expanse of the hilly plateau. In the distance, the snow-covered peaks of the sacred Tavan-Bogdo-Ula range bake in the afternoon sun. Since the Soviet days, a barbed-wire fence has cut through this remote mountain plateau. Running east to west, parallel to the Russian-Mongolian border, many of the fence's wooden posts have fallen down, succumbing to the fierce elements at work on the plateau. Nobody has bothered to fix or replace them.

We park our vehicle next to an old excavated kurgan that, after its contents were removed during a dig, was backfilled with dirt. A circle of boulders, strewn around a pile of rocks at its center, is all that remains of the burial mound. It looks like a giant stone target, a good twenty yards in diameter, scarred into the flesh of the Ukok Plateau. The highland is indeed becoming a target for many—from Russian Jeep enthusiasts tearing across the fragile wetlands in their mud-splattered four-by-four vehicles to archaeologists looking to unearth treasures to the state-run resource development companies planning a gas pipeline to China.

Arzhan's friend Maria Amanchina, whom we picked up after visiting Aktru, wears a traditional, long, and sleeveless kaftan over a warm gray jacket. Strings of multicolored beads and cowry shells dangle from a wide collar and tinkle rhythmically as she walks slowly around the kurgan's outer ring of boulders, overgrown with grass. Maria kneels by a large upright stone and lights her pipe. Her eyes are closed, as puffs of blue smoke rhythmically escape from the corners of her mouth. Bowing her head in silent prayer, she pinches the bridge of her nose with her free hand, as if trying to make a headache go away. Answering my whisper, Danil explains that it is Ukok's fate that is the source of Maria's pain.

A two-thousand-mile natural gas pipeline snaking southward all the way from Yamal—a project the Russian energy giant Gazprom planned, to deliver natural gas directly to China—will slice the Ukok Plateau in two, despite its being a part of a World Heritage Site. While Gazprom insists that the pipeline will be built and serviced from the air, Russian and international environmental groups, like Greenpeace and World Wildlife Fund, are concerned that the pipeline construction is just the first step in the Kremlin's agenda to open up this remote and relatively untouched region. The roads, power lines, and associated development, they say, will follow the pipeline, because it is the shortest route from Russia's overabundant Yamal gas fields to China. According to UNESCO, this "energy corridor" would pierce the heart of the Ukok Plateau, destroying unique wetlands, summer pastures, and other parts of the rich World Heritage Site, such as ancient burial sites, including the burial place of the Ice Maiden, named for the permafrost-encased sarcophagus in which she was discovered.

Twenty-four centuries ago, a noblewoman from the nomadic Pazyryk tribe, the ancestors of the modern-day Altai peoples, had been placed in an oversize sarcophagus hewn from a single larch log and lowered into an underground chamber at the bottom of a large kurgan. Six sacrificial horses, richly saddled and harnessed, were laid to rest on the northern side of the burial chamber. Ceramic jugs, dishes, an iron knife, and two portable wooden tables—all the implements the deceased would need on her horseback journey into the realm of her ancestors—had been set on the felt-covered floor. The woman's body was mummified with herbs, bark, and the fur of *kunitsa*, a European relative of the North American pine marten. Intricate tattoos of mythical animals adorned her shoulders and arms—a deer with an eagle's beak, its antlers blossoming into griffon heads, and a spotted panther with a long, up-curved tail, likely a snow leopard. The woman's three-foot-tall hairpiece was festooned with gold-plated wooden figurines of animals, as befitted one of Pazyryk's nobility.

In the summer of 1993, an expedition from the Novosibirsk branch of the Russian Academy of Sciences, led by up-and-coming archaeologist Natalya Polosmak, was searching for traces of Pazyryk culture on the Ukok Plateau. The researchers stumbled on the kurgan of the Ice Maiden, right where we are now standing. Without asking local people for permission, they dug up the remains and, in the name of science, shipped them out first to Moscow and then to Novosibirsk. The dig was hailed as one of the greatest discoveries of modern archaeology, providing new insights into Pazyryk culture: the clothing, food, horses, woven textiles, and art were well preserved by the permafrost that filled the burial chamber and the noblewoman's sarcophagus.

During the examination of the remains, the scientists recognized the noble traits of the woman, but the nature of her status in the Pazyryk society and her relationship with the modern-day Altai people eluded them. Was she a ruler or a healer? A warrior or a holy woman? Local people know her as Ukok Princess Ochy Bala, a legendary ruler of the Pazyryk people, and, unlike the scientists, have absolutely no doubt about her role in the past, present, and future of Altai. This daughter of Altai was buried on the sacred mountain plateau among her ancestors to ensure the peace and well-being of her people. The eerie nightmares reported by the archaeologists during the excavation, the near-crash of the helicopter as the sarcophagus was being airlifted from Ukok to Novosibirsk, and several powerful earthquakes during the ensuing years, have all been unequivocal signs to local people that the princess's removal from Ukok had unhinged the long-established equilibrium in the region. They were adamant that she must be returned to her rightful final resting place as soon as possible in order to restore the balance.

Without the princess on the Ukok Plateau, Maria explains, the Altai people are struggling to maintain the balance in their lives—whether they have to overcome daily strife, fight the planned pipeline, or deal with climate change. This is why, Maria says, she has been working so hard to bring the princess back to her Ukok home. After visiting the

Novosibirsk branch of the Academy of Sciences, where the princess's remains were kept under controlled temperature and humidity, Maria developed a deep, direct relationship—a friendship she says—with Ochy Bala. Maria swore to rescue her from the prison of the museum and return the Ice Maiden back home to Altai. She collected thousands of signatures petitioning Russia's president and the prime minister to grant the princess a safe return to Altai—first to a local museum and then to her original resting place on the Ukok Plateau. Maria came with us to Ukok to reaffirm her commitment to bring Ochy Bala back home, to restore her vital role of looking after Altai and its people. The Russian authorities, however, brushed off all local concerns about the princess, arguing that there was absolutely no evidence of any relationship, genetic or morphological, between the Ukok princess and the Altai people. This argument made little sense to the locals, for whom the Ukok princess and Altai were one.

In 2012, Maria's wish came partially true. The Ukok princess's remains were returned to Altai and put on display in a special sarcophagus in Altai's capital, an exhibit built with Gazprom funds as part of their campaign to pacify local opposition to the Ukok pipeline. Though pleased that the princess is now much closer to Ukok, Maria and other local activists continue their campaign to rebury the princess on the plateau. The increasing number of extreme-weather events over the last few years—tornadoes and devastating floods, with the most recent almost submerging the part of the Altai capital where the Gazprom sarcophagus with the princess is kept—made even the local politicians begin to serve up the idea of the princess's reburial as part of their election campaigns. But, even if Maria eventually succeeds in overcoming all these obstacles and manages to bring the princess's remains back to the Ukok Plateau to be put to rest, there is little apparent hope of the Ukok princess ever coming fully home. The permafrost that preserved her remains for thousands of years is disappearing, melting away in the Altai's steadily rising air and ground temperatures.

Permafrost in Altai has been relatively stable since the Late Pleistocene glaciation about eighteen thousand years ago. During the 20th century, however, the average ground temperature in the region has increased by about 1.4 degrees Fahrenheit total. At the lower edge of the permafrost, where many Altai kurgans are found, this slight warming is enough to cause permafrost to melt. As a result of the increasing temperature, more permafrost is melting away—the so-called active layer, where the permafrost thaws and freezes every year, has increased by 23 percent since the 1970s. During the same period, the lower edge of the permafrost has retreated upslope by about two hundred yards, while its total area shrank by 15 percent. Scientists predict that, as air temperatures continue to rise in Altai, the permafrost will disappear completely toward the end of the 21st century, leaving the ancient contents of Ukok kurgans thawed out and decaying.

After Maria's ceremony is completed, we get into our vehicle and start heading back. Approaching the edge of the plateau, we spot two Russian Jeeps bouncing down the mountain pass in the distance. When we catch up with them, several bearded men spill out of the vehicles to greet us. They are members of the UNESCO team Danil told me about, working on a plan to preserve the Frozen Tombs of Altai, the name of their project. During our short exchange, interspersed with handshakes and cigarette and lighter swaps, the researchers talk about their work and their fears for Altai's frozen kurgans. The team is made up of archaeologists and climatologists from UNESCO, the University of Ghent, and their Russian research colleagues, who have been monitoring permafrost temperatures and cataloging Altai's frozen tombs to develop a plan to rescue them from thawing. Some proposed solutions included constructing large umbrellas that would shade each individual kurgan from direct sunlight in order to stabilize its internal temperature and arrest the thaw. This, according to the UNESCO-Ghent report, would give researchers enough time to excavate and document the treasures, saving them for posterity in museum collections.

It all sounds like a well-meaning and worthwhile project, but, as snippets of lively Russian-English chatter whirl around our group like fallen leaves on the evening breeze, I wonder what local people think about the virtues of this new scientific endeavor on their traditional territory. For the UNESCO scientists, the disappearance of permafrost means the loss of precious scientific data, preserved in ice for generations, about human history in this part of the world. For the Altai people, the thawing permafrost potentially signifies a gradual irreversible loss of part of their heritage. It seems that UNESCO's efforts to save the frozen tombs of Altai from the impacts of climate change should be welcomed by the local people. But are they? I have to ask Maria about this during my visit to her place on the way back from Ukok.

SHAMAN'S VISION

T wo unblinking round eyes glare at me through the wisps of white smoke rising from a fire pit in the middle of Maria's *ail*. The sentinel's face is still, his stare fixed, and his thin lips, above a pointed goatee, are neither smiling nor frowning, as if he is uncertain of my true intentions. I shift uneasily on a stump by the entrance and try to shake off the feeling that I am being x-rayed. The eyes, I remind myself, are just a pair of brass half orbs protruding from the wooden effigy of a shaman carved into the handle of Maria's drum, which rests on her shrine by the hearth. Those eyes could not possibly see anything, I reassure myself.

The late-afternoon light seeps in through a smoke hole in the roof, sending shadows scurrying to the corners of the *ail*. Maria kneels by the hearth, her lips moving in a silent prayer, a small pot in her hand. With a few shakes of the wooden spoon, she spatters tiny pearls of milk over the fire, sending them jumping, popping, and hissing on the hot, soot-covered rocks. Puffs of steam, mixed with the trails of pale smoke, rise from the smoldering logs.

Maria packs the bowl of her pipe with tobacco and lights it with a twig pulled from the fire. We sit in silence as she pulls on the pipe, wafts of pale smoke slowly enveloping us. After a while, she snuffs the pipe out and slowly returns to her bed next to the shrine.

"I'm not feeling one hundred percent today—weak and achy all over," she explains apologetically. "That Ukok ceremony the other day really took a lot out of me. I need a couple of days to recover. I'll lie down now, okay?" she asks. "No-no-no! Please stay," she pleads, seeing me rising from my seat. "It's all right for us to talk a bit about Ukok." She gestures for me to sit back down and stretches out on the bed, head resting on the palm of her right hand on top of a blue-and-red-flower-print pillow. We talk for the next couple of hours, with occasional breaks for Altai tea.

Both of Maria's parents were shamans. Shamanism was strictly forbidden during Soviet times, but local people would still visit them in secret to be healed. Her mother was a clairvoyant, capable of sensing places, living beings, events, or things directly with her mind. Maria's uncle on her father's side was very good at seeing the future. When men from the village were sent to the front line during the Second World War, he had accurately predicted who would return home. Maria's great-grandfather, on her mother's side, had also been a powerful shaman. According to family lore, when the local police threw him in jail, he would easily escape his locked cell. Eventually the prison guards gave up and stopped arresting him. Powerful shamans like this no longer live in Altai, says Maria, because most of the lineages were decimated during Stalin's reign of terror, when hundreds of shamans were arrested, killed on sight, or sent to northern Siberia to die in labor camps.

A local shaman had predicted that Maria's mother would give birth to eight children and the seventh one would become a shaman. Fifty years ago, Maria was that seventh child. When she was a year and a half old, she fell ill. Her parents had to leave her with another traditional healer for three months until she was cured. Ever since, Maria has been able to see into the future and heal people.

"Once, when I was in my teens," Maria recalls, "I was looking after our sheep on a summer pasture and dozed off. In my dream, I saw a white-bearded man, all clad in white. He told me that it was time for him to leave Altai but promised to return in twenty years. He said that, as a proof of his promise, he would send my sheep back home. When I awoke, I saw a white rider galloping away in the distance. I returned home, and found my sheep already there. My father explained to me that it was an omen and that I had met the Spirit of Altai, our protector, who lives on Belukha Mountain." Sometime later, another healer told Maria that she had to heed that call of the Spirit of Altai and become a shamaness. Over the next thirty years, guided by her dreams, visions, and intuition, her relationship with the Spirit of Altai, and later the Ukok Princess, Maria has become the respected shaman she is today.

"In the past," Maria says, "the energy of the earth was so pure, because people didn't despoil it. Now, because of the pollution, many plants and animals and people are sick, dying, and disappearing. When I was little, airplanes were just starting to fly over our land. My father told me that a thousand years from now, the sky would get polluted and all the contamination would end up back on Earth with rain and snow and the earth would turn into sand and everything would disappear. If we don't want to end up living my father's vision of our future, we should not be going up in the sky [air and space travel] and digging things out of the ground [archaeology and mining]. We should be more respectful of our Mother Earth. Only in that way can we save the world for our children.

"Every tree, every flower, every blade of grass is alive, just like us," Maria continues. "We need to have a relationship with them. Because I respect them, all kinds of creatures—bugs and butterflies, squirrels and birds—come to me, asking for help. When I hug a tree, say, a birch, and if I have some negative energy in me, it pushes me away and I feel it intuitively at the energy level, whether it is positive or negative. We must find a way to communicate with nature. If every human being could feel nature, the world would be saved. We must save Mother Earth, so that we ourselves don't disappear." This is why, concludes Maria, Altai people oppose all human activities that harm the earth, whether it is the construction of a gas pipeline, or the disturbance of the ancestral remains at sacred sites—even if it is done with the best of intentions. All such acts ultimately upset the balance of life, disrupting local and global natural processes, including weather patterns and climate.

The *ail*'s door squeaks open and the driver pokes his head inside. He is apologetic—we have to leave now if we want to make it to Uch-Enmek tonight. Before heading back to Barnaul to catch my flight to Moscow, I want to see Danil, who had left for the park the day before. The driver's timing is perfect, as Maria is worn out by our conversation. I thank her, make her promise to resume our conversation when I return to Altai, and go to fetch my bags.

"Did you feel the energy of Ukok?" Maria asks me as I am about to step out the door. "It always feels so soft and gentle," she says, "as if swimming in a fresh mountain spring." Her tired face lights up as she sits upright in bed to bid me farewell. "I am glad you came," she says. "On our own, we have no hope of healing anybody or fixing anything. We can do this only by asking other living beings to help us heal the earth. We need to ask everybody—animals, plants, spirits, the land itself—and, of course, each other."

KEEPING THE BALANCE

Back at Uch-Enmek, Danil takes me for a drive around the park. We stop by a sacred tree to tie *kyira*, traditional white strips of cotton. Such trees can be seen around Altai at mountain springs and mountain passes—strips of white, yellow, or light blue cotton or light horsehair tied to tree branches to demonstrate reverence toward Altai. Danil does this to ask the spirit of Altai to bless my journey and to look after my family. The supplicant, he explains, never asks for anything for him- or herself.

From the top of a knoll, we watch specks of cars tumble down the dusty road below us. Farther up the valley, forested foothills rise in dark green swells to the cusp of the ridge, where they break into the foamy crest of the snow-capped Uch-Enmek Mountain. I share my impressions from this trip with Danil—glaciers melting, kurgans thawing, petroglyphs eroding, scientists worrying, global heritage disappearing, and development accelerating. And in the midst of it all, the Altai people trying to revive and hold on to their traditions, territories, and sacred sites.

"We cannot avoid our current predicament," Danil reflects. "Life unfolds according to its own laws, whether we comprehend them or not. It's impossible to go back to the way things were. We can only try and do our best under current circumstances." "Modern society," he continues, "may consider itself advanced in knowledge, but spiritually it's quite ignorant. To come up with any solutions to the ills of the modern age, we must find a way to cast aside our prejudices and build on our collective knowledge, whether it is derived from our spiritual traditions or from scientific inquiry."

"We shouldn't try to understand the value of the kurgans just by looking at what's inside of them," Danil continues. "Digging them up and documenting all the artifacts doesn't give us full understanding. We need to consider how they are put together, including their physical and magnetic properties, as well as their position on the landscape."

According to the Altai worldview, Uch-Enmek Mountain is sacred, but not just because it is a place to gather for ceremonies and rituals. Local people believe that, like any other living being, the living earth has tissues and organs that, when working properly, keep it alive and healthy. In the Altai worldview, the sacred Karakol Valley is the *umbilicus mundi*, or the earth's navel. They believe that through this navel, the planet receives vital energy from the cosmos, in a way similar to a fetus receiving nourishment from its mother. The valley nurtures and maintains the relationship between people and the land locally, but also throughout Altai and the rest of the world.

"The Karakol Valley and Uch-Enmek Mountain are important places that help keep our relationship with the earth and cosmos in balance," Danil explains. "I understand this now, not only through our traditional teachings but also as a geologist. Here at Uch-Enmek, and throughout Altai, we are trying to use modern technology and concepts to translate our traditional understanding into the language of science, so that we can communicate these important ideas to the larger society to help us all take better care of the earth."

Back at the park's office, Danil rolls out the Altai geological map. He points at a dark ring at the center of the Karakol Valley, six miles long and about two miles wide. According to the map legend this is a deposit of gabbro and dolerite rocks, which contain a high concentration of magnetite. Danil then pulls out another map, which shows most of the ancient kurgans in the Karakol Valley clustered at the bottom half of the magnetite ring. The proximity between the kurgans and the deposit, Danil says, is not a coincidence. This is where the Earth's navel is located.

According to science, Earth's magnetosphere, shaped by the movement of its molten core as well as the makeup of its crust, interacts with the energies of the sun and cosmos reaching our planet, and influences cloud formation, thunderstorms, and other atmospheric phenomena. Danil explains that Altai people have known of these relationships for eons. Certain geological features around their traditional territory that had strong magnetic properties they recognized as sacred natural sites. They built artificial structures, such as burial mounds, or kurgans, out of magnetite-rich rocks that often had to be brought in from a great distance. Danil believes that his ancestors constructed these kurgans to purposefully tap into, and amplify, the power of sacred landscapes. They carried out ceremonies at these sites to direct the energies of these places toward sustaining the well-being of Altai, its people, and all other living beings.

To investigate the properties of the Earth's magnetic field around kurgans in the valley, the Uch-Enmek Nature Park partnered with the Siberian branch of the Russian Academy of Sciences and Gorno-Altaisk State University. They documented the structure of the kurgans—a ring of magnetite and iron-bearing rocks encircling a burial chamber. Measurements around intact and dug-up kurgans showed that undisturbed kurgans maintained a strong, continuous magnetic field, while it was broken up around the excavated kurgans. The conventional explanation for some burial chambers being empty has been that they were prepared ahead of time, in anticipation of a death of a nobleman or -woman. Danil, however, is adamant that these structures are *meant* to be empty, their rings of magnetite-rich rocks repeating the configuration of the larger magnetite structure of the Karakol Valley, the *umbilicus mundi*.

At one kurgan, researchers discovered a small, highly dynamic magnetic field that was moving against the relatively uniform magnetic background. The field was moving around the kurgan and changing its behavior when people were present. The researchers also measured changes in the strength of the kurgan's magnetic field over time, discovering that it was very sensitive to thunderstorms and lightning outside the park, even as far as Mount Belukha, over a hundred miles from the Karakol Valley. Using Kirlian photography—a special method for capturing images of living objects in a magnetic field—researchers also documented how the kurgans had a restorative effect on human bioenergy fields. Disrupted electric conductivity of human skin became fully restored after individuals spent time at a whole kurgan. There was also a noticeable drop in blood pressure, indicating a calming effect of the place on a person.

"We don't need this scientific lingo for our people," says Danil. "We already know these things about the kurgans based on our traditional knowledge. We are doing it only to make outsiders pay attention to the role the kurgans play on the land, and the importance of keeping these sacred places undisturbed."

To Altai people, kurgans are not randomly scattered burial mounds packed with unique relics of cultures long forgotten. Instead, they are purposefully built structures, intricately assembled to enhance and propagate the energies of each site, like Uch-Enmek Mountain or Ukok Plateau. Once such a place is physically disturbed, for example as a result of archaeological work or pipeline construction, that sacred site can no longer perform its functions. And because sacred sites are part of a large interconnected network, such disturbances have consequences beyond the immediate vicinity of the site.

As their brothers and sisters in the East did, Altai people learned long ago about the energy flow in the human body. Disease, they learned, is a result of an imbalance in that flow, which could be fixed by stimulating certain spots along the energy meridians on human skin—acupuncture points. Altai people believe that, in a similar way, the Earth also has acupuncture points. Their ancestors recognized these places as sacred sites, which play exactly the same role for the living Earth as acupuncture points do for human bodies. Altai traditional rituals act on these sites in the same way as the needles stimulating acupuncture points on the human body, only at the scale of the entire region or even the planet. When sacred sites are well looked after and active, Danil explains, the energy flows through the area, keeping Altai and the cosmos in balance.

If the kurgans are left undisturbed, says Danil, even if the permafrost encasing the remains of Altai ancestors melts in some of them and their remains return to earth, such sacred places, together with the shamans who care for them, will continue to perform their millennia-old role of safeguarding Altai and its people, maintaining the balance of human-environment interaction.

"UNESCO's project is well intentioned," Danil muses aloud, "but it simply lacks the necessary understanding of our reality, and so all that energy and financial resources end up misplaced. A wiser and more practical approach would be to work with us to help take care of the land in the way we know is beneficial to our culture and our ancestral responsibilities of looking after this land. It's only through such collaborative and creative work between scientists and local people that real solutions to modern challenges can emerge. This is what we are trying to do in Uch-Enmek."

As we are finishing our conversation, two dark dots glide ahead of the approaching darkness—a pair of golden eagles. Tracing the contours of the forested foothills with their wingtips, the birds unhurriedly pull a white curtain of snow flurries over the sacred Karakol Valley. It reminds me of our meeting with Arzhan back at Uch-Enmek campground at the beginning of our trip. I wonder if this is the snow that he saw in his mind's eye.

On the way back to the car, I stop by the sacred tree to tie a *kyira*. I ask the great Altai spirit to help Danil and his people to look after their kurgans in the way they deem appropriate; I ask for the Ukok Princess Ochy Bala to find her way back home to the Ukok Plateau; and I wish for the Karakol Valley to remain the Earth's navel, the place where the boundaries between human, planetary, and cosmic realms no longer hinder our vision and we can see our path with crystal clarity.

CHAPTER FIVE

PACHAMAMA'S BLOOD

More than nine thousand miles west of Altai, on another continent, is Torimbo, a tiny community of the Indigenous Sápara people in the Ecuadorian Amazon. It is a world away, but this is where I am heading next to learn how Sápara stay resilient in the face of climate change and other challenges. Just like the Altai people do with their sacred sites, the Sápara keep a healthy relationship with their sacred forest—Naku—its spirits, and other living beings.

⚬⚬⚬

BLOOD

The slender and languorous Conambo River snakes through the lush rain forest at the western edge of Ecuador's Oriente region. This distant tributary of the mighty Amazon carries its silt-laden, tawny waters from the eastern slopes of the Ecuadorian Andes to the Peruvian border and beyond. For millennia, the Conambo River has brought the rich sediment from the Andean foothills, depositing it along the riverbanks and enriching the soil. During the monsoon season, the swollen river plays with fallen trees like toy boats, before discarding them in eddies along sharp bends. During the time of drought, it quenches the thirst of many rain forest creatures. Daily, the river brings gifts of abundant catches of many kinds of fish to the fishers of Torimbo village.

On a gray February day in 2013, the river carried something that hadn't stained its waters for decades. Suspended in its turbid waters was the spilled blood of a Sápara youth. At the water's edge, several yards away from the verge of the rain forest, lay the lifeless body of thirteen-year-old Emerson Ushigua Ruiz. The boy's neck had been broken by a blow from a thick and heavy tree branch discarded nearby. A set of human footprints descended from the forest down the sandy riverbank toward the motionless boy. Scarlet blood, oozing into the sand from the dead youth's mouth, mixed with the mocha-colored waters of the Conambo River.

Just a few miles downstream from Emerson's body, the river passed another crime scene—an old oil well. During the peak of oil exploration in the region in the 1980s, this oil well had spilled crude oil—known to Sápara as the blood of Pachamama, or Mother Earth—into the rain forest and the river. Many creatures died or fled. The area had remained devoid of fish and wildlife, and unfit for crops, for many years. But the oil reserves discovered at the time on Sápara territory were considered too small, the crude too heavy, and the place too remote for the oil companies to launch a full-scale operation. After polluting the area, the oil company left, capping the oil well to conserve it until more opportune, or desperate, times would make a comeback possible.

Four decades later, the bioculturally rich Sápara territory is back on the chopping block of the fossil fuel industry. Once again, the long-brewing conflict between two opposite ways of seeing the world is flaring up. On the one hand, the Indigenous Sápara people see their rainforest as a living and breathing conscious being that must be cherished and cared for—the sacred Naku, who is a source of precious life, and a foundation of their wellbeing. The Ecuadorian government views the forest as a resource to be exploited in order to generate revenue. The government's view resonates with some of the settler communities in the region that, for years, have been encroaching on the Sápara territory and looking to cash in on resource extraction. This clash of worldviews escalated into violence, leading to the murder of Emerson Ushigua Ruiz.

I learn all of this from Alcides Ushigua Armas—the grieving father of Emerson—when I come to the Ecuadorian Amazon to learn about the Sápara's efforts to address climate change under the escalating threat of oil development on their traditional territory. The Sápara worry that should Pachamama's blood spill again, their Naku may not recover, putting their own future in jeopardy.

⸙

NAKU

S ápara's Naku lies at the western edge of the Amazon rain forest, a globally recognized hot spot of biological diversity. About eighty miles north of it is the Yasuní National Park and Biosphere Reserve—arguably the most biologically rich place on earth. "Home to an estimated million living species, most of them yet to be identified,"—clarified and confirmed with Dr. Swing, the Yasuní National Park in the Napo moist tropical forests ecoregion of northeastern Ecuador is considered to be one of the best-known symbols of global biodiversity.

Before leaving Ecuador's capital, Quito, for Torimbo, I met Dr. Kelly Swing, a director of the Yasuní's Tiputini Biodiversity Station, in his Spartan office on the sunny campus of Ecuador's Universidad San Francisco de Quito, where he teaches environmental science. A respected authority on biodiversity conservation, Dr. Swing has spent his career studying biodiversity in the Ecuadorian Amazon and has developed a deep appreciation for the uniqueness and global importance of the region.

"The highest levels of biological diversity are found along the equator, within one or two degrees latitude—a seventy- to one-hundred-and-forty-mile-wide band," Dr. Swing explained to me. "The further away you move from the equator toward the poles, the fewer species you encounter. Here, the intersection between the Andean uplands and the Amazonian lowlands forms a transitional zone of overlap between both latitudinal [north-south] and altitudinal [up-down] gradients of biological diversity, creating an astounding abundance of distinct life-forms. In eastern Ecuador, both the Yasuní park and Sápara territories are within this band."

Dr. Swing first came to South America in the late 1970s on a one-year Fulbright Scholarship. Twenty-six years later, he continues his research in the region. His thick white beard and mustache make him look more like an Arctic explorer than a tropical biologist. As he takes me on a brief tour of Ecuadorian biological riches, there is no doubt he is an expert at conveying these important ideas to a layman. Settled comfortably in his chair behind a sunlit desk, Dr. Swing proceeds with the lesson.

"Throwing around big numbers is not very meaningful if we can't compare them to something else. So, consider that there are estimated six hundred species of birds in Yasuní, spread around an area approximately the size of New Hampshire State. In comparison, both the United States and Canada—with their combined area being six hundred and fifty times larger than the Yasuní territory—have a grand total of eight hundred bird species. The park is also home to about two hundred species of mammals, half of the total number in the entire United States and Canada, and includes ten different species of primates and five species of large cats—an unprecedented number of felids living alongside each other. In both the United States and Canada, there are about twenty-five species of bats, while Yasuní has over a hundred.

There are about four hundred species of fish and one hundred and fifty species of frogs, compared to eight hundred and ninety, respectively, in the United States and Canada combined. One hectare of Yasuní forest may contain up to six hundred species of trees and over one hundred thousand species of insects! Not individuals, but *species*! That's as much as all of the species of insects in the United States and Canada combined! Obviously, microbial diversity is even more overwhelming. So, when you put it all together, the grand total exceeds a million species in this New Hampshire-sized park! This is what we call in conservation science a biodiversity hotspot."

Over the last two and a half centuries, scientists have described a total of about 1.5 million species on our planet. The best scientific estimate of the total number of species living on Earth is somewhere around 9 million species, most of these are yet to be found and described. "And over one-tenth of all possible species, described or not, live just over there," Dr. Swing said, motioning toward the window, in the direction of the Yasuní park.

"Our biodiversity research station sits on the north bank of the Tiputini River, now part of the Kichwa territory," continued Swing. "But a hundred years ago, it was the territory of a different Indigenous group, the Huaorani." The Huaorani still occupy a large swath of rain forest cradled by the horseshoe-shaped Yasuní park, south of the Tiputini River, partially overlapping with the territories of the uncontacted Tagaeri and Taromenani tribes, who have been living in voluntary isolation to seclude themselves from the Western world in the remote inaccessible part of the rain forest since the 1940s.

"The Indigenous peoples of the Amazon have proven to be the best guardians of their traditional territories, which they've managed for thousands of years, without destroying the biodiversity," continues Dr. Swing. "The fact that the Amazon ecosystems are as rich as they are today is proof of how successful these cultures have been living in balance with their environment. Occupying one area for centuries, they coevolved with the land, the rivers, and the rain forest in a way that didn't destroy the environment and, in doing so, ensured their own survival. Those Indigenous groups who have managed to achieve this, including Huaorani and Sápara, have endured and even thrived. That is, until the 'civilized' world blundered in, with all its missionaries, military, and an unquenchable thirst for oil."

∝∞∝

CHILDREN OF ARITIAKU

Though it is located near Yasuní, the Sápara territory is less known, despite suffering virtually none of the disturbances—roads, pipelines, and logging—besieging the Yasuní. Out of Ecuador's seven Indigenous nationalities that have historically inhabited the Western Amazon, Sápara is one of the smallest in size. There are about two hundred Sápara remaining in Ecuador, and approximately the same number still live just across the border in Peru—after the 1941 war with Peru, Ecuador split their territory in half.

For a long time, researchers assumed that small, dispersed Indigenous groups still living in the Amazon are the survivors of the Stone Age, whose hunting and gardening strategies allowed them to survive in the vast, largely hostile, rain forest. But recent historical and archaeological research suggests that the contemporary small groups of Indigenous peoples are actually the remnants of large Indigenous communities that existed until the Spanish conquest of the 16th century, and which were decimated by the epidemics of measles, smallpox, and yellow fever, and other European "gifts." Over the ensuing four hundred years, the surviving remnants of the original Indigenous cultures shifted territories, adopted simpler technologies and subsistence practices, and formed new ethnicities and communities, giving rise to the image of small "bands of natives."

Historical records of Sápara's original size, culture, and language, and the extent of their territory, are scarce. The first notes on Sápara date back to the 17th century, when missionaries and early explorers entered what later became known as the Pastaza province. Several early accounts describe a strong Sápara nation of twenty thousand to thirty thousand made up of more than two hundred peaceful tribes that differed in name but shared a common tongue. They lived in temporary settlements made up of a few *malocas*, or round leaf-roofed houses, surrounded by small *chacras*, or fields, cleared in the rain forest. They built dugout canoes, wove hammocks and nets from plant fibers, hunted with bows and arrows and *pucunas* (blowguns), fished with *barbasco* poison, and gathered wild plants. Whether Sápara have ever built anything bigger than their seasonal camps is unknown, but there is no doubt that, like the rest of the Indigenous groups in the Amazon, they were devastated by the contact with Europeans.

According to their story of origin, Sápara are the children of Aritiaku, the red howler monkey. The very first Sápara, their ancient hero Tsitsano, was born of the union of the two Aritiaku that transformed into the first man and woman while traveling throughout the region. The Sápara oral history and rare historical records explain the collapse of the Sápara nation as a result of many factors, from wars with other tribes to missionization, from forced settlement to the epidemics of smallpox and yellow fever brought about by increasing contact with the advancing world of white men. By adopting different survival strategies—fleeing the persecution, adopting a new language, intermarriage—Sápara managed to withstand the plagues that besieged them.

Even though there are no written records of the impact of the 1941 war between Ecuador and Peru, Sápara remember well how their relatives were attacked, harassed, robbed, their homes destroyed, and their women kidnapped and raped. The war ended in 1942, with the signing of the Protocol of Rio de Janeiro that ceded seventy-seven thousand square miles of Ecuadorian territory to Peru. The Sápara nation was physically divided, with many relatives ending up on opposite sides of the border. In 1952, the evangelical missionaries of the Summer Institute of Linguistics, a global US-based Christian nonprofit, arrived under the pretext of studying native tongues to translate the Bible into local languages. Their work meant to help missionaries transform Sápara from "wild heathens" into good Christians, and do the bidding of the government and oil companies to get rid of those Indigenous peoples that "interfered" with their development agenda. The missions offered Indigenous peoples a seemingly secure life with all the necessities of civilization—health care, education, and a guaranteed passage to the promised land. All the Indigenous peoples needed to do was to stop being who they were—give up their freedom of movement throughout their territory, neglect their traditions, abandon their language, and forget their spirituality and connection with their land.

All of these factors, combined with the elusive semi-nomadic life-style and inter-ethnic marriage alliances with their numerous Kichwa neighbors, ultimately created the perception that the Sápara culture and language had disappeared. But although many Sápara got swept away by the tide of missionization, settlement, and development, a few of them vehemently opposed the advances of the evangelical missions and acculturation. Though the dominant Kichwa language has largely replaced their native Sápara tongue—there are just a half-dozen fluent speakers remaining—the "true" Sápara, as they like to call themselves, have not relinquished their cultural identity, which for them is insepa-rable from rejecting Christianity, maintaining their spiritual beliefs, and taking care of their sacred Naku. A group of Sápara families led by a powerful *shimano*, or a shaman, Blas Ushigua, would not betray their intimate spiritual connection with their life-giving Naku to an alien

ABOVE: Tero Mustonen, head of the Snowchange Cooperative, paddles across Ylinen Lake, near his village of Selkie, Finland. BELOW: Like every Skolt Sámi, Vladimir Feodoroff is as much of an expert at steering his boat on a lake as he is at lassoing reindeer during a seasonal roundup.

The land around Rautujärvi Lake, more than 250 miles above the Arctic Circle near the Norwegian and Russian borders, is home to the Skolt Sámi—reindeer herders and fishermen whose traditional ways are closely intertwined with the northern climate.

Ex-president of the Sámi Council and Tero's longtime friend, Pauliina Feodoroff coordinates the Skolt Salmon Co-management Project and leads the local nonprofit Sámi Nue'tt.

ABOVE. Reindeer winter roundup—when animals are counted, marked up, vaccinated, and some slaughtered for food or other uses—is an important part of the Skolts' annual reindeer herding cycle. BELOW: Jouko Moshnikoff (left) and his friend Teijo Feodoroff (right) set nets under the ice to catch predatory pike and burbot, in order to help Atlantic salmon, their traditional food, recover.

ABOVE: Semion Khudi, a Nenets, guides his reindeer team out of the waters of the Seyakha River, one of many rivers that Brigade #4 has to cross on their summer migration. BELOW: Inside a Nenets herders' traditional *chum*, Gosha Khudi is taking a break from his daily chores and checks text messages on his cell phone. A young reindeer doe, a survivor of the 2013–2014 "rain-on-snow" extreme weather event, hides from mosquitos inside the tent.

The next generation of Nenets herders practice their lassoing skills daily on everything in sight—sleds, dogs, and each other.

ABOVE: Nyadma Khudi (right) and his son Gosha (left) wrestle a young bull to the ground to cut off its velvet antlers, or *punty* (*p-an-ti*). A buyer from Bovanenkovo will pay them 750 rubles (about 11 USD) per pound of blood-filled antlers destined for the Chinese traditional medicine market.
BELOW: *Argish*, a caravan of reindeer sleds, passes under an elevated pipeline at the Bovanenkovo gas field in Yamal. When the pipelines first appeared, the reindeer would not go under them. Today, as the herd crosses the gas field on its annual trek to summer pastures, they do it without hesitation.

A Nenets herder seeks a safe passage through the Bovanenkovo gas field—an ever-growing tangle of gas rigs, pipelines, roads, and buildings—sitting smack in the middle of Brigade #4's traditional migration route.

For centuries, the Altai people have herded their livestock across the plateaus and through the mountain passes of the Altai Mountains in Central Asia. With its outstanding landscapes and rich diversity, the region gained international recognition when the Golden Mountains of Altai were designated a World Heritage Site by UNESCO in 1998.

ABOVE: Alexander Dibesov, a warden of a mountaineering camp, scans the scree slopes for signs of mountain sheep around the Aktru glacier. Just sixty years ago, the glacier came down all the way to where Alexander is kneeling. Today, it is barely visible up the slope in the distance. BELOW: On sacred Ukok Plateau, Maria Amanchina, a traditional Altai shaman and healer, lights a pipe to send her prayers with the smoke to the Sky, the Land, and the Spirit of Altai.

ABOVE: Custodians of sacred sites in Kyrgyzstan, Samankul Azyrankulov (standing) and Kadyrbek Dzhakypov (lying down), came to Altai to reconnect with the sacred landscape that nourished their ancestors, including Manas—the hero of the longest Kyrgyz epic poem, who was born in Altai over a thousand years ago. BELOW: En route to Aru-Kem Lake in the Uch-Enmek Nature Park, Uchural Nonov, a park warden, ties a *kyira* of horse hair to a sacred tree.

Called the "Pastures of Heaven" by the ancient Greek historian Herodotus, Ukok Plateau is dotted with hundreds of burial grounds, or kurgans.

ABOVE: The Indigenous Sápara territory in the Ecuadorian Amazon is a vast and rich biocultural landscape that, unlike the famous Yasuní National Park and Biosphere Reserve, remains mostly unmolested by roads and oil development. BELOW: For Ecuador's Indigenous Sápara people, being able to move around their traditional territory is essential to climate change adaptation.

ABOVE: Gloria Ushigua, the leader of the Ashiñwaka, the Association of Sápara Women, is lighting a fire to prepare a simple but nourishing meal of fish, yuca, and greens. BELOW: Alcides Ushigua Armas fishes the waters of the Conambo River for some barbudo, a foot-long catfish abundant throughout Sápara territory. According to Alcides, his son Emerson Ushigua Ruiz was killed in 2013 for their opposition to the oil development.

In Lago Agrio, oil development had been gnawing away at the environment and local lives for decades. An Ecuadorian court ordered Chevron to pay US $9.5 billion in compensation to local residents for contaminating the water used for fishing, bathing, and drinking. The Sápara definitely don't want this to ever happen on their traditional territory.

ABOVE: Juan Carlos Ruiz, an elected leader of the Sápara traditional territory, is ready to defend his ancestral land from oil development with his spear and, if necessary, his life. BELOW: Every November, the extended families of Hin Lad Nai Karen villagers harvest dry upland rice in the mountains of present-day Myanmar.

ABOVE: After one or two seasons of cultivating a swidden field, it is fallowed, or set aside to rest, for the forest to return. After six, ten, or even twenty years, the tall trees of the fallow are cut down again, as the swidden-fallow cycle continues. BELOW: Along a narrow trail winding through the thick foliage of a ten-year-old fallow, a large green snake (likely a Red-Tailed Racer) is devouring a bat. According to Karen, animals and birds use fallows for shelter and the villagers occasionally hunt them here.

ABOVE: A young Karen woman deftly guides a shuttle across the warps of a traditional back-strap loom, turning cotton thread she bought at a town market and dyed black with natural dyes into cloth. BELOW: A young Karen villager from Hin Lad Nai is playing a traditional Karen musical instrument—a reeded horn made of wood.

Assam tea tree flowers are highly valued and, just like tea leaves, are dried and sold. But even more valuable is their role in attracting wild bees.

In the spring of 2013, to celebrate the survivors of the residential school system, the Tla-o-qui-aht people raised a striking totem pole in front of the Tin-Wis Resort and called it Tiičswina, or "We survived!" The crests of the twenty-foot pole represent all of the Tla-o-qui-aht groups affected by the tragedy of forced assimilation.

ABOVE: A Tla-o-qui-aht Master Carver, Joe Martin has spent his life crafting and paddling canoes, an art he learned from his late father, Chief Robert Martin. BELOW: Islands of Clayoquot Sound are reluctant to get out from under the cover of morning fog. But later in the day, the summer sun often burns through the mist, and the light throws land- and seascape into sharp, vibrant relief.

ABOVE: The mythical green sea serpent adorning the Tla-o-qui-aht Tribal Parks uniforms, says Joe Martin, "reminds us of all the creatures that fly and walk in the world, and the laws of nature by which we all live and die." BELOW: It is predicted that air temperatures will rise by 2.5 to 7 degrees Fahrenheit during the 21st century in this part of British Columbia, consequently increasing ocean and fresh water temperatures.

Eli Enns, the codirector of Tla-o-qui-hat Tribal Parks, embraces his people's traditional territory. The Tribal Parks are managed by Tla-o-qui-aht people for future generations in a way that is respectful of their ancestral principle of Hishuk ish tsa'walk—Everything Is One. According to Josie Osborne, the mayor of Torino, a settler community in the territory of a tribal park, Tla-o-qui-aht teachings even provide the Tofino city council with a framework for thinking about the ways to derive local livelihoods from the land and sea, without depleting them.

All photographs © Gleb Raygorodetsky

God. "Clothes wear out, books get old, but what will save us is our culture," Blas Ushigua instructed his people, as these Sápara groups decided to stay away from the missions. They continued their seminomadic way of life of hunting, fishing, and gathering, called *purina* (literally "to walk around"), from one seasonal shelter, or *tambo*, to the next, throughout the Sápara territory, well into the 1980s. Eventually, however, the growing encroachment from settlers, missionaries, and oil companies forced the Sápara to establish their own communities independent from the Christian missions. They wanted the government to finally acknowledge that the Sápara were not extinct but still looked after their traditional territory—and they were determined to keep it that way.

In 1992, the Ecuadorian government formally recognized 251,503 hectares of the Traditional Sápara Settlement Area, later adding more, for a total of 322,029 hectares—about 8 percent of their historical range along the Conambo River watershed. The 1990s linguistic work by Dr. Carlos Andrade, with the remaining half-dozen Sápara speakers, helped rescue significant parts of the Sápara linguistic legacy, resulting in UNESCO's recognition of the Sápara language as an "Intangible Cultural Heritage of Humanity" on May 18, 2001. Today, the Sápara territory has more non-Sápara families than Sápara. Established by the missionaries, Conambo is the largest village, with about three hundred inhabitants, most of them are descendants of various Indigenous groups of the Western Amazon—lowland Kichwas, Andoas, Cofáns, Achuar and Shuars, among others—whose traditional worldviews were subverted by the Christian tradition that arrived on the hills of missionaries, rubber barons, and traders. Making up just a quarter of the territory's population, the "true" Sápara live in small communities of approximately thirty to forty people, mostly in the western corner of the Sápara territory. We are on our way to one of them, the village of Torimbo.

AN AMAZON

I first met Gloria Ushigua, coordinator of Ashiñwaka, the Association of Sápara Women, in New York City, at the UN Permanent Forum on Indigenous Issues—a high-level UN advisory body on economic, cultural, and environmental issues of importance to the world's Indigenous peoples. She was one of the delegates that Land is Life brought to the annual gathering at the UN headquarters that year. It was a gray, damp mid-May afternoon in Manhattan, and I had spent most of the day inside the UN Headquarters, listening to presentations from Indigenous delegates, their partners, and UN agencies, on issues ranging from the United Nations Declaration on the Rights of Indigenous People (UNDRIP), to extrajudicial killings of Indigenous activists in the Philippines, from conservation refugees in the Democratic Republic of Congo, to climate change refugees in the South Pacific. These were very informative, but soul-sapping sessions, and in late afternoon, feeling a little numb, I drifted outside to share a pint with Land is Life's intrepid director, Brian Kean. He had arranged my participation at the Permanent Forum and was now spending his days organizing training sessions, meetings, and press conferences for the Indigenous delegates his organization had brought to the UN.

Land is Life was founded at the seminal Kari-Oca World Conference of Indigenous Peoples on Territory, Environment and Development, held in Brazil in the lead up to the historic UN Earth Summit in Rio de Janeiro, where critical global agreements, including the Convention on Biological Diversity (CBD) and the UN Framework Convention on Climate Change (UNFCCC) were adopted. After finishing school, Brian had dabbled in boxing, studied anthropology, and worked as a bricklayer before immersing himself fully in the global Indigenous rights movement after traveling extensively throughout Latin America. During those travels, he had helped several Indigenous leaders from the Global South to prepare for the Earth Summit. They asked Brian to create a

US-based NGO that could promote a dialogue between Indigenous peoples and international development institutions, help increase the participation of Indigenous peoples around the world in international policy making, and support the on-the-ground struggles of Indigenous peoples for their rights around the world. Guided by several respected Indigenous advisers from North America, Africa, Latin America, and Southeast Asia, Land is Life has been working tirelessly to respond to these requests and to help Indigenous peoples around the world address their needs and voice their concerns. Land is Life has been helping Gloria for several years with a variety of issues important to Sápara, from demarcating their traditional territory to bringing Gloria to the UN to share her peoples' story, to helping Sápara with a climate change adaptation work.

"Long day," Brian croaked hoarsely when I reached him on his cell and asked how things were going. "Just wrapped up our training session on UNDRIP. Wanna grab a bite? There's a good, cheap Chinese place just a couple of blocks from the UN. I'll see you there. Gloria's coming too." Checking Google's directions at every intersection, I soon found the diner. A bell jingled when I entered, and the heater blasted back the damp, cold air trying to sneak in with me. Land is Life's team—delegates from Alaska and Kenya, the Philippines and Ecuador—were sitting at the rear of the long and narrow dimly lit room, next to the warm kitchen. Everybody's jackets and coats were piled up on chairs at one side of the long table of deep-green faux granite. Talking quietly and sipping lager, everybody was preoccupied with generous servings of fried rice, Chinese noodles slathered in vivid orange sauce, steamed vegetables, and various fried meats.

Brian gave me a firm handshake and introduced me to Gloria. Her broad face broke into a warm smile as she got up from behind the table to give me a hearty hug. She wore a faded green jacket and cargo pants. Her long hair, amazingly soot-black for a 55-year-old, fell loosely over her broad round shoulders from under a jaguar-skin headband. She looked like an Amazon of Amazonia—a rebel warrioress, who, for a brief moment, had stepped out of the jungle she was defending to scan the horizon and get her bearings. I remarked to Brian that she was quite formidable and that I was grateful for her warm and gentle smile. With a chuckle, Brian translated what I said to Gloria and she broke out in shy laughter, shaking her head and covering her mouth with the back of her hand.

Though merry, she no doubt was beat—New York City is a long way from her homeland. Yet, every spring, since the Permanent Forum's first session at the UN headquarters, in 2002, Gloria has made this grueling trip from the heart of the Amazonian rain forest to the belly of Manhattan's concrete jungle. Her goal has always been to share with the UN global agencies, NGOs, and broader public her people's worry about the future of their culture, their rain forest, and all of Pachamama.

"When Gloria came to the forum for the very first time," Brian said, motioning for me to sit down across from Gloria and next to him, so that he could help with translation, "she was a bit overwhelmed by the Big Apple. She'd point at the skyscrapers and grumble that there's just too many big houses blocking the sky. She'd also complain that she had trouble dreaming." Sápara's dreams are firmly rooted in their territory and are the key parts of their worldview that defines their cultural identity, explained Brian. It is through the dreams that Sápara maintain their strong connection with the spiritual world—the realm of their ancestors, powerful spirits, and Piatsao, their creator. Dreams at night, or those induced through the use of hallucinogenic plants, such as ayahuasca or floripondio, help Sápara interact with other levels of reality in order to explore and better navigate their own world. Sápara say that they dream their way to the future, because their dreams are a way of experiencing, knowing, and interpreting the world around them. Being aware of the dream world, and recalling and interpreting the dreams on waking, is second nature to Sápara, just as meditation is to Tibetan monks. For example, a man's power, or *paju*, which defines the hunter's success, depends not only on what his dream is about but also how his wife interprets it afterward. To have a successful hunt, one must dream, because without it, Sápara say, one might as well go fishing instead of hunting. Without the *paju* power, the hunter cannot use the blowgun properly, because he will be short of *samai* (breath).

"When I dream in my sleep," Gloria explained, "I connect with all the spirits of the Naku. I don't see mountains—I see human beings. In my dreams, a tree doesn't look like it does in the waking world—with a trunk, branches, and leaves. It's revealed to me as a person, just like you and I, with whom I am linked through a sacred relationship that can't be broken." Absorbed in her story, I ordered another round of beers and snacks and, as Manhattan wrapped itself in a night blanket and most of the delegates trickled away, Gloria talked about her life, her people, and their many challenges.

She grew up in the selva, the lowland Amazon rain forest, along the Conambo River, a distant tributary of the Amazon. Trekking through the jungle and paddling up and down the river were her fondest childhood memories. "We used to be many," said Gloria. "But by 1970s, everybody—government, explorers, anthropologists—said that we no longer existed, gone extinct, finished. That didn't really matter to us at the time, as long as we could still continue to live peacefully in our Naku. But, when the oil developers and settlers started to push into our territory, we had to let the world know that we weren't extinct and this was still our rain forest, our home. So, we created our own settlements," Gloria explained, readjusting her headband and pushing back her long hair.

"The prospectors came in, dug holes along the river, and blew up explosives to see if there was any oil in the ground. This scared off our boas, who control the power of the jungle, because they are the *owners* of freshwater, and the water animals." Brian explained to me that for Sápara, "owners" are animals, plants, or spirits that define and monitor the rules by which humans must behave toward these living beings. They determine the rules for hunting, fishing, and gathering, and must be negotiated with. "When the oil exploration companies finally left," continued Gloria, "My father, Blas, a strong *shimano*, called the boas back. Then, the fishes returned. For many years since then, you'd hear only laughter in our village. We were quite content," Gloria reminisced.

"But now, the oil companies are trying to come back, once again, to get the oil from under our forest. We don't laugh as much now. With the threat of oil and mineral exploitation, logging, and road construction, the spirits of the forest are suffering. They tell us about what's happening. That's why I come here to New York, to the UN, to tell the world that our sacred rain forest and our culture are in danger. We are fighting to protect our future and our sacred Naku from oil development." Brian praised the Sápara's resolve to preserve the integrity of their sacred *Naku* in the face of formidable odds. "It has been scientifically demonstrated that Indigenous territories are key to maintaining the integrity of rainforests, conserving biodiversity, and [sustaining the] ecosystem services they depend on. These are important elements of the Indigenous peoples' ability to cope with a changing climate. The best way to mitigate climate change is to strengthen Indigenous peoples' rights to their ancestral territories, because, among other things, the rainforest absorbs a lot of carbon dioxide from the atmosphere, contributing to climate change resilience," Brian stressed. "But, territories like Sápara's also hold the promise of big money from oil, gas, and other resource development, pushed by the national governments. This has divided local communities and attracted fortune hunters from outside the Indigneous territories. Inevidably, this leads to vilonece."

According to Brian, several Sápara had been killed or seriously hurt over the last few years. As is the case with most Indigenous leaders struggling to defend their lands against the onslaught of development projects across the world, the lives of activists like Gloria—who have been threatened and beaten up in the past–are in constant danger.

YUCA GARDENS AND MEDICINE TRAILS

R *elax and rest to get over the shock of the crash!* advises a laminated sheet
of emergency-landing instructions the pilot hands to me when I
squeeze into a seat next to him and buckle myself in. Briefly inclining
his graying head, he quickly waves a cross over his chest and mouths
a short prayer, inaudible behind the din of the roaring motor of the
single-engine, five-seat Cessna. Putting on a cloud-white flight helmet,
he lowers the tinted visor and flips a few switches on the flight control
panel before spitting a request for a go-ahead into the black sponge of
the helmet microphone. We wait for a few minutes for the flight control
tower to green-light our takeoff from the Río Amazonas Airport—a
single airstrip along the Pastaza River, at the edge of the town called
Shell. As the name suggests, the settlement was established by the Royal
Dutch Shell company during its early days of oil exploration in the region.
After a decade of operations, however, Shell abandoned the airfield and
the town in the mid-1940s, but a Christian missionary group took over,
allowing the community to linger for decades.

The Cessna's windows are covered with the yolky smears of squashed
insects and smudges of the brickred mud from the airplane's earlier flight
to one of the communities in the vast selva. In the blue above, over the
rim of the distant rain forest, giant charcoal clouds balloon rapidly, like
ink drops spreading on blotting paper. Our Cessna taxies out to the end
of the runway and spins around for the liftoff. I have to tuck my feet
under the seat and shift my photo camera to the side in order to avoid
bumping into the rudder pedals and the yoke, which move constantly
in front of me. My knees are knocking a bit, and I wonder if it is the
excitement of the trip, the rattling plane, or the preflight jitters. It must
be all those things.

It's been a couple of years since our first meeting in New York, but I am finally on my way to Torimbo, one of the Sápara communities where Gloria Ushigua has been working on a climate change adaptation project. In the back of the plane, my Sápara guides are jammed in between backpacks, camping gear, and boxes of dry food and sweets that we picked up last night at the local market—our gifts for the community. The guides are Gloria; Rosa Dahua, Gloria's colleague and partner; and Juan Carlos, one of the elected leaders of Sápara territory from Torimbo, about a 45-minute flight east of Shell. I am hoping to learn about Gloria's work on climate change adaptation, as well as to better understand the challenges Sápara people are facing at a time when Ecuador's president, Rafael Correa, is rolling back progressive reforms his government launched at the beginning of his tenure a decade ago.

In 2007, Ecuador endorsed UNDRIP. In 2008, it developed a new constitution that recognized the collective rights of Indigenous peoples, their right to be consulted on development projects, as well as the rights of nature. Over the last few years, however, the cash-strapped government has been desperately pushing for oil development in the Amazon rain forest in order to pay off its considerable US $15.2 billion debt to the Chinese government. In doing so, it has turned a blind eye to the immediate and future impacts of these projects on Indigenous peoples and the rain forest, going against its own progressive pro-Indigenous and proenvironmental constitutional obligations.

The engine revs up and we lurch forward, gathering speed along the pot-holed tarmac toward the rain forest, looming ahead. As the plane lifts off and banks over the river, I give a thumbs-up to my travel companions in the back of the plane, "Here we go!" Below us, a few cars and loaded trucks wait at a closed gate, guarded by the military from the nearby garrison, to cross the tarmac from the highway toward the scattered farms along the Pastaza River. Our Cessna veers eastward and, gaining in elevation, leaves the trucks, roads, scattered farms, and clearings behind until there is nothing but the giant waves of the emerald-green Naku rolling beneath.

Perched on a high bank over the Conambo River, Torimbo is a collection of several clusters of leaf-roofed huts scattered around a grassy airstrip cleared in the rain forest along the river. A couple of more conventional tin-roofed houses sit right next to the runway. A windowless, blue, cubical shack on stilts has a small solar panel and a radio antenna perched on its roof. A larger stilted house with a single room and shuttered windows is the village school. A short walk away from the runway is a gazebo-like community meeting place, recently constructed with government funds. We set up our tents along the edge of a tennis court–size square of packed soil, under the gabled tin roof resting on tall and roughly hewn posts. Juan Carlos sits on a thick stump in the middle of the floor, talking to a dozen or so villagers who came out to greet us. A quick round of introductions is followed by the distribution of supplies and gifts we have brought with us. A gaggle of kids—from toddlers to teenagers—rummage happily through bags of candies and cookies that Rosa passes around, shooing away a pet scarlet macaw that flew down from the edge of the forest and is now edging along the railing, closer to the bag of treats.

Before nightfall, we amble along a muddy trail through the rain forest to Juan Carlos's place for dinner. His traditional leaf-roofed *maloca* is built on a high bank, overlooking a lazy branch of the Conambo River. When we arrive, he grabs a hefty ax and marches off into the forest to get some firewood. His wife throws a large aluminum pot of yuca on the fire to boil, as a couple of kids scamper down the bank to the family's long dugout canoe, eager to test the new fishing lines and lures that Rosa brought for them. As the daylight fades, we sit by the star-shaped fire under the stars emerging above us. We savor briny fish soup with starchy boiled yuca, and Juan Carlos and Gloria talk about their climate change work.

The climate of the Ecuadorian Amazon, where Sápara live, is tropical—warm, humid, with a lot of rain. The temperature ranges from

60 degrees Fahrenheit to 100 degrees Fahrenheit, averaging 75 degrees Fahrenheit. About ninety-five inches of rain fall every year, and humidity is relatively stable at 88 percent. Though not as dramatic as the Arctic, the increase in the average annual temperature in the Amazon due to climate change has also been significant—about 1.4 degrees Fahrenheit over the last three decades. The average annual temperature in the Amazon is expected to increase by 3.6 to 5.4°F by 2050. (a couple degrees Celsius) This would lead to less rainfall during the dry season and widespread drying of the rain forest, turning it from a "carbon sink," an area that absorbs carbon from the atmosphere, into a source of carbon, which releases it. The frequency and intensity of forest fires is also predicted to eventually go up, transforming the Amazon from a tropical moist forest to a fire-driven savannah-like landscape covered with drought-tolerant vegetation and depleted of biodiversity. Changes to rainfall and surrounding landscapes alter the flow of the Amazon River and its thousands of tributaries, which regularly pour over 15 percent of the total global freshwater into the Atlantic Ocean. Lately, the increasing floods, due to the erratic rainfall, have affected hundreds of thousands of people. In Sápara territory, increased floods created landslides that destroyed hunting areas, like the sandbanks where the *charapas*, river turtles, lay hundreds of eggs, a delicacy that Sápara relish. It is against this backdrop that the Association of Sápara Women of Ecuador, Ashiñwaka, and Land is Life have been working on developing a climate change adaptation project.

"Several years ago, we started noticing that our yuca plants were not growing as well as before—they were getting smaller and their flesh was getting covered in black spots, like some sort of sickness," Gloria says. "We thought about how we could fix it. Land is Life helped us get some funding to connect with a global climate change adaptation initiative, run by our Quechua neighbors in Peru."

Currently on hold because of a shortage of funds, the Indigenous Peoples Climate Change Assessment, or IPCCA, is a global partnership of several Indigenous communities from India, Thailand, Finland, the

Philippines, and Panama developing culturally appropriate strategies to cope with climate change and to inject local voices into the global climate change discourse. The very same partnership that the Skolt Sámi have participated in, the initiative was conceived of and coordinated by the Association for Nature and Sustainable Livelihoods, or ANDES, an NGO created in the mid-1990s by Indigenous Quechua communities living near Cusco, Peru. They established and managed the mountainous Potato Park in order to protect more than six hundred traditional varieties of potatoes and associated traditional knowledge. Since 2004, ANDES, in partnership with research institutions around the world, has been working to restore and exchange disease-free potato varieties between the Potato Park communities experiencing different effects of climate change.

"Following the Potato Park example," explains Gloria, "we brought together Sápara people from several communities to share different varieties of yuca plant to see which one was doing better under what conditions, and in combination with what other plants. We selected some that were still healthy and growing large, and shared them among our communities, to help them keep their yuca harvest strong. They're pretty good now," Gloria says, spooning up the boiled chunks of a white yuca tuber from her fish soup, and taking a satisfied bite.

"Another thing we are finding now is that there are more snakes around than in the old days," Gloria continues. "Having access to anti-venom medicine is really important for us, but it's hard to get Western medicine here. Luckily, Naku is our best pharmacy," she explains. Traditional medicines abound in the rain forest and help keep Indigenous peoples healthy. Without the traditional medicinal knowledge of the healing properties of the bark of the cinchona tree, the modern antimalarial medicine, quinine, would not be available. Without the knowledge of local healers of the curative properties of the Madagascar periwinkle, also known as the rosy periwinkle, many drugs for treating such cancers as lymphoblastic leukemia and Hodgkin's lymphoma, would not exist today. Traditional forest medicines known to Sápara help treat various diseases, including snakebites, but are getting hard to find near their settlements. "So as part of our climate change adaptation work with ANDES and Land is Life, we focused on our traditional medicines. We gathered some medicinal plants around the forest and planted them in medicinal gardens, so that we have them near our communities without having to wander all over Naku looking for them, especially when there was flooding," Gloria concludes. A much more dependable strategy in the middle of the Amazon than relying on expensive western medications that have to be flown into the community.

Sitting on a log by the fire, Juan Carlos is rocking his baby son, who spent most of the evening trapped in a traditional hammock made of the fibers of chambira, a wild palm tree, stretched between the house posts. Freed now, he is all smiles, gumming his father's thumb, when Juan Carlos joins the conversation.

"After we established the medicinal gardens, we began restoring our traditional trails to reconnect with as much of our territory as possible. The first trail we built was here in Torimbo," he says, motioning into the darkness. He explains that, until about thirty years ago, Sápara maintained their traditional annual *purina* cycle of movement throughout their ancestral territory, traveling along an established network of trails cut and kept up throughout the rain forest. They moved between seasonal camps, where they would stay for weeks or even months at a time. Along the way, they hunted, fished, gathered wild fruit and medicinal plants. They also planted some of the plants in their kitchen gardens near their campsites. Their cyclical movements throughout the territory were never random but were dictated by the seasonal availability and distribution of plants, fish, and game. Some resources could be tapped into throughout the year, like fishing for eels and piranha, but others were seasonal, such as fruits, turtle eggs, birds, and ants. Some fishing was also seasonal, dependent on the timing of fish migration either upriver to feed or downstream to spawn, with the period between October and November, considered to be the best fishing season, because the fish are fat then.

The *purina* system enabled Sápara to have access to their entire territory, creating a mosaic of diverse resources of food and medicines that have helped Sápara to adapt to changes when some parts of their territory became unavailable because of heavy rains, droughts, or settler encroachment. "When we had unexpected flooding, or some other extreme weather event," explains Juan Carlos, "we could always move to a different part of our territory where, we knew, we could find food, shelter, and medicines."

As Sápara began settling into permanent hamlets—with schools, airstrips, radios, and other trappings of civilization—the *purina* system withered. Though some of its elements remained, like the hunting and fishing *tambo* we are going to visit tomorrow, the trail system largely disappeared, making it harder for Sápara to access different parts of their territory. Gloria described how some fruit trees and medicinal plants that used to be common along the traditional trails of her childhood could not be easily found, because people no longer move through their land, planting fruit trees and distributing seeds or cuttings of medicinal plants. Recognizing that without traditional trails they would not have as many options available to them to deal with change as before, Sápara decided to begin restoring some of the trails as part of their climate change adaptation project.

"We felt really festive when we were cutting the trails and building the medicine gardens," Gloria chimes in. "It was just us and Naku. We'd drink ayahuasca to talk to the plant and animal spirits, and commune with our ancestors. My brother, Manari, visited with our late *shimano* father, who told him that he was really happy to see us restoring the old trails on our land. It was hard work cutting trees and *some men*"—she raises her voice to poke fun at Juan Carlos—"whined that they wanted to go back home. But we stayed with it and kept going. It all felt just right."

"These days," says Juan Carlos, "the trails are important not only for connecting our communities with fruit and medicinal gardens, hunting and fishing areas, but also for monitoring our territory to prevent intruders from harming our Naku." One of the main concerns for Sápara is the oil development that is threatening their territory. They are convinced that the point of entry for the Andes Petroleum will be the old oil well, a day's walk from Torimbo. To keep an eye on the site, they cut a trail to it, cleared a patch of rain forest around the capped well, and built a "peace camp" with a *tambo* in the middle. Every few days, a couple of Torimbo Sápara walk the trail to spend the night at the camp, making sure that the oil companies have not sent their crews to uncap the well, and that Pachamama is not "bleeding" again.

⸎

"KEEP THE OIL IN THE GROUND"

The fossil fuel industry arrived in Ecuador in 1878, when M. G. Mier and Company received exclusive rights to extract petroleum, tar, and kerosene from the Santa Elena Peninsula on Ecuador's Pacific coast, near the city of Guayaquil. A few years later, a Standard Oil subsidiary was granted a similar concession to look for oil in the Ecuadorian Amazon. In 1937, a Royal Dutch Shell subsidiary received a permit for exploration and extraction of oil from a 38,600-square-mile swath of the Oriente, near what later became the town of Shell. In the years that followed, an airstrip was built, workers brought in, oil wells drilled, and military bases raised to guard company workers from "savages." The first oil began to flow from Shell's operation in 1940, but in just a few years, citing poor returns, Shell left the Oriente. This was a heavy blow to the debt-burdened Ecuadorian state that had counted on the oil revenues to bolster the country's economy. "The Oriente is a myth," declared Ecuador's president, as development in the region came to a halt. Many settlers who originally moved here from the west, attracted by the prospect of good-paying jobs in the oil patch, stayed behind and farmed, cut timber, and continued to build the road to the country's capital, Quito, the most lucrative market in the country. It took another two decades before the road was finished and Big Oil returned to the region.

The Ecuadorian government has always wanted to transform what it perceived to be the savage, diseased, and impenetrable jungle of the Oriente into an orderly, useful, and productive part of the state. Its resolve to settle the region was strengthened after a military invasion by Peru in 1941, when Ecuador lost a significant portion of this territory. In response, Ecuadorian officials enacted a number of laws, including the Oriente Law, the Agrarian Reform and Colonization Law, and the Vacant Land and Colonization Law, in order to open up the region to farming and ranching. In 1967, new oil deposits were discovered in the northern part of the Oriente, and the government seized this opportunity to pry the region open. Building both the oil extraction infrastructure and roads to access it created links between the Oriente and the economic center of the country. The roads brought settlers from the Sierras, and other poor regions in the west of Ecuador, into the "unoccupied" Amazon rain forest that the government was parceling away for free. With few exceptions, the traditional territories of the area's Indigenous peoples were treated as "vacant" and, therefore, available for settlement. To get a free parcel of land, a settler had to simply cut down at least half of the standing rain forest and transform the plot of "wilderness" into a "managed agricultural system." For the government, the Indigenous subsistence agriculture was too chaotic and unmanageable because it was based on a vast diversity of crops and swidden-style agriculture that included clearing and burning small patches of rain forest, growing crops for a couple of years, and then allowing the rain forest to come back. The state preferred a more structured system, where the rain forest was clear-cut and replaced with agriculture, to make it easier to exert its control over the rain forest and its Indigenous peoples.

When we first met at the UN Permanent Forum, Gloria explained to me that Sápara remember the devastating impacts of oil exploration on their land in the past. They also visited other Indigenous communities in northern Oriente, including the infamous Lago Agrio, where oil development had been gnawing away at the environment and local lives for decades. Here, an Ecuadorian court ordered Chevron to pay US $9.5 billion in compensation for a class-action lawsuit against the corporation for contaminating the water used by the local communities for fishing, bathing, and drinking. The Sápara saw that the water was polluted, the people sick, and the kids hungry, because the wild animals and fish had disappeared. Sápara definitely didn't want this to ever happen to their own communities, said Gloria. They also recognized that the damage from the oil being syphoned out of their territory would harm not just their communities but would be damaging to the rest of the world.

"The more oil we pump and burn," Gloria said to me then, "the more the climate changes. If we really want to stop climate change from getting worse, we must leave the oil where it belongs—in the ground. Not because we want to be paid for it, like our government tried to do with Yasuní, but because the Naku and Pachamama need to be left in peace so they can heal."

Fresh off Correa's first presidential victory, the Ecuadorian government proclaimed that it was ready to deliver on the progressive agenda high-lighted in the new 2008 constitution—the first such legal document in the world to grant rights to nature and recognize the collective rights of Indigenous peoples. Ecuador just needed some help from the global community, it said. From the grand podium of the UN in New York— the same platform that Gloria has used to call attention to the threat of oil development and the fate of her people and the Amazon—President Correa proposed that Ecuador would "keep the oil in the ground," by permanently abstaining from oil development in the southern portion of the Yasuní National Park known as Ishpingo-Tambococha-Tiputini, or ITT. According to its proponents, the so-called Yasuní-ITT initiative would conserve biodiversity, protect the Indigenous peoples in voluntary isolation inside the park, and avoid the emission of large amounts of greenhouse gasses, such as carbon dioxide, from oil production and consumption. To make it all work, Ecuador would need US $3.6 billion by 2020, to cover approximately half of what the state would otherwise earn from the sale of the ITT's crude oil, at 2007 market oil prices. The funds would be spent on renewable energy jobs and protecting biodiversity.

But somehow the government's appeal fell on deaf ears, failing to entice the international backers, mainly the rich northern developed countries, who could not quite see, despite their climate change mitigation and biodiversity conservation rhetoric, what they would gain in return for their investment. It could have been Ecuador's troubled history with lenders, after it decided to annul a large portion of its US $10.3 billion foreign debt in 2008. It could also, quite possibly, have been the misleading messages the government was sending about its intentions regarding the Yasuní-ITT initiative. On the one hand, it was campaigning to "keep the oil in the ground," but on the other, the oil production continued in other parts of Yasuní, and at the same time the government was auctioning off multiple new oil blocks in the Amazon rain forest south of the park, including the Sápara territory. Whatever the reasons, during the six-year incubation phase of the initiative, the Ecuadorian government managed to secure financial pledges for just US $336 million, out of which a mere $13.3 million, or less than 0.4 percent of the requested total, actually reached Ecuador.

In August 2013, citing poor buy-in from the global community, President Correa scrapped the Yasuní-ITT plan and invited oil companies to bid for the ITT oil. "The world has failed us," Correa declared, pointing his finger at the greatest greenhouse gas emitters, who expected small nations, like Ecuador, to put the environment ahead of their development and poverty alleviation. According to Acción Ecológica, a respected environmental NGO in Ecuador, President Correa's decision to open up Yasuní-ITT to oil development sacrificed the area's incomparable biological and cultural diversity in exchange for a mere ten days of global oil supply that would release around four hundred million metric tons of carbon dioxide into the atmosphere, equivalent to the emissions produced by 57 million cars driven for one year. At the end of 2016, the first oil began to flow from the ITT block inside the Yasuní National Park. This is definitely not how the Sápara people want to "keep the oil in the ground" on their traditional territory.

While still promoting the Yasuní- ITT initiative, at the end of 2012, the government launched the eleventh oil round for the area south of Yasuní, including Block 79 and Block 83 that cover more than 50 percent of the Sápara traditional territory, including the village of Torimbo. Though the government generated a lot of publicity around the eleventh oil round, only two companies, both already working in Ecuador, made initial offers and even then, according to some sources, only because the Ecuadorian government asked them to do so, in order to entice other bidders. When no other backers materialized, Andes Petroleum—an Ecuadorian consortium of two state-run companies, Chinese oil firm SINOPEC (China Petrochemical Corporation) and CNPC (Chinese National Petroleum Company) that were already working in Ecuador—got leases for both oil blocks. Despite the significant drop in oil prices and the public outcry, the contract with the Chinese company was signed in January 2016, igniting new protests from Indigenous peoples throughout Ecuador. The day the contract was signed, Sápara people, in protest of the impending invasion of their territory and violation of their constitutional right of being consulted, organized multiple rallies, public protests, and press conferences.

"We built the trail and the 'peace camp' by the old oil well for a very simple reason," concludes Juan Carlos. "We need to make it crystal clear to the government and the oil companies that this is *our* land, and they cannot enter, unless we give them permission."

ALCIDES'S TALE

The next morning, an old and narrow dugout canoe pushed by a chugging longtail motor carries us down the Conambo River for about twenty miles, as the scarlet macaw flies. Hunting and fishing along the way, Alcides Ushigua Armas and other Torimbo villagers regularly travel to this *tambo*—a vestige of the traditional *purina* system—at the southern boundary of their territory bordering the Shiviar people's land. We spend the entire day on the river. Sometimes we are baking in the sun. Other times we are soaking in a cloudburst swooping down on us, with little warning, except a sudden darkening of the sky and a thunderous swoosh of approaching torrents pummeling the foliage to the ground. Along the way, we are shadowed by screeching flocks of scarlet macaws and green-winged macaws, chased by flocks of prattling parakeets, monitored by stealthy guans, and watched, almost in bewilderment, by an occasional toucan. A harpy eagle passes high above us, veering off to look for its lunch, likely a woolly or a howler monkey that we have heard chattering in the canopy. We come ashore and hike to a large oxbow lake, formed when one of the Conambo meanders was cut off from the main channel, to look for the birdlike tapir tracks imprinted in the sticky clay of salt licks. As we examine the footprints sunk deep into the mud, a large freshwater stingray glides past us through the murky waters of the lagoon.

Our skipper occasionally pulls up along a shady bank to let Juan Carlos, the other lads, and Rosa snag some barbudo, a foot-long catfish abundant throughout Sápara territory. Every time Jose Carlos lands one—the fish's long barbels wriggling like giant earthworms—he expertly slaps his catch on the side of the boat to snap off its spiky dorsal and pectoral fins to avoid getting impaled on the sharp barbs. A few times, he grabs his *pucuna*, a nine-foot-long blowgun made of the stem of a chonta palm. From a short wooden quiver, he pulls darts dipped in curare—a strychnine-containing muscle relaxant from the bark of a liana *Strychnos toxifera*, and tries, unsuccessfully, to shoot down birds sitting on low overhanging branches as we drift by. It is hard to do it from a moving canoe, but maybe he just had too much chicha—a traditional beer-like drink made by chewing boiled yuca tubers and leaving the mush, called *pikak*, to ferment over three to four days. Throughout the trip, our skipper, Juan Carlos, and another Torimbo youth have huddled up in the back of the canoe next to *mucahua*, a large traditional clay pot filled with the fermented corn-yellow brew. Giddy with the joy of the journey and a bit tipsy on chicha, they toss the bowlfuls of the thick mushy drink at each other and, every time we pull ashore, plunge in the river to wash the yellow stains off. Toward the end of the day, as we drift downstream, Gloria is passing around foot-long finger-thick *guaba* seedpods called "ice-cream beans" for the sweet vanilla flavor of the white, cotton candy–like pulp around the black seeds. Sucking on the sweet beans, I marvel at the giant blue morpho butterflies flickering in and out of sight, against the jade of the jungle around us. A few bends of the river before we reach our destination, Juan Carlos and his friend grab the *pucuna* and the shotgun and, when the boat passes by a muddy bank, jump out of the boat, landing waste-deep on a shoal, and clamber up into the forest—it is hunting time.

Sápara hunt for food throughout the year, but especially during the "fat-monkey season," between May and August, when wild guava and cocoa trees bear fruit that feed many forest animals. This is the best hunting period, but Sápara never abuse it, and take no more than a couple of monkeys from each group. A *pucuna* is the weapon of choice, though noisy shotguns are also used, when the Sápara manage to get cartridges from Puyo. The chonta spears come out when hunting peccaries and tapirs, as well as armadillos. The Sápara menu is supplemented with other gifts of the rain forest, including parrots, toucans, *ukui*—the flying ants, *yuyo*—palm heart, and much more.

Sápara view their prey as human beings, with different spirit "owners" protecting different species. The *amunkui*, the hawk, is the owner of the boas, who are in turn the owners of river and lake animals. The *amasanga* is the owner of monkeys, but, more importantly, it rules over the entire rain forest, kitchen garden, and hunting activities. The sacred task of hunting an animal begins with the hunter asking the spirit owner to grant its permission, which could be negotiated with the use of special hunting amulets. Sápara also believe that it is the great spirit protector of the jungle, Piatsao, who always watches over the hunt and intervenes if the people are not following the rules. Many of their traditional stories teach Sápara to hunt with restraint and avoid overhunting. The lessons of the story of the first Sápara, the cultural hero Tsítsano, killing the last female turtle and dooming the turtle clan to extinction is used to teach children not to hunt female turtles. The central message of all such myths and stories is that hunting or fishing should be done only to provide for one's family and community, never for amusement or profit.

"It was a nice day, and six of us went fishing along a tributary of Conambo River," recalls Alcides Ushigua Armas. "When we made it to our fishing spot, we got out of the canoe and started fishing from the shore." Alcides's sleeveless overshirt, made of the pounded fiber of *llanchama* tree bark, is drying by the fire. He got caught in a downpour on the river, midway through our boat trip. The steam from his shirt mixes with the smoke rising from the smoldering fire and fades into the gathering dusk. Alcides's wiry frame is clad in a T-shirt of undetermined color, which hangs loosely over tattered black slacks tucked into a scuffed-up and muddy pair of rubber boots. His jet-black mop of hair makes it hard to guess his age. Only his poor teeth and deeply furrowed face, the color of the Conambo River, betray that he is fifty-six years old, all of them spent here, in the rain forest on the Sápara traditional territory.

We are standing next to a makeshift dining table—long, thin branches lashed together with strands of bark—in the center of a *tambo*. The shack sits in the middle of a large clearing in the rain forest at the top of a knoll overlooking the Conambo River. An old shotgun leans against a supporting post of the shelter, next to the blowgun. A *kapok*-filled gourd and a short quiver, packed full of blow darts, are tied to the blowgun's long and slender black shaft. Alcides and his companions spent the day on the river hunting and fishing, and now a chicken-size mottled guan with an ocher-colored neck and a brown woolly monkey as large as a hare, lie by the fire waiting to be cleaned for tomorrow's meal.

As the daylight fades, and the darkening Naku draws closer to the camp, Gloria and Rosa serve us a dinner of boiled yuca and *maito* fish—a local method of baking food wrapped in broad leaves, of either the *bijao* or banana plant, over hot coals. Alcides gingerly pulls apart the charred leaves of one of the *maito* wraps and digs into a steaming barbudo.

"My boy Emerson wandered off from us, looking for a better fishing spot," Alcides recalls. "We lost sight of him when he disappeared behind the bent, and called after him. When he did not reply, I went looking for him." Alcides pauses, still picking at his fish, but forgetting to eat it.

"I found him sprawled at the water's edge." He continues gazing into space in front of him. "He wasn't moving. Blood gushed from his nose and mouth when I tried to pick him up. He was dead." Alcides's voice catches slightly. He rubs his twitching cheek with the back of his calloused hand. We sit in silence, as the static of the cycads in the forest around us grows louder. "These are the six o'clock cycads," Alcides remarks. "They're early." The sparks from the crackling ambers drift through the gathering night, morphing into fireflies pulsating in sync with the random flashes of the distant lightning—known to Sápara as the playful Supay spirits—before finally settling on the heavy curtain of the night as the first stars. A lifetime passes.

Eventually, Alcides continues his heart-wrenching story. He brought his son's lifeless body back to Torimbo. For several days he tried to radio the town of Puyo for help, calling the police and the parish council, but no one responded to his calls. A couple of days later, when Alcides's two other sons, Jonás and Jaime, went hunting near the village, they were chased through the forest and barely made it home alive. Jonás, the younger brother, was so terrified by the experience that he fainted as they were trying to escape. Jaime had to drag him through the forest all the way back home. The terrified boys were certain that it was Emerson's killers who were after them. For days later, they would not leave the house. Emerson's body remained in an old abandoned *maloca* that used to belong to Alcides's late mother. A couple of weeks went by before Alcides managed to catch a passing flight to Puyo and make an officially notarized statement to the police. A few more days passed. Finally, a police officer and a medic flew in from Puyo to the community to examine Emerson's decomposing remains. Without visiting the murder scene, and based only on the examination of a decomposing body, they quickly wrote up a report concluding that the boy's death was accidental, when he fell from a tree and broke his neck.

"Why would he climb trees?" Alcides asks, shaking his head in frustrated disbelief at the action of the authorities. "He was fishing. And there are no trees near the water at that place anyway. My son was murdered, end of story! And I know who did it—the Conambo people. How do I know? Because just a couple of days before the murder, they threatened our lives." Alcides pauses to wrap the fish bones back into the *bijao* leaves and tosses the bundle of leftovers onto the smoldering coals. He proceeds to recount how, before his son's murder, he, Emerson, and a couple of other Sápara families from Torimbo traveled by boat to Conambo to attend a community assembly about oil development on their territory. The main speaker at the meeting was Basilio Mucushigua, the president of the NASAPE (La Nacionalidad Sápara de Pastaza del Ecuador), the local organization, recognized by the Ecuadorian government as a representative of Sápara's interests. But NASAPE, says Alcides, is nothing more than a front that Mucushigua and his Conambo cronies use to their own advantage. "He is not even Sápara, but an Andoa who came to our territory many years ago," explains Alcides.

Mucushigua signs agreements with the government to sell natural resources, such as oil, from Sápara traditional territory in exchange for payments that are supposed to support the local people, but these funds never reach the Sápara communities. He signed the recent agreement for the oil development in Blocks 79 and 83 with the Ministry of Petroleum, without consultation with the Sápara people.

At the community meeting, Alcides stood up and declared that the village of Torimbo would never have anything to do with oil development, because they know it would destroy their rivers and their Naku, just as it had done in other parts of Ecuador, and just as they remember it did when the company drilled the first oil well on their territory in the 1980s.

"Basilio and his thugs had their shotguns in full view. They told us that if we continue to interfere, we'll be brushed aside one way or another, whether with shamans or shotguns. This is why I know what happened to my boy and who did it," Alcides concludes defiantly.

"After this," Juan Carlos says, "we decided to replace NASAPE and create a Sápara-only organization that would represent our own interests and make decisions that are good for our people and Naku, without interference of Christianized Kichwas. We called it the Zápara Nationality of Ecuador, or NAZAE. We held an assembly among the true Sápara, and decided to elect our leaders from those who live by our traditional values, who see the forest as a living, breathing, and feeling being, full of spirit. The government, of course, doesn't want to recognize us as legal representatives of our territory, because we reject their oil development plans. They keep working with Basilio. I was elected by our people to represent this part of our territory around my community of Torimbo. We elected Gloria's brother, Bartolo Ushigua, as our president. With Gloria, he's been leading our push against the oil development."

OF DRAGONS AND SPIRITS

I met Bartolo Ushigua, the president of Sápara's NAZAE, in Quito, the day after I arrived. Bartolo's traditional Sápara name is Manari—a powerful alligator that is the caretaker of the water world—after his *shimano* father. There is no doubt Manari is powerful—sturdy of stature, kind of face, and fierce of gaze that penetrates into the innermost crevices of your soul. Along with Gloria, Manari has been at the front lines of the battle for the recognition of his people and their ancestral territory. We sat at a café near the office of Terra Mater, formerly Pachamama Alliance, which has been supporting the Sápara's fight to stop extractive industry from returning to their territory, and talked over a cup of coffee.

"The Kichwas came to our country with my father's permission," explained Manari, sipping his cappuccino. "This is the only reason why they live on our territory. Their true intention, though, has always been to take over our land for their own benefit. They are now in bed with the government, signing contracts for the promise of money, whether it comes from oil or so-called conservation."

Manari recalled how, several years ago, without real consultation with the communities, Mucushigua signed a twenty-year contract with the government for a forest conservation program called Socio Bosque, or the Forest Partners Program. The program was intended to set aside a portion of the rain forest, in the Sápara territory, to reduce deforestation in exchange for cash payments made to the communities for not cutting down trees. This sounded good on paper and, according to Conservation International, a prominent international conservation NGO and the Socio

Bosque's architect, would deliver significant conservation gains. Manari explained, however, that Sápara territory has never been threatened with deforestation, though for generations Sápara have cut trees throughout the entire territory to build houses, canoes, and clear *chacras*. Unlike the northern Amazon, forests in Pastaza are still largely undisturbed, free of commercial logging. Still, the agreement Mucushigua signed prohibited Sápara from using the forest in their traditional way within the Socio Bosque area. They were told that they would even have to return the funds already paid to them, if the government were to find out, from satellite images, that a small patch of their rain forest had been cleared.

"There was no real consultation," said Manari. "Basilio just threw together a token community meeting to tell the villagers that they had signed the Socio Bosque agreement with the government and that it was a good thing for them, because it protected the rain forest *and* they got paid. But nobody's seen the promised thousands of dollars, besides Basilio and his people," Manari fumed. "It's got nothing to do with saving the forest. It's all about the government controlling our territory. How can they talk about protecting the forest and then let the oil companies right in?" Manari asked angrily. Soon after the Socio Bosque agreement, Manari explained, the government knocked on Mucushigua's door again, but this time with an agreement for oil development. Another mock "consultation" followed. Many Sápara couldn't come, either because it was just too far away for them to travel to Conambo, or because when they found out about the meeting, it was too late to make it there. At the consultation, there were mostly people from the Christianized communities, with just a few "true" Sápara. "Nobody even asked us if we wanted oil development or not," said Manari. "Basilio got up and simply told us that if we didn't accept oil development, the military will come and the government would take the oil anyway. The government decided that this farce constituted a successful consultation, and Basilio signed the deal for the oil blocks, this time for the promise of millions of dollars."

Sápara have been protesting this deal ever since the Ministry of Hydrocarbons signed the agreement with Chinese Andes Petroleum for oil blocks 79 and 83 in early 2016. Manari, together with Gloria and their various Indigenous and non-Indigenous partners, like Terra Mater and Amazon Watch, have been at the forefront of the protests. At some point during their campaign, Manari met a representative of the Chinese Embassy overseeing activities of Chinese companies in Ecuador. The bureaucrat, according to Manari, laid it out plainly— because the Chinese company holds permits for the oil blocks 79 and 83 in lieu of the US $17.5 billion in Chinese loans to Ecuador, everything on and in these blocks now belongs to China. Essentially, the Sápara people must just keep quiet, while China takes whatever it needs to recoup its investment from the Sápara territory. If the oil is going to be insufficient to pay off Ecuador's debt to China, said the bureaucrat, they will take other resources, like gold, copper, or uranium.

"He even talked about taking our traditional medicines and timber," Manari exclaimed in frustration, banging his hand on the table and rattling our empty coffee cups. "He said that they would take everything, even the soil, if they have to. If we become a problem for them, he said, they will buy some land in Puyo, build houses, and move us there." Manari leaned forward at the table across from me. "What can you say to somebody like that?" he asked in exasperation, looking me straight in the eyes. Answering his own question, he continued, "Well, I simply told him that if they enter our territory, they'll encounter serious problems. The government, I said, can give you all sorts of permits, but it's our forest, because we've lived here since time immemorial. Our history's here. The spirits of our ancestors are here. Still, he didn't seem to hear me," Manari recalled, shaking his head incredulously. After a pause, he raised his index finger, with a mischievous grin and continued, "then I asked him, 'What about your Chinese dragon? What does it mean to your people?' I could see right away that I got his attention. He went on telling me how it was a powerful spirit for them, and how their dragon was awake now, and this is why their country is doing so well. Good, I thought to myself. Speaking of spirits, I said, what would happen if your dragon spirit was in danger? Would you get mad? At last, I saw that I was getting through to him. 'If you extract oil from our land,' I said, 'You will disturb *our* spirits Tsamarow and Piatsao that look after us and our territory. And believe me, you wouldn't want that.'"

Tsamarow is the spirit whose essence is a spear that transforms into a person, and who keeps balance between people and the forest. Piatsao is the incorruptible Creator who always challenges Sápara by sending both good and bad things their way. He is the supreme spirit of the jungle and the air, the wind and birds, animals and the whole of nature. In ancient times he lived in this world with Sápara and gave them their language.

"I described to the Chinese man the world within the earth, beneath the top layer of the soil. I told him that our spirits maintain the energy of the Blood of Pachamama—the crude oil—underground. All trees, crops, animals, and medicinal plants are connected to that energy through the sun, stars, and the moon. Our sacred spirits maintain this balance. 'If you hurt our spirits,' I said, 'we'll break your spirit and we'll win. You won't even realize it.' The man stopped saying that Sápara should stay quiet. Instead, he promised to relay all this information to the oil company, so that they understood exactly what would happen if they begin oil extraction," Manari concluded. "Meanwhile, we continue with our protests and press conferences. We are doing it for all the living beings of our Naku. They are part of nature, they can feel and think, and we, Sápara, hear their voices and feel their pain. We are sharing their message with the world: 'Keep the oil in the ground, where it belongs!'"

NOT IN VAIN

Gloria, Rosa, Juan Carlos, and I return to Puyo on the same airplane, which has a large harpy eagle painted on its mud-splattered side. Aero Sarayaku is an Indigenous airline company created first and foremost to provide emergency medical services to isolated Indigenous communities in the region. It was established with a US $600,000 portion of a payment that the Indigenous people of Sarayaku received from the settlement of their lawsuit against the government of Ecuador. In 2012, the Inter-American Court of Human Rights ruled in favor of the Sarayaku in the case of *Sarayaku v. Ecuador* for violating the Sarayaku people's right to Free, Prior and Informed Consultation, as guaranteed by the Ecuadorian Constitution, when the government awarded an Argentinian oil company exploration rights to the Sarayaku territory without consulting the Indigenous community. The ruling ended a decade-long legal battle the Sarayaku had been fighting since the oil company was permitted to enter their traditional territory in the 1990s.

Franklin Gualinga, the lanky ponytailed Aero Sarayaku's managing director, greets us outside his company's hangar. He gives Gloria and Rosa a hearty embrace and shakes my hand when we get off the plane next to a gigantic Sikorsky sky-crane helicopter dwarfing our Cessna. As we wait for our luggage to be unloaded, I ask Franklin why they need such a giant aircraft.

"It's not ours," Franklin says, kicking the Sikorsky's tire with a grimace. "It's for mining and oil exploration projects. We're against oil development, so we don't work with these guys, just renting the same hangar for now." The massive chopper looks like a menacing long-legged hornet—pinched waist, widespread wings, bulging eyes—ready to pounce.

"Back in the 1990s, they used this kind of helicopter to bring explosives to our territory for seismic testing," Franklin says. "Though we won in court all right, and even got an official government apology and some money, there's still over a ton of explosives left on our territory that they refuse to take out. It's a festering wound on our land—the mere presence of the explosives affects the entire forest! When they did the seismic tests, it was like they were destroying the spirit of our Pachamama.

"To a stranger in the forest," Franklin continues when we walk inside the office, where our luggage is being unloaded from a cargo cart, "it wouldn't seem like a big deal—just a bunch of trees that must be cleared. But like Sápara, we know the forest is a living being, we feel Pachamama's heartbeat here. For us, that seismic work was like a murder, a crime against life. So, our goal now is to make sure that the outsiders understand what's at stake here. This is what we've been working on. Our victory in the Inter-American Court is just one part of our larger strategy. Now it's a tool that all Indigenous peoples in Ecuador, including Sápara, can use. We share a boundary with Sápara, and we are allies. What happens on their land affects us just as much. The battle *against* the oil companies and *for* the living forest is being fought everywhere. We're working together with Sápara because we've got lots of experience resisting the oil development. When the time comes, the government will bring in military and police, and try to make us, the Indigenous peoples, fight among ourselves for the money they are offering us, or some other resources. So we all must stand together with Sápara to face the threat of oil development for the sake of our forest, our Pachamama, our children."

In my mind, I hear Alcides's words on our canoe trip down the Conambo River. "The government and the oil companies are trying to intimidate us," he says. "But we are not scared. Without our sacred Naku, we cannot survive. We must keep it healthy, and no amount of money can do that. I am prepared to die protecting it, so that my grandchildren always know their Naku as well as we do. So that my boy's blood wasn't spilled in vain, and Pachamama's blood is never spilled again."

CHAPTER SIX
SWIDDEN HONEY

———&———

Sápara not only hunt and fish but also rely on swiddening, or swidden agriculture, to maintain a healthy and culturally appropriate local diet. Also called shifting cultivation, swiddening is viewed by the governments and many researchers around the world as harmful—a backward practice that devastates forests and biodiversity and is a significant contributor to climate change that must be abandoned. This is why Sápara were not allowed to practice their traditional land use in the part of their territory set aside for the Socio Bosque program of forest conservation. But a growing number of experts increasingly agree that swiddening is arguably one of the most sustainable forms of agriculture known to man. To learn more about this ancient practice, I traveled to northern Thailand, where the Indigenous Karen and their research partners have demonstrated that shifting cultivation helps them adapt to climate change and mitigate its impacts—something we all benefit from.

JAR OF LIGHT

In the dark, unfurnished room, a sunbeam falls through a single paneless window and fills a glass jar with amber light. Sitting on the planked bamboo floor in a house on stilts, Chaiprasert Phokha leans his wiry body into the light, pops the vacuum-sealed lid open, and, with an encouraging nod, passes the eight-ounce container to me. The sweet aroma of rain forest blossoms fills my nostrils, making me think of the large flowering trees I passed with Phokha on our morning walk along one of the many trails fanning out into the rain forest from the village. A loose faded polo shirt of undetermined color hanging over his lanky frame, Phokha arranges a half-dozen glass jars on the floor in front of me. All are filled with amber light.

"We've harvested three thousand jars [fifteen hundred pounds] of wild honey this year," he declares, not without pride, and his face spreads into a satisfied grin. "All of it came from the wild bees living in the rain forest around our village," Phokha explains with the help of Dr. Prasert Trakansuphakon, my guide and translator, who brought me to Hin Lad Nai—an Indigenous community of Pgakenyaw Karen in northern Thailand.

I first met Trakansuphakon at a workshop organized in 2012 in Australia by the United Nations University—Institute for Advanced Studies' Traditional Knowledge Initiative, where I worked at the time, and the UN's IPCC. Our workshop was focused on traditional knowledge and climate change mitigation and governance and Trakansuphakon described how, in northern Thailand, the Karen people were keeping their land-use traditions alive, despite the government's attempts to ban them because their traditional practices supposedly made climate change worse. The Karen have been collaborating with researchers, like Trakansuphakon, to demonstrate just the opposite, that their traditions are good for the biodiversity, local economy, food security, and a viable climate change mitigation strategy.

A Karen himself, Trakansuphakon has been working with the Hin Lad Nai community, helping them document their traditional ecological knowledge, while bringing undergraduate students and researchers from Chiang Mai University to study the Karen land-use practices. He arranged my trip here and introduced me to Phokha, the elected headman of Hin Lad Nai village, who organized our stay and meals with one of his relatives. I followed Trakansuphakon to Hin Lad Nai because I want to understand how the Karen people have been dealing with climate change, while navigating government policies and development strategies.

According to Trakansuphakon, climate in Thailand is expected to become warmer. The summers will be longer, and winters shorter. During the wet season, rain will not fall as often, but it will be more of a torrent than a shower when it does occur. The total amount of rain will likely stay the same every year, but it will not be distributed throughout the seasons as predictably as in the past. An increase in heavy storms, the ensuing floods, and mudslides will lead to more erosion, especially in deforested areas. After such downpours and floods, the oversaturated soil fails to absorb all the standing water, creating a fertile breeding ground for mosquitoes, leading to increases in waterborne diseases, like malaria and dengue fever. At the same time, periods of drought will be longer and more intense, devastating Thailand's rice paddy agriculture, the third largest global rice producer.

Pressured by the government to abandon their subsistence agricultural traditions in favor of intensive farming of major cash crops, like paddy rice and corn, many rural farmers in the region can barely earn enough to feed themselves while repaying the loans they must take to buy seeds, pesticides, and fertilizers for growing these cash crops. When the farmers switch to permanent agriculture focused on a few high-yield cash crops, they abandon the diversity of traditional crops that have sustained them in the past and proved resilient to pendulum swings in the weather. When the crops fail because of extreme-weather events—such as floods, droughts, hail, or tornadoes—farmers have few options available to them. Unable to grow their own food, and having to pay off their loans, many farmers quit farming and move to the city to seek menial employment to support themselves and their families.

It took us just over two hours to drive the eighty-five miles from Chiang Mai, a provincial capital in northern Thailand, to Hin Lad Nai. Most of our route was along a well-kept highway. Only toward the end, as we left the floodplain and began a gradual ascent into the forested foothills of Chiang Rai, did the paved road begin to swing from one narrow valley to the next, down one ridge and up another. At the end of one climb, several broad planks nailed between two tall wooden posts covered with curly Thai lettering announced: AN ECOLOGICALLY SUSTAINABLE VILLAGE AND A RECIPIENT OF THE GREEN GLOBE AWARD FOR 1999–2009. The sign directed us off the main highway toward our destination—the village of Hin Lad Nai. Our Toyota trundled on a bumpy dirt road down a steep hill, and, in a few minutes, we were bouncing on concrete slabs, entering the village. The road tapered off at a tiny village square in front of a two-story community hall used for public meetings and hosting visitors, like the Chiang Mai University students Trakansuphakon regularly brings here. Tucked into the folds of a wooded valley, Hin Lad Nai is a cluster of blue-roofed stilt houses scattered on both sides of a shallow creek that, joined by dozens of small streams, flows toward the main Lao River. For centuries, this watershed was known as the traditional land of Pgakenyaw Karen.

Inside Phokha's stilt house, perched on a steep slope, I peer into the daylight through a glass jar full of viscous honey. The sun has just crested over the valley and the lush forest outside melds into a golden honey-like shimmering mass. The afternoon is hot and sticky, but it's nice and cool inside. In the back of the shaded room, behind the sooty pots and pans hanging from the ceiling over a cold fire pit, Phokha's teenage daughter sits on a woven plastic mat covering the dark wooden floor. She deftly guides a shuttle across the warps of a traditional back-strap loom, turning cotton thread she bought at a town market and dyed black with natural dyes into a cloth. After a week of work, she will make a traditional Karen shirt, either to wear or sell. On the floor next to her, a large round tray of woven straw is overflowing with fresh greens, fruit, tubers, and nuts she collected on her way back home from Phokha's rice field. The second tray is filled with drying flowers of the native variety of Assam tea. The villagers have been caring for and harvesting this native tea for generations, despite several attempts by the government to introduce the more profitable, but also fertilizer-intensive, oolong tea. The Assam tea tree flowers are highly valued and, just like tea leaves, are dried and sold. But even more valuable is their role in attracting wild bees.

Three kinds of wild bees live in Hin Lad Nai's forest, explains Phokha. The giant *kenae* bees plaster their honeycombs over thick branches high up in the canopy. The medium-size *kwae* hide theirs in the underground cavities or old trees. And the small *kenae pho*, the stingless bees, build honeycombs inside bamboo trunks. Traditionally, the Karen would only collect honey from the colonies of the giant *kenae* bees. The honey hunters would climb fifty to sixty feet high up a tree to harvest the sweet forest nectar. But several years ago, one local Karen family decided to try their hand at beekeeping with local wild bees. Along a forest trail, they set up beehives made of short hollowed-out trunks of local trees. To entice the wild *kwae* bees to settle in the hives, they smeared the insides of the trunks with the beeswax from the wild *kwae* honeycombs. The experiment was a success, and today most of the Hin Lad Nai families put out dozens of beehives along forest trails, harvesting hundreds of pounds of wild honey every year. They keep some for themselves, but sell most of it at the market, putting 10 percent of their earnings into a village fund that supports diverse communal activities—from purchasing a truck to deliver harvested tea to a nearby processing plant to paying for the costs of clearing a firebreak around the Hin Lad Nai forest.

I am impressed by the villagers' ingenuity in finding ways to make a living from their forest without destroying it, because, regrettably, deforestation has been a common outcome of most of the income-generation programs, and not just in Thailand. But what I find even more remarkable is the fact that wild bees are so plentiful around Hin Lad Nai. As the global collapse of bee colonies over the last several years makes it abundantly clear, these wild pollinators are very sensitive to environmental pollution and disturbance. They do not fare well when bombarded with pesticides, or when their habitat is destroyed because of large-scale land conversion to industrial agriculture. It is therefore quite extraordinary that the wild bees of Hin Lad Nai are doing so well. After all, this forest is no "pristine" wilderness.

—⦿—

SHIFTING CULTIVATION

The landscape where Phokha's wild honey comes from has been managed by the Karen for generations following time-tested traditions of shifting cultivation—an ancient set of agricultural practices that involves clearing forest patches to plant crops for one or two seasons, and letting the surrounding woodland return, before repeating the cycle. Today, the wooded hills of Hin Lad Nai look just as verdant as the slopes of the Khun Chae National Park we drove through on our way here—diverse and thick vegetation, trees of different sizes and ages under a multistory canopy. The village of Hin Lad Nai is recognized by the government of Thailand as a model of a low-carbon, environmentally friendly lifestyle, and yet most Thai and global environmental experts and government officials continue to regard shifting cultivation as anathema to biodiversity conservation and healthy ecosystems.

Graphic images of hewn-down trees and scorched earth shock us easily. Our visceral, though largely uninformed, reaction is to think that any land-use traditions leading to such apparent devastation are backward and primitive practices that must be abandoned. Slash-and-burn agriculture is the commonly used derogatory misnomer that epitomizes the supposedly heinous nature of swidden agriculture.

Thai authorities consider the Karen traditions of shifting cultivation to be the most primitive and unsustainable type of land use. And they are not alone. According to the International Work Group for Indigenous Affairs (IWGIA), a Copenhagen-based nonprofit organization championing Indigenous peoples' rights worldwide, the view of shifting cultivation as a land-use practice that devastates forests, destroys biodiversity, and, more recently, contributes to climate change, has its roots in the Food and Agriculture Organization of the United Nations (FAO) 1957 report, which describes shifting cultivation as a "backward type of agricultural practice" and "a backward stage of culture in general." Though FAO later tempered its rhetoric about shifting cultivation, their outdated sixty-year-old statements still influence international and national discourses, policies, and decision making about agriculture and shifting cultivation.

It seems improbable that a forest so "misused" could provide a suitable habitat for any creature, let alone such environmentally sensitive pollinators as bees. The honey in my hand, however, tells me a different story of shifting cultivation, and the Karen, stewards of this ageless tradition. It is a tale of a forest with rich soils and abundant wildlife, including that key indicator of a healthy ecosystem—wild bees. A myriad of things must coalesce to fill Phokha's glass jars with the rich, wild honey. Sunlight, water, and soil must provide energy and nutrients for the plants to grow; wild bees—an important bioindicator of environmental health—have to pollinate the flowers; and wildlife and birds need to eat and distribute the fruit and seeds, enriching the soil and structuring the forest. For the Hin Lad Nai rain forest to be healthy, this intricate dance must take place year after year, ad infinitum, despite the Karen tradition of shifting cultivation. Or could it be *because* of it?

"For the wild bees to do well, the forest must have lots of shade from big and small trees of different ages. It all depends on the year, of course. Sometimes there's more honey, and sometimes there's less. But we harvest and sell it every year now," explains Phokha. "Our neighbors in the next valley, though," Phokha continues, motioning toward the window, "decided to sign up for a government rural development program and converted most of their forest to permanent fields to grow corn for sale. In the past, they'd never spray any pesticides or fertilizers on their fields, just like us. But now, their soil is so poor without the swiddening that they have to do it. There's no wild bees left there." As he talks, I recall seeing a parched landscape stretching on both sides of the highway just before we entered the Hin Lad Nai forest—copses of trees sparsely scattered over mostly denuded hills carpeted with corn.

Trakansuphakon expands on Phokha's story. "Intensive agriculture permanently converts rain forest into vast corn fields or oil palm plantations, creating dead zones. Hin Lad Nai forest, on the other hand, has remained remarkably healthy, despite centuries of shifting cultivation. And, at a time when numbers of honeybees are declining worldwide, local wild bees are thriving." It seems that the conventional disparaging view of shifting cultivation, promoted by government bureaucrats and development agencies, doesn't reflect the true nature of this tradition.

To better understand the controversy surrounding shifting cultivation, I met with a Thailand-based agricultural anthropologist and leading expert on shifting cultivation, Dr. Malcolm Cairns, before coming to Hin Lad Nai. After years of learning about the shifting cultivation practices of the Naga people in northern India, and an extended stint at the World Agroforestry Centre (ICRAF) in Indonesia, he settled in Thailand. He had just edited and published a weighty volume, his second on the topic, called *Shifting Cultivation and Environmental Change: Indigenous People, Agriculture and Forest Conservation*. Halfway through editing the book, Cairns suffered a debilitating stroke that partially paralyzed his left side. Yet he persevered and finished revising the thousand-odd-page manuscript by typing on his laptop with one hand. When I sought him out, Cairns was immersed in editing the next volume on shifting cultivation but was kind enough to pull himself away from his desk and arrange for dinner at one of his favorite local spots.

A small paper sign, propped up with a tome of Buddha's teachings on a desk in my hotel room, read: PETS, SMOKING OR DURIANS ARE FORBIDDEN! The large and thorn-covered durian, regarded as the "king of fruit," is praised for its taste but not for its foul smell. Because of the odor—reminiscent of rotten onions, turpentine, or raw sewage—certain hotels in Southeast Asia ban its use. Specks of ants were chasing one another around the desk and inside the cracked screen of my old MacBook, when the phone rang, summoning me to the hotel lobby to meet Cairns. On the veranda, geckos scurried up the walls after insects or plastered themselves on top of the giant glass balls of outdoor lights, stalking their next prey.

Cairns was determined not to allow such a "trivial" matter as a stroke to get in his way. The lanky bearded Canadian expat carried on, albeit at a lot more deliberate and slower pace, with the help of a Thai chaperone and a "red truck"—a cab fixture in Chiang Mai. Both were now on hand to take us out to a dinner place where we could talk about shifting cultivation.

"The diversity of shifting cultivation traditions around the world is overwhelming," Cairns said over dinner. "While it's a testament to the effectiveness of these practices, such variety also breeds confusion, contributing to the bad rap these traditions get. Though one of the most ancient and widespread agricultural practices, shifting cultivation is also one of the most misunderstood." A big problem, Cairns explained, is that the term "shifting cultivation" is used too indiscriminately to describe both the beneficial and harmful land-use practices. Sustainable traditions of "rotational" shifting cultivation, like those in Hin Lad Nai that allow for the forests to return, are lumped together with destructive practices of "pioneering" agriculture, when farmers, ranchers, or corporations permanently clear the forest to convert it into agricultural plots, pastures, or plantations. Slash-and-burn is one example of the "pioneering" land-use practice being wrongly associated with the sustainable "rotational" practices.

I first heard of shifting cultivation during my graduate coursework at Columbia University's Center for Environmental Research and Conservation, or CERC. A unique interdisciplinary program that was launched at Columbia in the mid-1990s, CERC integrated social and natural sciences to mold the minds of aspiring biodiversity conservation researchers like myself. One of the interdisciplinary classes, called People and Environment, was taught by Dr. Miguel Pinedo-Vasquez, a balding middle-age Peruvian with tired eyes and a warm smile behind a dark walrus mustache. The tiredness and shadows under his eyes, I was convinced, were cast by his incessant, rarely successful, and often stressful struggle to make the conservation community recognize the shortcomings of a worldview in which people are believed to be separate from, and ultimately bad for, nature. Such a paradigm—dominant in conservation science for decades—postulates that the only way to ensure that nature has a future is to keep it safely away from people, behind some kind of a fence, like a national park.

Harvard biologist E. O. Wilson's pronouncement that "nature needs half!" means that "only by setting aside half the planet, or more, in reserve, can we save the living part of the environment and achieve the stabilization required for our own survival." This strict stance, however, does little to help get to the root of our destructive behavior. Allowing development to destroy habitat in one area with a promise of "offsetting" this destruction by conserving another place actually perpetuates humankind's assault on the environment. It creates an illusion that as long as a portion of nature is put away and locked up in some sort of a park, we can rape and pillage the rest of the planet. In this "nature," says Pinedo-Vasquez, people are mere spectators rather than active participants directly engaged in nourishing a lasting and respectful relationship with the Earth. If a couple of rooms in our house are kept nice and tidy, while the rest of it is totally trashed, we would not consider it to be a healthy living space. Yet this is exactly what has been promoted as the best option for managing our collective house—planet Earth. Instead, we need to do our best to remember, learn, or invent ways to live well throughout the *oikos*, our house—the foundation of both our *eco*logy and *eco*nomy.

What Pinedo-Vasquez had learned firsthand during his Amazon childhood and over the decades of his fieldwork with local Indigenous and non-Indigenous stewards of tropical agro-biodiveristy in the Amazon was that people are not separate from but are an integral part of nature, deeply entangled in a multitude of relationships with all its elements and processes. It is this understanding of the inextricable interdependence of culture and nature that Pinedo-Vasquez sought to share with the aspiring Columbia students of conservation science, when he introduced us to shifting cultivation.

For millennia, shifting cultivation traditions, also known as swidden agriculture, have been practiced on every continent humans have ever called home. The term "swidden" derives from the Old English word for a "burnt clearing." It is a far more neutral descriptor than the value-laden term "slash-and-burn," which is often mistakenly used to describe these practices in a derogatory way. Worldwide, there are thousands of swidden cultivation traditions, depending on the constellations of crops, growing season, planting period, climatic conditions, and many other factors. These systems are as diverse as the peoples who have practiced them for generations. Whether it is *chacras* in Ecuador, *jhum* in India, *milpa* in Mexico, or *chitemene* in Zambia, such swidden systems have some common elements. To begin with, most of the trees and shrubs in the selected small patch of forest, typically around one hectare, are cut down and left to dry for a few days. To help the forest regenerate down the line, roots and tall stumps are left untouched in the ground. Then, the now-withered vegetation is burned to release nutrients into the soil in preparation for crop planting, which makes the use of artificial fertilizers unnecessary. Fire also destroys weeds and pests, so no herbicides and pesticides are needed during the short period of crop cultivation. One or two growing seasons later, the field is fallowed, or set aside to rest, for the forest to return. After six, ten, or even twenty years, the trees of the fallow are cut down again, as the swidden-fallow cycle continues.

Shifting cultivation is typically thought of as an agricultural practice specific to tropical ecosystems, and most contemporary reports of swiddening stress how different it is from the Western system of permanent agriculture. However, these accounts omit the fact that shifting cultivation was used until very recently to clear forests and grow grain throughout Europe. In 1749, while journeying to Skåne, or Scania, in southern Sweden, the Swedish naturalist Carl Linnaeus (1707–1778)— the father of binomial nomenclature, the modern classification system of naming organisms—offered detailed observations of a type of shifting cultivation called burn-beating, which originated in eastern Finland, where it was practiced until the 1900s and included the cultivation of rye and turnips in the ashes of burned out spruce forest patches.

"Burn-beaten areas are everywhere," Linnaeus wrote in his account of the Scania expedition. "If the inhabitants of Småland were not allowed to have burn-beating, they would want for bread and be left with an empty stomach," he declared in his notes. In parts of France, some form of shifting cultivation was practiced until around 1890. In Germany, Austria, and northern Russia, swiddening was still practiced in the 1960s. Finnish immigrants brought burn-beating cultivation all the way to the New World, where, in Eastern Woodlands and other places, it blended with shifting cultivation traditions of Native Americans, flourished through the 19th century, and persisted well into the 20th century.

In Southeast Asia, shifting cultivation has been practiced for thousands of years, mostly by Indigenous peoples living in marginal environments, like the Karen in northern Thailand's highlands. According to IWGIA, in Asia alone, about four hundred million people, mostly Indigenous, practice some form of shifting cultivation. For these peoples, shifting agriculture is not just a mode of production, but a spiritually rooted way of life that ensures their well-being, food security, and environmental sustainability. Shifting cultivation maintains patchy landscape of fields, fallows, and natural forests, which in turn supports high biodiversity and provides families with fish and game, crops and medicines, construction materials and firewood—all important to local subsistence and cash economies.

COOL EARTH

Those seeking solitude, peace, and quiet should not have the village of Hin Lad Nai on their bucket list. I discover this during our first night here. Local roosters (and there is more than one in every yard) begin testing their vocal cords well before sunrise, around four in the morning, according to my watch. Their crowing, amplified by the absence of daily village clamor, bounces from yard to yard along the valley for a good half hour until, finally reassured that they still possess the prowess to entice the sun to rise above the horizon, the cockerels relax and calm down. A few snorts from the stirred-up hogs follow, and the village sinks back into predawn slumber. I crawl out from under a mosquito net, kindly strung up over my sleeping bag by our host, Niwet Siri, Phokha's brother, in the largest room of his two-story stilt house. I tiptoe downstairs, heading for the village toilet, just a few yards from the Siris house. A huge rusted sickle of the moon hangs over the dark smudges of treetops, like a gorget of hammered copper. The din of cicadas has died down and I can almost hear the distant hum and crackle of starlight brushing against the earth's stratosphere, but there is no aurora borealis in this part of the world.

An hour later, roosters launch the next volley of crowing and now it doesn't weaken. Before too long, the staccato of a knife on a wooden block rolls in from the kitchen, as our hostess chops up meat for breakfast. As I learn later, it is a *lu lu*, or a rice field rat, a rodent regularly caught around rice fields with an ingenious spring-loaded noose made of bamboo and string. I get up and look out our paneless window. The bluish-rose band of dawn wells up along the valley's rim, as the earth turns its Thai flank toward the sun. Hin Lad Nai is waking up—a muffled chatter of the villagers preparing for the day ahead, the tinkle of ducklings and chicks rushing to the creek for a morning bath, snorts of pigs and whining of dogs eagerly awaiting scraps of food, children's laughter, and the occasional sputter of a motorbike.

We break our fast in the adjacent room by a fire pit—an earth-filled rectangle cut into the floorboards near the window—surrounded by stacks of blackened tin cooking pots. A few rows of drying corncobs hang from a bamboo drying rack, while wafts of steam float above a large pot of freshly cooked rice, like the morning fog above the Hin Lad Nai rain forest. Our hostess dishes out the steaming rice on plastic plates, set among numerous small bowls of fragrant forest greens, stewed vegetables, minced *lu lu*, and pork crackling. Her two grown-up sons devour breakfast before heading out to the family field, as she wraps their lunch of rice, greens, and pig rind into large bamboo leaves, expertly tying them with a piece of twisted vine. Having inhaled their morning meal, the strapping lads splash hot Assam tea into bamboo cups and pass them around.

Our guide for the day appears in the kitchen doorway just as we put our empty teacups down. With a timid chuckle, Pu Nu—a village healer and wisdom keeper—pulls off a stretched woolen hat from his straggly mop of gray hair. A respected village elder, at seventy-two, Pu Nu is withered but agile. An oversized canary polo shirt and a pair of tattered shorts hang loose on his lean frame. Nodding and grinning, he chats to Siri in a soft monotone, stammering once in a while, his tongue struggling to keep up with his thoughts, making him squint in frustration.

Pu Nu will take us to his swidden field in the next valley, where he grows dry upland rice, a variety that doesn't require flooding as does the lowland variety grown in paddies. On the ground floor, a dingo-like mongrel stirs from its morning nap under the house ladder, as we pull on rubber boots to protect us from snakes in the forest understory and rice fields. We head uphill and the mutt trots behind us, all smiles, tail wagging—possibly glad of our company, but more likely hoping to get some food scraps. The dog stays behind at the first switchback, as we leave the road and cut to a footpath heading upslope toward the adjacent valley.

The trail traverses the slope along a contour line, then jumps over the ridge and dips down toward an old logging road along a shaded creek. We ford the stream in ankle-deep water and pause on the other side. Morning light drips from the forest canopy over the old road in big blotches of sunlight and shade. The cool air is infused with the strong aroma of fermenting citrus. Pomelos the size of handballs—deflated and covered with patches of mold under clouds of tiny fruit flies—are scattered along the shallow creek crossing. Pointing the fruit out to me, Trakansuphakon first recites and then translates a Karen *hta*—a traditional short poem:

> The village my father settled, is traced here,
> The pomelos they planted are still here.
> Look and observe the many fruits up in the trees.
> Their delicious taste remains unforgettable in our heart.

"For centuries," Trakansuphakon says, "pomelo trees have been a symbol of the close relationship between the Karen and their forest. Generations of Pu Nu's people have been born of this forest, nourished by it, and returned to it when they passed. And all that time, they have been looking after the pomelo trees planted along the forest trails by their ancestors."

Pu Nu flips one of the pomelos in the creek with his boot. "Many people really like them, but I don't care for the taste," he says almost apologetically. "It's good to have them around, though. It reminds us of our ancestors, who planted these trees for us. It's reassuring to have some things stay constant for generations." He looks up into the sunlit canopy, parchment-thin skin stretched taut over his sinewy neck. "But many things aren't the same anymore, like in the old days, when these pomelos were planted." He sighs, lowering his gaze to the shaded understory.

"We never used to have hailstorms," he explains, "but a couple of years ago, we had a really bad one. Lots of damage. We lost our crops in many fields. In the village, all traditional roofs made of leaves were destroyed. The government gave us some money to rebuild, so we now all have new blue metal roofs," Pu Nu explains as he readjusts a satchel over his shoulder.

"It is easy to fix the roofs, but it's all together different with the forest," he sighs. "For several days after the storm, we kept finding dead birds and animals in the woods, all killed by the hailstones. I even found dead hornbills and gibbons." His stammer returns, as if, overcome with emotion, he struggles to express his feelings about what took place here.

Reciting another Karen *hta*, Trakansuphakon helps explain the special relationship between the Karen, hornbills, gibbons, and other creatures of the forest:

> One gibbon dies—
> Seven forests cry in grief;
> One hornbill lost—
> Seven Banyan trees are found in solitude.

Long ago, the Karen were true children of the forest, a thread in the web of relationships between people, plants, animals, and spirits. Once, a hostile tribe plotted to take over the Karen territory, to subdue them. The Karen found out about the plans and asked their forest brothers and sisters—gibbons, hornbills, loris, and other animals—for help. The animals did not hesitate, and agreed to help the Karen fight off their enemy. Gibbons and hornbills made a huge racket that sounded like troops of warriors assembling throughout the forest, getting ready for a battle. The long-limbed and big-eyed loris, Karen's other forest ally, sharpened war arrows until their arms were worn to the bone. This is why, say the Karen, loris have very thin limbs. Confused and frightened, the enemy fled without a fight. Since that battle, the Karen do not hunt gibbons, hornbills, and loris, and are always sad to see their forest relatives suffer. Pu Nu worries that the hailstorm was just a taste of the suffering that the changing climate will bring to their extended forest family.

As we keep walking to the swidden field, Pu Nu talks about other signs of climate change his people have observed. In the old days, seasons used to always be the same. Because the northeast monsoons would not reach this far north in Thailand, November through February was a cooler dry period. It would start warming up from March through May, and the southwest monsoon would bring heavy rains to this part of the country between May and November. But over the last twenty years or so, these ancient weather patterns have been shifting, becoming less predictable, and making it harder for the Karen to plan their shifting cultivation and other traditional activities.

For example, the increase in temperature may be better for growing dry rice, but when this warmer weather brings strong rains, diseases in rice increase. When the rains come later than normal, planting season has to be delayed, which means that harvest season must also be postponed. Pu Nu describes how they used to pick tea leaves in March, but because of late rains, they now must wait until April for the plants to be ready.

Trakansuphakon explains that Hin Lad Nai Karen know that their ability to deal with climate change has been, and will continue to be, inextricably linked to their agrobiodiversity-rich swiddening traditions.

They feel that government schemes promoting cash-based intensive agriculture, like corn or tobacco, are too dependent on fertilizers and pesticides, which makes their communities much more vulnerable to climate change. The money they can earn from selling these cash crops—the measuring stick of the industrial market-based agriculture promoted by the government—can never replace the diversity or resilience of locally adapted crops. The villagers are certain that relying on local Indigenous crops makes them more resilient to change than the cash crops. Growing tea and bamboo, and harvesting honey for sale at the local market, are all part of the age-tested holistic swidden-fallow tradition, which provides the Karen with a great variety of cultivated and wild plants for subsistence and sale. Moreover, it also sustains local forests and biodiversity. The richness of the rain forest that their traditional swidden-fallow system sustains is the ultimate source of their food security and their ability to adapt to climate change.

In about an hour, we arrive at a small hut made of split bamboo trunks set on stilts at the upper edge of Pu Nu's swidden field. The shack has only two low walls that support a palm-leafed roof covering a large platform of springy bamboo planks, tightly cinched together with strings of bark. From the shelter's cool shade, we have an unobstructed view of the steep slope carpeted with tall green-and-gold rice plants, almost ready for the harvest. The field stretches down to an overgrown creek at the edge of the lush forest on the opposite side of the valley. It is getting hot and muggy and, pointing to the thunderheads bunching up above the opposite ridge, Pu Nu notes that we are in just the right spot to have a meal and wait out the afternoon downpour. We unwrap our bundles of rice, greens, and pork rind and settle in to rain-watch.

"We need about 1.2 tons of rice per person every year, and I get enough for my family from this and a couple of other swidden fields," Pu Nu tells me. "After this year's harvest, I'll rest this field again for seven or maybe even ten years. I won't plant anything, just let the forest come back. Next year I'll clear another old fallow. It all depends on how well the soil recovers from the previous swidden and what signs I get from the spirits of the forest and rice.

"See that field?" he asks, pointing toward what looks to be an impenetrable hedge. "It's been resting for a couple of years. And that one over there hasn't been touched for over a decade," he says, waving his hand in the direction of what looks like a forest—thick understory mixed with tall trees, their crowns forming a multistory canopy. It is hard to believe that it is only ten years old.

Pointing at the charred trunks protruding from the thick green-and-gold carpet of ripening rice, Pu Nu explains that the long stumps from cut-down trees are not uprooted, because leaving them in the ground is better for the soil and helps the forest come back faster.

"Trees give shade and collect water, which is good for wild bees and the soil," Pu Nu says. "We say, cool soil—full stomach." Back in Chiang Mai, Cairns explained to me that that the charcoal produced from burned plants through shifting cultivation, increases soil's nutrient content and removes carbon dioxide from the air, making the soil richer in organic matter compared to the tree plantations or permanent agricultural fields that depend on fertilizers. I also recall that this topic is at the very heart of the latest controversy surrounding shifting cultivation.

A major global campaign to address climate change, known as Reduced Emissions from Deforestation and Degradation, or REDD, has focused on conservation, management, and enhancement of "carbon stocks" in the forest. The core idea of REDD is that in order to reduce greenhouse gas (GHG) emissions, carbon must be kept locked up in standing trees and other vegetation. Hence, shifting cultivation traditions that periodically release carbon into the atmosphere through burning are considered an anathema to carbon conservation practices and must be eradicated. But according to Cairns, this logic completely ignores the simple truth that shifting cultivation is not only indispensible for carbon conservation, it also supports local livelihoods.

"Over millennia, forests like Hin Lad Nai have been influenced, and likely formed, by shifting cultivation," remarks Cairns. "We know from many studies in the Amazon and other tropical forests that areas often considered 'pristine wilderness' are, in fact, a product of human manipulation over centuries. The REDD program is trying to 'protect' the forests from the very thing that has made them what they are."

It is not the rotational shifting cultivation that contributes to increased GHG emissions, argues IWGIA. It is government-backed, large-scale permanent land conversion programs for industrial agriculture and tree plantations in Southeast Asia. The acrid haze that has enveloped Southeast Asia in recent years—because of the fires set to clear the land for oil palm and pulp and paper plantations—is a telling example of the impacts such large-scale land-use changes have on climate. To show clearly that their shifting cultivation traditions are not to blame for the increase in GHG emissions, Hin Lad Nai Karen, along with two other Karen communities, partnered with scientists on a multiyear research project documenting their communities' carbon footprint. Supported by IWGIA and Oxfam, a well-known global aid and development charity, the project demonstrated that the area under shifting cultivation absorbs *significantly* more carbon annually than it releases during field clearing and burning.

The IWGIA-Oxfam study found that the greenhouse gases—such as methane from paddy fields and carbon dioxide from burning—released during shifting cultivation around Hin Lad Nai, are fully absorbed by the surrounding vegetation of the fallows and the forest. The researchers calculated that the entire 3,700 hectares of community forests, fallows, and fields store a little more than 17,600 tons of carbon, which is about ten times as much as a comparable area of tree farms or pasturelands would contain. The village uses less than 10 percent of that area for shifting cultivation, releasing just under five hundred tons of carbon into the atmosphere every year from various agricultural activities, like growing paddy rice and Assam tea. This makes the annual carbon emission from swiddening less than 3 percent of all the carbon stored in their traditional territory. Instead of being considered a culprit behind the increase in GHG emissions, argues IWGIA, the Karen shifting cultivation practices should be viewed as an important strategy for keeping carbon locked up in the forests and out of the atmosphere.

"Here it comes," Pu Nu observes, brushing the last grains of rice from his mouth with the back of his sinewy hand and motioning toward the top of the opposite ridge. Like a bird of prey, the downpour swoops across the valley toward our shack. The sky darkens, the wind comes in strong gusts, and the static of rain on leaves fills our ears. When it reaches our shelter, all we can see is the thick gray curtains of rain thrashing around us. Not a single drop, however, finds its way through the simple but rugged traditional roof of interlaced palm fronds. As quickly as it comes in, the rain moves on farther down the valley. The clouds part, and the green-gold rice field sparkles in the sunlight. At the end of the valley, a rainbow arches between the ridges.

"That forest is part of our ancestral territory," Pu Nu says, sticking his knobby finger toward the densely forested hillside across the valley. "We used to clear fields and grow dry rice there. It was full of animals. Then the government gave permission to a logging company to cut it down. Before clear-cutting the forest, the company workers set fires to the woods and killed every deer, boar, bear, and even tiger that tried to escape. A few years later, the government declared that this area was going to be protected as a forest reserve where we were no longer allowed to practice swiddening. It's been close to forty years now, but most of the animals still keep away from that place." Pu Nu shakes his head in frustration.

On our way back to the village, Trakansuphakon tells me a story of a Karen farmer in another community. Like his father and his father's father before him, the villager cut down some trees that cast a shadow on his rice field. But, according to the new government regulations, these woods were no longer his traditional territory but were part of a recently established forest reserve. This made it now illegal for the villagers to practice shifting cultivation. The man was arrested and thrown in jail for several years. By the time he was released and returned to his village, both his wife and son had died. There are many such stories of the Karen and other ethnic minorities, says Trakansuphakon, being persecuted by the government, which believes that local people—whom it disparagingly calls Chao Khao, or Hill Tribes—are incapable of looking after the forest and that they only spread deforestation, communism, and opium.

KARL MARX, POPPIES, AND FORESTS

The centers of culture and power in Southeast Asia—densely populated with farmers practicing rice paddy agriculture—were historically spread along the floodplains of Irrawaddy, Mekhong, Lao, and other major river systems. On their margins, along forested slopes and uplands, lived a number of ethnic groups practicing shifting cultivation. Despite the lack of common identity or linguistic similarity, they became collectively known as the Karen, from both the Burmese and Siam (pre-modern Thai) condescending terms for the people of the forest. Though not part of either the Burmese or Thai societies, the Karen were entangled in a web of symbiotic relationships with the elites, who relied on the Karen knowledge and skills to gain access to highly valued and traded forest products, like wild meat and timber. During the early colonial times, faced with the likelihood of losing its northern and western territories to British and French empires, the Thai government relied on the Karen to guard the country's frontier. With the authorities trying to ensure Karen's loyalty to the state at the time, Karen communities were granted high autonomy, and even exempted from paying tribute to the king.

Eventually, however, as the modern Thai state asserted greater authority over the northern regions, the Karen lost their privileges. The state's concept of Thai-ness was based on the idea that the "modern" way of life is inseparable from living on floodplains and practicing paddy agriculture. Karen's mountain living and traditions of shifting cultivation, on the other hand, were signs of backwardness and anti-Thai-ness. The Thai term *"rai luan loy,"* which literally means a drifting field, was used by authorities to describe Karen traditional land-use practices as "nomadic," "temporary," and inferior to the purportedly far superior "permanent" agriculture of the lowland Thai communities. Moreover, local press portrayed Karen as wild, timid, and slow, with no interest in improving their primitive ways. Increasingly, the Karen people were being viewed as a hindrance to the country's progress.

In the aftermath of World War II and the onset of the Cold War, the Thai government chose an economic development path based on greater integration into the global market through boosting rice production. All major floodplains were turned into a checkerboard of paddies growing rice for export. The arable land in the lowlands became a precious commodity and the state encouraged lowland farmers to expand their reach into the foothills and the highlands—traditional territories of many Indigenous groups, including Karen. Where the shifting cultivators saw fallows, critical for forest regeneration, biodiversity conservation, and their food security, the state authorities—just as ignorant of the local shifting cultivation as the government of Ecuador is ignorant of the Sápara people's swiddening traditions—saw only underpopulated swaths of forest, open for the taking. As the area available for swiddening shrank, some local families had to seek other ways to compensate for their land loss. They switched to growing cash crops or looked for other ways to make a living outside of their community.

The jurisdiction and control over Thailand's forests, a valuable natural resource, belongs to the Royal Forest Department (RFD), established by the then newly fledged state of Thailand on the cusp of the 20th century. Today, RFD maintains authority over half the country's territory. RFD's initial focus was on controlling the harvest of high-value timber (such as teak) for British companies, which left the majority of other tree species standing and the forest, by and large, undiminished. Since RFD had no capacity, nor desire, to assert its control over its entire dominion, there were few restrictions on how local people used the forest. Wood clearance for agriculture was even encouraged, and Karen swidden cultivation continued to thrive.

After World War II, international organizations guiding global and national forest policies, such as the Food and Agriculture Organization (FAO), viewed Thai forests as key to the country's modernization. The demand for all types of wood increased worldwide and logging accelerated exponentially. The 1954 Land Code marked a significant shift in the Thai state's forest policies, restricting local forest use, asserting state's control, and encouraging logging. The forests that covered almost two-thirds of the country in the 1950s shrank to less than a third by the 1980s. At some point, the remaining forested areas were much smaller than what was marked as Forest Reserves on government maps. In only five years, between 1973 and 1978, Thailand (an area just a little larger than California) lost a territory of forest the size of Connecticut to logging alone. Mining and agricultural expansion made the forest loss even worse. By authorizing large-scale deforestation in the northern regions, the Thai government believed it killed several "birds" with one stone. Not only did it assert much greater control over the area, it cleared large swaths of territory for industrial agriculture, and at the same time displaced local farmers, who had little choice but to provide a labor force for the new agricultural fields and urban areas.

Meanwhile, Thailand was also becoming a strategic battlefield in the Western world's war on communism that was sweeping through Southeast Asia, from China to Vietnam to Burma.

"Religion is the opium of the people," wrote the father of communism, Karl Marx, stressing the abhorrent nature of both, which was incongruent with the communist ideals. But in the highlands of northern Thailand, part of the infamous Golden Triangle, both communism and opium thrived together. At least this is how the government saw it. In the 1970s, the Communist Party of Thailand established bases in the highland forests where some ethnic minorities, like the Hmong people, grew opium poppies for trade. The area soon became a refuge for the opponents of the Thai military regime fleeing political repression, as well as some ethnic minorities displaced as a result of government implementing its development agenda. Not poppy growers themselves, and initially indifferent to the communist cause, Karen joined the government opposition in protest of the indiscriminate violence against them by the border patrol police. In the public eye, the inferior and poor relatives of the Thai, these Karen, suddenly were transformed by the progovernment press into fierce red rebels who spoke strange tongues, destroyed the environment, were ready to take on government forces, and sold opium to support their revolutionary cause.

To stymie the "red tide" in the region, the United States backed the Thai government's economic development aspirations, but on two conditions—root out the Thai Communist Party and eradicate opium production on Thailand's side of the Golden Triangle. To do this, Thai authorities pushed ahead with asserting greater authority over the northern part of the country. They labeled Karen and nine other ethnic minorities living in the forested highlands of northern Thailand—Akha, Hmong, H'tin, Khmu, Lahu, Lisu, Lua, Mien, and Mlabrithat—as Chao Khao. These "troublemakers," the government claimed, undermined national security by growing and selling opium, supporting communism, and destroying forests with their primitive swidden agriculture, and were now officially a national problem that had to be "solved." Though the literal translation of Chao Khao is Hill Tribes, it is also understood to mean the "other," or non-Thai people, hostile to Thai interests. The government's designation of Chao Khao fed into public perception of Karen and other ethnic minorities as outsiders to the Thai nation-state. Thai national laws, policies, and programs focused on Chao Khao have been developed based on these prejudices and misconceptions of the ethnic minorities that continue to this day.

"When, after World War Two, the Thai government asserted its control over the northern region," explains Trakansuphakon, "shifting cultivation was declared illegal by the government because it was considered to be environmentally destructive. This has defined Thai public perception of Karen's traditions as backward and inferior. Today, the majority of the public still believe this to be true, without really understanding the first thing about the history or traditions of these ethnic minorities."

The fight against opium cultivation and communist insurgency dominated Thailand's Chao Khao policies in the 1960s and 1970s. Because the northern highlands provided a refuge to the opponents of the Thai military dictatorship, the government promoted the settlement of the area by lowland farmers. The colonization was accompanied by road construction, with Thai's road network increasing sixfold between 1950 and 1980. The influx of settlers that followed undermined Karen traditional land use, and eventually led to an increase in conflicts between lowlanders and the hill tribes.

By the mid-1980s, communism was collapsing worldwide, and the Golden Crescent was rising in the mountains of Afghanistan, Iran, and Pakistan to eclipse the Golden Triangle of Burma, Laos, and Thailand as the global opium hub. Soon, the Thai government's anticommunism and antiopium campaigns petered out. When, in November 1988, a massive mudslide carried away two villages in the south, causing the death of 251 farmers and affecting the livelihood of another 300,000 thousand, logging and tree plantations that replaced the original forest above the villages were blamed. The realization of the scale of devastation caused by logging under the banner of modernization finally began to sink in. Thai authorities focused their attention on dealing with deforestation. The leading environmental ideas of the time were those of "fortress" conservation, based on the Yellowstone National Park model of "parks without people." The official response to the forest destruction, which the very same government had sanctioned earlier, was to create a network of protected areas covering close to 30 percent of the still-forested parts of the country and to make them free of human disturbance. The Indigenous peoples whose territories ended up inside these protected areas were caught between a rock and a hard place. First, their forests were logged with the government's approval. Then, the local people were forced from their ancestral lands so that the government could "protect" the forests it didn't completely destroy. Since two-thirds of the remaining forests were on the Chao Khao territories in northern and western Thailand, the ethnic minorities became the scapegoats in the government's search to assert its control over the forests. Resettlement of Chao Khao and protection of watersheds against encroachment became the focus of the government's activities.

When in 1992 the Khun Chae National Park was established in the area and the Karen people of Hin Lad Nai were ordered to leave, the villagers decided to fight for their rights to stay on their traditional lands. They joined forces with other ethnic groups in the region who faced similar threats and formed the Northern Farmers' Network, which managed to fight off the government's push to resettle them. Though still not recognized by the government as traditional owners of the forest, they were allowed to stay in their ancestral settlements and continue their swiddening traditions in some parts of the remaining forest. To stay on their ancestral territory, they had to agree to a number of restrictions placed by the government on their traditional practices—including limiting their swiddening, which was still viewed as detrimental to biodiversity.

※

OF SNAKES AND BATS

From the village hall, the road follows the creek for a few hundred yards, bringing us to the village school. Several whitewashed single-story buildings crowd a small school yard. At one end, a Buddha statue is flanked by two large solar panels—part of the government's alternative energy program. Several kids surf the Internet on their cell phones outside the school's Wi-Fi hub—the only one in the village. We cross the yard and begin climbing out of the valley along a narrow trail snaking up the forested slope. Eventually, as we continue to gain elevation, the track merges with an old logging road. Though large swaths of Hin Lad Nai forest were logged more than thirty years ago, the forest is brimming with life again. As we gain the ridge, we are overtaken by a farmer on a motorbike heading to his field, his wife perched behind him, a woven basket on her back and a hoe in her hand. Here, the footpath narrows and starts to snake its way down into the valley through stands of bamboo trees.

"This is a two-year-old bamboo fallow," explains Phokha through Trakansuphakon, when we stop for a drink. "Another eight years or so, and we'll be able to plant here again."

The slope levels off and we enter a young forest. Fifteen- to twenty-foot trees shoot up from the thick understory that is almost impassable, but for the trail. We slowly pick our way forward, pausing once in a while for Phokha to clear the path with a few well-placed slashes from his machete.

Suddenly, Phokha points to a stealthy shadow, zigzagging in complete silence along the path before us—a bat. I blink, and it is gone behind the next bend. Few moments later, ahead of us by a few steps, Phokha freezes in his tracks and signals us to stop. He points to a spot ahead, a few feet above the trail. At first, I can't see anything. When my eyes adjust, I spot a small and dark angular wing, twitching against the dappled backdrop of the foliage. Only then I notice a large green snake wrapping its sleek and muscular liana-like coils around the dying bat.

Phokha and Trakansuphakon step away from the snake and backtrack up the slope. I linger a little longer, transfixed by this glimpse of life-and-death spectacle, unfolding throughout the Hin Lad Nai forest. This must be the very bat we flushed out from the understory just a moment ago. The snake's coils tighten, the bat croaks with the last gasp, its bulging eyes glaze, and, a few more seconds of this lethal embrace later, the bat expires. The snake eases its grip and begins to meticulously examine its prey. Its tongue darting in and out, the serpent slowly probes its own coils with its nose, until it finds the bat's head. Like a piece of magnetic putty engulfing a metal object, the snake swallows the prey whole—first the progress is slow, almost tentative, but after reaching some tipping point, it is quick and final. The bat's wings are the last to disappear. After snapping a few shots of this jungle feast, I head back along the trail to catch up with my companions.

As I walk along the trail, I wonder what other creatures choose fallows to hide or rest. Siri, our host, told us earlier that villagers find fresh tiger tracks fairly regularly throughout Hin Lad Nai territory. Earlier this year, a tiger killed a cow near one of the remote swidden fields. Once, trying to clear grass around a tree near his rice field, Siri himself ran into a sleeping tiger. Thankfully the giant feline fled, but Siri has been carrying a shotgun with him to the forest ever since. It is the more numerous and troublesome Asiatic black bears that apparently cause the villagers more grief. Nine villagers have been attacked by bears wandering through the forests over the last few years. Luckily, nobody has been killed yet. Then there are wild boars roaming through the woods, swiddens, and fallows. Though the main damage is to the crops, Siri described stumbling on a patch of churned-up earth along one of the trails, with clear signs of a battle between a boar and a tiger, and, judging by the amount of tiger blood spilled on the ground, the felid didn't fair well.

Camera in hand, I hike up the slope along the trail twisting through the thick understory. What would I do if there was a tiger on the trail behind the next bend? Run? Play dead? I spent much time in cougar country in the North American Sierras and Rockies and know my mountain lion safety protocol—look large, make lots of noise, fight back. I am not quite sure whether it applies to tigers, though. But in all likelihood, my reaction should definitely not be "take a picture" if I were to see the king of the jungle, which is what is on my mind right now.

Back at the top of the ridge, Phokha and Trakansuphakon are resting in a small bamboo shack we passed on the way down to the fallow. This one is even more basic in construction than Pu Nu's rice field shelter—no walls, just a raised platform under a slanted roof, big enough to cover a dozen people from the afternoon sun or rain. It sits at the intersection of our footpath and what looks like an old road following the top of the ridge in both directions. "A firebreak," explains Phokha. "We cut it around the entire Hin Lad Nai forest to help us monitor fires so that when we burn fallows during the spring months to create new fields, flames have no chance of spreading." In the shade of the shelter, the light breeze cools me, as I stretch on top of the pliant bamboo planks and listen to Trakansuphakon describe the local swiddening calendar.

Around Hin Lad Nai, after a patch of forest is cleared sometime in February, villagers let the slashed vegetation dry, before setting it on fire just before the first rains. This is usually done sometime in March, but, lately, the beginning of the swiddening season has been harder to predict, as the climate has been shifting. The entire community discusses their plans for burning the fields and monitoring the fires. The best time to burn is in the late afternoon, before sunset, so that the vegetation can burn easily but the fire is not too strong. To prevent the fire from spreading, the flames are directed downslope and toward the center of the field. The burn lasts only a couple of hours at the most and, after about a week, villagers collect the unburned firewood from the field.

Rice is the Karen people's staple crop, and it is normally sown in May, after the villagers perform a special ceremony to ask the rice spirit for a good harvest. Holes are poked in the ground with digging sticks and rice and vegetable seeds are planted. While dry rice is maturing, quick-growing crops, like taro, tapioca, pumpkin, sugarcane, and corn, are planted so that the villagers can have access to different sources of food until the rice is ready to be harvested at the end of October to early November. After the rice is sickled and threshed, animals are allowed to graze on the remaining vegetation in the swidden. Then it is left to rest, until the forest reclaims it.

"Fallows are important for us in many ways," Phokha states. "Here, we gather fruit and nuts and collect firewood. As you saw, many birds and animals look for shelter here, and we come here to hunt and collect medicinal plants that don't grow in the old forest but grow here, because there is enough light for them."

Hin Lad Nai Karen livelihoods are closely dependent on the forest that provides people with food, firewood, and timber, as well as income, like from the harvest and sale of bamboo shoots and bamboo worms, a valuable commodity. The precious gifts of the forest are harvested with care. When clearing fields, the Karen use only a small part of the forest on the slopes, leaving the forested hilltops untouched, which prevents devastating mudslides that are common in deforested areas. In addition, they recognize these landscape features as important for regulating local weather and ensuring the area has enough water. When harvesting bamboo, farmers do not cut down the entire bamboo copse, but leave a pair of shoots in the ground to speed up regrowth in the next season. In the same way, when hunting wild honey, the Karen do not disturb the brood, but take only honey.

Thai authorities, however, still view fallows as merely abandoned land contributing little to the local subsistence economy and community well-being. In Thailand, like with Sápara in Finland and Nenets in Russia, the government does not recognize Karen's rights to their traditional territories. The state has full control of land-use management decisions and designates these "abandoned" areas of the forest either as protected areas to be conserved or as economic forests destined to be logged and replaced with tree plantations or industrial agriculture. This makes local ecosystems, as well as biological and crop diversity, more vulnerable to external shocks, such as climate change, limiting options available to the Karen to adapt to change. Most of it, says Trakansuphakon, is because the authorities do not understand the nature and value of shifting cultivation. They fail to grasp the positive contributions that shifting cultivation makes to food security, conservation, and climate change adaptation. This is despite the growing global recognition that shifting cultivation is essential for supporting both agro- and biodiversity.

Dr. Miguel Pinedo-Vasquez, my former Columbia professor and now a director for International Programs at Columbia University's Earth Institute Center for Environmental Sustainability, argues that integrating swidden agriculture into biodiversity conservation, as well as climate change adaptation and mitigation, is essential for reducing GHG emissions, sustaining local biodiversity, supporting local livelihoods, and contributing to the food security of local communities. Together with his wife and coauthor, Dr. Christine Padoch, director of the Forests and Livelihoods Research of the Indonesia-based Center for International Forestry Research, or CIFOR, Pinedo-Vasquez argues that, when managed properly, swidden-fallow systems create forest "supermarkets," where villagers can harvest a broad range of vegetables, herbs, and fruits from the fields as well as wild medicines, edible wild plants, fruits, and nuts from the fallows and natural forests around them. In one Karen village in northern Thailand, for instance, nearly 370 plant species were found in the swidden fields, home gardens, paddy fields, and surrounding forest patches that made up the village territory. Research findings from northeast India show that high crop diversity—over forty crops in a shifting cultivation landscape—and diversity within crops are fundamental to building climate change resilience and ensuring adaptation. Shifting cultivation creates a landscape-level "carbon sink" that keeps carbon locked up as organic biomass and out of the atmosphere, where it would further exacerbate climate change.

Before leaving Hin Lad Nai, I buy a few jars of wild honey from Phokha to share with family and friends back home in Canada. I imagine them smacking their lips and relishing the rich floral flavor, and think of a day when this amber distillation of the rain forest goodness may become as coveted as the organic and local wild honeys we in the West now crave. It could be marketed as swidden honey, similar to shade-grown coffee, and endorsed or certified by an enlightened conservation or development organization that would recognize the value of the Karen peoples' shifting cultivation for biodiversity conservation, climate change mitigation, and human well-being. Perhaps this could even be the FAO, which, according to Yon Fernandez de Larrinoa, FAO's advocacy officer on Indigenous Peoples and Gender, is now reevaluating its long-standing unease toward shifting cultivation—a hopeful sign of better things to come for the Karen and their traditions in Hin Lad Nai.

Today, every mouthful of Hin Lad Nai honey reminds me of the rejuvenating air along the shaded paths through the rain forest—the loamy scent of the soil, the fragrant aroma of dewy vegetation, and an occasional sweet whiff of rain forest flowers. And in my mind's eye, I see the timeless view from the top of the ridge—the village of Hin Lad Nai cradled gently in the motherly embrace of the earth.

CHAPTER SEVEN

EVERYTHING IS CONNECTED

——∞——

The Karen's aspirations to continue their traditional stewardship of the rain forest while earning a living from it without destroying it are shared by many other Indigenous people, including the Tla-o-qui-aht people in British Columbia, Canada. From the land of Karen, I journey to the other side of the Pacific, where the Tla-o-qui-aht are developing a *conservation economy* that does not undermine but supports local livelihoods and enhances resilience of both communities and ecosystems in the face of changing climate.

When a few years ago I first came to the ancestral territory of the Tla-o-qui-aht people—most of us know it as Clayoquot (pronounced *KLAH-kwat*) Sound on the west coast of British Columbia's Vancouver Island—I immediately fell in love with the land, the sea, and the people. Some of it brought back memories of my own childhood on the Kamchatka Peninsula. It also reminded me of my fieldwork on the Alaskan coast, the Seward Peninsula, when I was a graduate student at the University of Fairbanks. Now I have returned to the area to reconnect with the place and my Tla-o-qui-aht friends, and to learn about the current challenges they are facing.

———

SURVIVORS

The thin, undulating bands of waves lap at the beach behind my back. The gray and damp morning seeps into the sand under my feet, turning it into a sticky paste, like wet raw sugar. The setting is anything but sweet, though. Looming over me, a giant index finger of a totem pole—stacked with black, red, and white animal-shaped rings—stabs the low-hanging gray sky, calling it to witness.

I stand in front of the Tin Wis Resort Lodge, owned and operated by the Tla-o-qui-aht First Nation just outside of Tofino, a modest-size town of almost two thousand at the southern end of Clayoquot Sound. This was the site of a government-funded and church-run Indian residential school, one of several operating in the area, until it was shut down and reclaimed by the Tla-o-qui-aht Band Council. For decades, under the banner of "nation building," the Canadian government made every effort to assimilate First Nations into mainstream Canadian society throughout the country, or as this policy became known later, "kill the Indian in the child." As if the phrase weren't gruesome enough, the means to achieving this goal were even more so—forcibly separating children as young as two years old from their families for up to fifteen years, forbidding the use of their language, and punishing them if they dared engage in any traditional practices. At its peak in the early 1930s, the residential school system operated eighty such facilities across Canada.

Until the last school closed its doors in 1996, the lives of more than one hundred and fifty thousand First Nations children were irreversibly changed through systematic psychological, cultural, physical, and often sexual abuses. Only in 2008 did the Canadian government make an official apology to the victims of this cultural genocide, to their families, and to all First Nations, and set up the Truth and Reconciliation Commission in order to document testimonies and inform all Canadians about what happened in the residential schools, in order to ensure that it would never happen again.

For decades, there was little here to remind anybody of this tragic chapter in the history of the Tla-o-qui-aht First Nation—one of thirteen Indigenous groups that make up the Nuu-chah-nulth (pronounced *new-CHA-nulth*) Nation, called Nootka by the European traders and settlers, who have been living along the west coast of Vancouver Island for millennia. The only two buildings remaining from the original sprawling residential school complex were remodeled into the Tin Wis Resort Lodge conference center and a repair shop. But in the spring of 2013, to celebrate the survivors of the residential school system, the Tla-o-qui-aht people raised a striking totem pole in front of the Tin Wis hotel. They called it Tiičswina: "We survived!"

Hewn out of a single western red cedar log, the twenty-foot pole is a black-red-and-white pyramid of crests, or living beings, from the tiniest mouse to the imposing bear, representing all of the Tla-o-qui-aht groups affected by the tragedy of forced assimilation. Standing next to me is Joe Martin, the lead Tla-o-qui-aht carver for the Tiičswina project. He explains that for the Tla–o-qui-aht people, a totem pole is much more than a piece of art but rather an embodiment of their traditional laws—their constitution. "It represents our rights and responsibilities based on the natural law of Mother Earth," says Joe. "It is a reflection of *hishuk ish ts'awalk*—our understanding of the world where everything is connected."

Standing next to the bear crest at the base of the totem pole, Joe reminds me that the idea of "totem pole" in Western culture suggests an individual's status, importance, and power depending on how high up or down she or he is in relation to others. In the traditional worldview of Joe's people, however, the totem pole is all about interdependence, inclusion, and integrity, where each animal crest depends on the others, all the while being valued for its own function and significance. The crests at the very bottom of the totem pole often symbolize the fundamental role that those animal or spirit beings play in the functioning of the Tla-o-qui-aht universe. Take one of them out—the entire totem pole crumbles.

"The top crest of the totem pole, in our tradition," explains Joe, "always represents the sun or the moon. Those things are very important, because everyone's life is influenced by them. Doesn't matter where we live in the world, we're all affected. This is the first natural law and it teaches us respect—self-respect and respect for other living beings. The second crest is a fundamental part of each totem pole in our tradition. This is one of the most important crests—the wolf who upholds the natural law. "The next crest is of two serpents and it has several meanings. It is the lightning in the sky as well as a mythical sea serpent. It represents our teachings about being aware of everything around us. It reminds us of all the creatures that fly and walk in the world, and the laws of nature by which we all live and die. This includes our gratitude and responsibility to our past and future ancestors. We are the link between them because we have inherited all of the medicines that sustain life both physically and spiritually, and are responsible for passing them on to the future. We are accountable to them and all living beings to live in accordance with the natural law.

"All of this was taught to our people through our *ha-ho-pa*, traditional education, from the moment we were conceived, and all throughout our lives, by our parents, relatives, and elders. This was the thread connecting us to our past and future ancestors, anchoring us in this world. But the residential schools did us real damage by cutting this thread—and it'll take generations to recover what's been lost."

Joe reflects that the only way Tla-o-qui-aht people have coped with—and will continue to adapt to—dramatic changes in the past, cultural, social, and/or environmental in nature, is through maintaining their relationship with their traditional territory, while remaining firmly rooted in the ancestral teachings of the natural law. It carried them through the vagaries of the forced assimilation and relocation schooling, and now they are drawing upon it for the new challenge ahead.

A Tla-o-qui-aht master canoe carver, Joe has spent his life crafting and paddling canoes, an art he learned from his late father, Chief Robert Martin. He is also a skilled fisherman and is just as proficient at handling motorboats as he is at paddling canoes. An unrivaled guide to the Clayoquot Sound, he often takes visitors around the Ha'huulthii, their traditional territory, and shares his deep knowledge of the lore of the land, sea, and traditions of the original peoples of the Clayoquot Sound—the wolves, orcas, salmon, trees, Tla-o-qui-aht, and others. Today, Joe generously agreed to take me on a tour.

Like many Indigenous communities around Canada and throughout the world, the Tla-o-qui-aht people have suffered greatly at the hands of the dominant society from colonization, missionization, development, and assimilation. But over the last two decades, slowly but surely, they have made significant progress toward restoring and sustaining their ancestral relationships with, and responsibilities toward, their traditional territory. More recently, however, another significant variable—climate change—has been added to the equation of challenges that the Tla-o-qui-aht people have been trying to balance for generations.

It is the middle of July now, the peak of tourism season, and Vancouver Island is on its way to breaking a record of consecutive days without rain, one of many signs that the weather and climate are drifting away from their historical norms. Air temperatures are predicted to rise by 2.5 to 7 degrees Fahrenheit during the 21st century in this part of British Columbia, consequently increasing ocean and freshwater temperatures.

According to Ecotrust Canada—a Vancouver-based NGO and a long-term partner of Tla-o-qui-aht people working on developing economic alternatives to benefit local people and places—summers on the island are predicted to be drier, while winters will see more rain and less snow. Less summer rain will make freshwater a precious commodity here during the warm months, even though it is one of the wettest places in North America. And the winter storms will continue to get stronger, pummeling the Clayoquot coast more often, as the sea level continues to inch up the shoreline, eating it away. I want to understand what these new transformations mean to the Tla-o-qui-aht people in the context of past changes they have experienced—abrupt social shakeups, like assimilation into industrial society; environmental changes, such as deforestation and overfishing; and unfolding climactic shifts, like warming air and water; and sea level rise.

Over the next few days, I hope to learn from Joe and his Tla-o-qui-aht relatives and friends, like his nephew and the tribal parks codirector, Eli Enns, and a tribal parks guardian, Cory Charlie, how they are navigating these challenges not of their own making. But to even begin a conversation, I first need to reacquaint myself with the place and the people. So, today, Joe is taking me to some of the most significant places in Tla-o-qui-aht people's territory. Our first stop is Echachist.

⚬⚬⚬

ENCHANTED ISLAND

At first, there is nothing, just shades of gray. The grayness brightens in places only to dim moments later. Some lighter patches rise and merge, darker ones swirl and fade. They are seeping into every pore of my exposed flesh. Ahead, a darker shape precipitates out of this almost primordial grayness. With no reference points, it is hard to judge the scale—is it a smudge on my glasses or an enormous mass looming in the distance? The *put-putt*ing of the ninety-horse outboard motor is almost inaudible in the thick fog as our twenty-foot fiberglass fishing boat rides the glassy swell toward the obscure shape ahead.

"Echachist!" Joe Martin's muffled voice comes from behind me, as the shadow condenses into the recognizable shape of an island. I hear *Enchanted!* instead. Suspended above the ocean—like Laputa, the flying island of Miyazaki's *Castle in the Sky*—Echachist, our destination, is swaddled in the rolling waves of dense morning mist. The fog has enveloped us since early morning, when Joe first pushed his boat away from a dock in Tofino—a nature lover's mecca. The town's small resident

population swells tenfold as whale-watchers and bird-watchers, surfers and anglers, storm trackers and kayakers, flock here throughout the year from around the world. Like a kid lingering in bed, pulling the quilt over her head when it's time to rise and get ready for school, Tofino always seems reluctant to get out from under the cover of morning fog. But later in the day, the summer sun often burns through the mist, and the light throws land- and seascape into sharp, vibrant relief. Joe is certainly counting on that today.

From under a full head of thick black hair with only a few streaks of white at his temples, Joe's penetrating dark eyes quickly scan the distance between the boat and the emerging coastline. Standing behind the navigation console and donning a crimson flotation jacket, Joe slowly turns the boat's wheel, cautiously guiding the vessel around large rafts of bull kelp toward the craggy coastline now in full view. In a few minutes we reach a rocky point on the island's southeastern shore that forms a natural breakwater, sheltering a sandy beach on the opposite side.

Joe kills the motor several feet from the rocks and nimbly runs to the front of the boat to grab a mooring buoy bobbing on the surface among the bladders of the bull kelp. With a few slashes of his fishing knife, he clears a patch around the boat from the large kelp blades and stipes, or stems, to make it easier to secure the boat to the mooring line with a couple of deft knots. Joe jumps onto the rocks and holds the boat as I climb out. "Welcome to Echachist, the home of Tla-o-qui-aht people," he says, and then adds, grinning, "And my home!" Where Echachist's ancient forest reaches the beach stands a house that Joe built more than twenty years ago.

Coastal temperate rain forests, like those of Clayoquot Sound, are as breathtaking as they are unique. Covering less than 1 percent of the planet's land surface along the coasts of western North America, New Zealand, Tasmania, Chile, and Argentina, these forests are rare and getting more so, as the timber industry continues to log the old growth woods, even though at reduced rates. A sixty-mile stretch of Vancouver Island's west coast is one of the few remaining places on earth where such rain forests endure.

The giant western hemlocks, Douglas firs, western red cedars, and Sitka spruce are some of the earth's most ancient living beings. More than a thousand years old and reaching three hundred feet tall and sixty feet in girth, these giants have stood witness to the region's history, both ancient and modern, geological and ecological, natural and human. The very presence of the old-growth rain forests here along the coast signifies that fundamental shifts in the earth's environment have already taken place, for the trees could only take root when the glaciers and the sea had retreated as the climate warmed.

In geological, and even human, terms, the climate and forests of Vancouver Island we know today are fairly young. The millennia of glacial advances and retreats between 29,000 and 15,000 years ago carved out the 865,000 acres of watershed that drains into the sound. When glaciers finally retreated, around 15,000 years ago, the climate became colder and drier compared to today. A warming period between 12,000 and 11,000 years ago allowed Douglas fir to take hold and expand, but about 8,000 years ago, the onset of a wetter and cooler climate helped western red cedar thrive and the entire ecosystem gradually transformed into the coastal temperate forests we know today. The Clayoquot Sound shoreline dropped from about one hundred feet to just ten feet above today's sea level, between 13,000 and 7,000 years ago. After remaining unchanged for another 1,000 years, the sea then continued to recede to its present levels.

With the glaciers' retreat, the coastal waters, the land, and its forests became home to a rich diversity of life-forms. The warm North Pacific Current brings moist air from the western Pacific to the western shores of Vancouver Island, where the rising slopes of the steep coastal mountains check the eastward progress of the ocean and air flows. Having used up every iota of energy carrying its burden of moisture this far, the clouds spill the rain and snow over the large tracts of coastal rain forest. Sometimes it rains as much as 120 inches a year here, giving it a reputation of one of the wettest spots in North America. The lakes, bogs, and aquifers absorb this deluge, while the countless rivulets, rills, streams, and rivers bring it back to the ocean. In the estuaries dotted with rocky skerries, or small islands, the sediment carried by the water from the forested mountain slopes settles into mudflats. The sea and forests, streams and mountains, fjords and mudflats—all form the rich matrix that creates abundant and diverse habitats that shelter and nourish a wide variety of local and migratory species.

Dungeness crabs scour the shallows in search of clams with such exotic names as manila, butter, varnish, and razor. En route from South America to the Arctic, flocks of western sandpipers make a stopover at the Tofino mudflats to feast on the profusion of polychaete worms and other invertebrates. Herring converge on beds of eelgrass along the shores to spawn, their eggs and milt mixing with seawater, attracting thousands of birds, whales, and seals. Cruising along the coast, gray whales dive to the bottom of shallow bays to gulp up the sediment teaming with mud-dwelling clams, ghost shrimp, and marine worms, which they filter out through the baleen plates suspended from their palates. Black and brown bears feast on salmon spawning in the streams and forage on salal, thimble, huckle- and salmonberries abundant in the forest understory. Roaming the mountains and coasts are wolves and cougars in search of black-tailed deer and Roosevelt elk that thrive on the nutritious grasses and lichens flourishing throughout the old-growth forest.

But it is the Pacific salmon that is the life thread of the Clayoquot ecosystem that stitches the land and sea together through its life cycle. Every summer, after traveling for nearly nine thousand miles away from their nursery streams, fattening for years in the open ocean on herring, pelagic amphipods, and krill, the salmon return to fresh water to spawn and die, unlike their Atlantic cousins, which the Skolt Sámi depend on. The Pacific salmon return to their birthplace, following scents and waypoints known only to them. They brave the rapids and waterfalls on the way to their spawning grounds—the gravel bottoms of creeks and springs—where they lay their eggs. Along the way, their bodies—battered and scarred by obstacles and predators—change. They transform into ancient warriors wearing the war paint of their distinct tribes—red sockeyes, purple chums, and rosy pinks. Though their fearsome headgear of hooked jaws and protruding teeth may be effective at keeping their own kin at bay as they battle for spawning partners, it fails to repel other foes, such as eagles, bears, and men.

More than 190 different species of plants and animals—from killer whales to giant cedars, from insects to lichens, from loons to bears—depend on the yearly arrival of this remarkable constellation of Pacific salmonids. By dragging the still-thrashing fish or the carcasses of spawned-out, dead salmon into the brush, predators transport precious nutrients, particularly marine nitrogen, into the riparian ecosystem. Along large watersheds, where bears are common, the traces of marine nitrogen of salmon can be found in plants growing as far as twenty-five hundred feet away from the stream. But even near small salmon streams, plants five hundred feet from the water are still "made of salmon," or of its constituent nutrients dispersed by predators and scavengers throughout the area and absorbed by the plants through their roots. Such an intricate entanglement of life's vital elements creates inalienable relationships between the open ocean and the old-growth forest. The salmon bring back with them precious nutrients to nourish the old-growth forests that provide cool, shaded waterways with ideal conditions for salmon eggs, as well as for *fry*, the freshwater life stage of salmon, that mature into smolt, the life stage that heads out into the open ocean.

Over millennia, this vibrant web of relationships has also supported human societies as rich and diverse as the ecosystems on which they depended. According to their lore, the Nuu-chah-nulth people have thrived all along the western shores of Vancouver Island since time immemorial. Nobody knows for sure, but it is estimated that before the smallpox epidemics introduced by European settlers decimated the region's communities in the mid-1800s, the Nuu-chah-nulth tribes living on Vancouver Island numbered close to one hundred thousand people. Today, less than eighty-five hundred Nuu-chah-nulth remain, thirteen hundred of which are Tla-o-qui-aht people. For thousands of years, flora and fauna of ocean and land—whales and salmon, halibut and berries, herring and ducks, clams and springbank clover—shaped their lives.

Echachist used to be a major seasonal hub for Tla-o-qui-aht whaling and fishing. Before the arrival of Europeans, it was a thriving center of Tla-o-qui-aht culture, serving as a major summer seat of the leading Chief Wickaninnish. The island's location, at the mouth of the Clayoquot Sound, where it meets the Pacific, made it an ideal site to launch whaling canoes. The island's even gravel beaches were also well suited for the landing of harpooned whales—gray, right, or humpback—as thousands of animals migrated past Echachist every year.

As I follow Joe to his house, my feet slide on rocks slippery with algae exposed by the receding tide and I stumble. At sixty, Joe moves up the steep rocky beach with the agility and surefootedness of a young man who knows every pebble on his land. The faded one-story building at the edge of the forest overlooking the landing has a wide unfenced deck under a big window facing the beach and the ocean.

Sun-bleached mussel shells, skulls, bones, and unusually colored and shaped pebbles adorn the top of a weatherworn low bench and a couple of small rickety tables under the window. Inside, the gray light, still struggling to break through the fog, seeps into the cabin through the window, creating a framed image of Echachist's coastline, like in a vintage photograph. Just like the faded archival photo that Joe is holding in his hands.

Wrapped in a traditional bearskin blanket, a Nuu-chah-nulth whaler stands on the beach. A pair of sealskin bladders is hoisted on his shoulders, tethered with a coiled leather thong to the whaling harpoon he is holding in his other hand. "In those days, our people mostly preferred to hunt for humpback whales," Joe says with a hint of nostalgia in his voice. "But there were other whales that were taken as well, like the finback, which is the second largest whale in the world, and the right whale, which also used to be here. They also went after the gray, minke, and sperm whales in their large whaling canoes."

Joe's Spartan house is spacious but sparsely furnished. There are a couple of old chairs and a table in the middle of the room. By the window, there are a bed and several shelves packed with tattered books, stacks of papers, carvings, and a medley of souvenirs from his various voyages.

"In the old days, our people would spend several weeks living on the island during the spring season," Joe explains. From a wall nail he lifts a hand-size hook made of hard wood. "This is a traditional halibut hook I made from the base of a spruce branch. I didn't quite finish it, because the wood had a weak point, but it's good enough for you to see how we used to catch halibut."

Holding one end of the wooden hook in his left hand, Joe places his right index finger across it to indicate where the missing barb and the bait would go. "The halibut fishing spot isn't too far from here," Joe explains. "In the old days, they'd bait the hooks with octopus caught on the reefs, and paddle out to set them on the ocean floor. We still go fishing in the same spot, but there is much less halibut nowadays and it doesn't grow as big as in the past."

I follow Joe out of the house and we walk to the opposite side of the beach. Countless mussel shells, crusted-over with sea salt and bleached by the sun, crunch under my feet. Joe stops at an opening to a wide channel leading through the rocks from the beach all the way to the open water. Large boulders piled up high on both sides signify the hard work Joe's ancestors put into clearing the beach to make it easier to beach harpooned whales centuries ago. The whales were butchered right on the shore, and the meat was cut up and smoke-dried for the winter, while the blubber was rendered into oil. Many whalebones were left behind in ever-growing heaps.

Joe points toward a grass-covered knoll about 15 feet tall and 150 feet long at the edge of the forest. "This is one of the spots where the bones were left," he says. "In fact there's this fella I'm to meet here in the next few days—Dr. Jim Darling. He's a whale biologist living here in Tofino. We're supposed to make a plan about where to begin digging for whalebones. Basically, he wants to be able to tell what kind of whale, how long ago it was, and also to see, perhaps, even what kind of a diet that whale had. For me, the general idea is to get our own youth interested in this history, so that they learn about our traditional territory and our way of life. Especially about the history of whaling, which used to be so important to our people but had to be abandoned because of what commercial whaling did to the whales."

Commercial whaling came to the Pacific Northwest in the mid-1800s, and, in less than a century, unleashed the same devastation on the migratory populations of whales that the fur trade had inflicted upon the furbearers a few decades earlier. Between 1905 and 1967, when commercial whaling was finally banned, whaling stations along the west coast of Vancouver Island alone killed and processed a total of over 24,800 fin, sperm, gray, humpback, and blue whales. The collapse in numbers of whales passing through Tla-o-qui-aht traditional territory during the first half of the 20th century made it increasingly difficult for Tla-o-qui-aht people to continue their annual subsistence cycle. As the whaling on Echachist came to an end, the island ceased to be a seasonal hub for Tla-o-qui-aht hunting and fishing. Joe's house is the only permanent Tla-o-qui-aht dwelling remaining.

Tla-o-qui-aht whaling technology was far from primitive—on the contrary, it was quite lethal. A thirty- to forty-foot oceangoing whaling canoe made of a single cedar log and manned by an eight-person crew allowed for quick pursuit of the migrating giants. Sitting side by side, six paddlers propelled the boat, with a steersman at the stern. In the bow, a harpooner captained the canoe, directing the hunt based on his knowledge of whale behavior and his ability to read subtle signs to predict a whale's movements. In the hands of a master harpooner, an eighteen-foot-long spear—its head hewn out of two interlocking pieces of hard yew and tipped with a sharp mussel shell glued into the shaft with rock-solid spruce sap—was a formidable weapon capable of making a significant dent in the numbers of whales migrating past Echachist. Still, despite this advanced technology, the Tla-o-qui-aht people managed to harvest whales for centuries without diminishing their numbers.

Joe explains that each Tla-o-qui-aht house, or clan, followed a set of traditional, time-tested rules governing their relationship with the entire Ha'huulthii, including how many whales they could take during the annual whale hunt. "I come from the house of Eewas, which means a wide land, and we were allowed to take ten whales every year," Joe states proudly and looks at me to see my reaction. With several thousand Tla-o-qui-aht people living around the Clayoquot Sound at the time, I imagine that unregulated whale harvest could be quite devastating. "Still"—Joe pauses here to emphasize the point—"they would never kill more than what they needed to provide for themselves, and every year they had whales to hunt. One of our teachings is that Mother Nature will provide for our needs, but not our greed. And it's our greed that's destroying many things nowadays."

We continue for a few minutes along the beach, climbing over rocks to the edge of an open grotto the size of a small swimming pool. The tide is beginning to come in, but there is still enough room for the waves to take a quick run across the cavern and slam with a timpani-like *BOOM!* against the underside of a low ledge. For Tla-o-qui-aht, as for other Nuu-chah-nulth tribes, whaling was not just a matter of subsistence, but it was a culturally and spiritually significant activity.

"Our whale hunters would come here to dive and prepare themselves for the hunt," says Joe, his bronzed hand reaching toward the pool.

"With the waves moving in and out like this, it kept them in practice so that they would never, ever be afraid of the water. They would come here and do this ritual the night before the hunt or early in the morning, just before leaving." We stand by the pool for a few minutes, listening to the pulse of the Clayoquot.

"Well, the fog's lifting," Joe finally says, pulling himself away from this window into his people's past. "Now's a good time to go to Meares Island—it'll be a nice ride." As we head to the island, the last wisps of fog dissipate and Clayoquot Sound around us bursts forth in brilliant hues—the deep malachite of forests, the almost translucent whalebone of the distant mountain peaks with puffy clouds floating above the deep sapphire of the ocean and the sound. Called Wah-nah-jus Hilth-hoo-is in Nuu-chah-nulth, Meares Island is the place where Tla-o-qui-aht people would traditionally spend their winters hunting, socializing, and holding important coming-of-age ceremonies, like the rites of passage into the wolf clan, when boys became men.

The ancient temperate rain forests covering Meares Island bear witness to longtime human presence, like the tree scars left by Tla-o-qui-aht ancestors who peeled off the bark for their baskets and carved out boards for canoes and long houses, harvesting the trees without cutting them down and killing them. Over centuries, these scars healed, leaving a permanent record of people's past use of the area. Today, such ancients are known as culturally modified trees, or CMTs. The markings in other parts of Clayoquot Sound rain forests are more recent, and much less benign. They are the scabs of clear-cuts left by the logging industry during recent decades, still healing on the mountain slopes and valleys around Clayoquot. These wounds would be much more extensive and threatening to life here had it not been for the unwavering resolve of the Tla-o-qui-aht people who took a firm stand against the logging industry in the 1980s and again in 1993, during one of the largest, peaceful, civil protests in Canada's history against clear-cutting of old growth forests.

—◆◆◆—

ANCIENT WOODS

On a sunny summer day, the view from Tofino's First Street dock, across the Van Nevel Channel, is stunning. The 2,400-foot-tall Wah-nah-jus, or Lone Cone mountain, arches above the tranquil surface of the Clayoquot Sound like the hump of a giant whale going into a deep feeding dive. A few small skerries break through the blue sapphire glass of the sound around the island, like a school of porpoises frolicking alongside the whale. At the foot of Lone Cone mountain, bright red, white, and blue Lego pieces of one-story houses line up along the water's edge. This is the village of Opitsaht, or a gathering place in the Nuu-chah-nulth language, the millennia-old winter village of the Tla-o-qui-aht people. The community is reachable only by water, and there is a steady trickle of fishing boats, water taxis, and cruise charters of different shapes, sizes, and colors streaking back and forth across the channel.

From Joe's boat, the vista looks like a fresh painting that is yet to dry. The air is crisp, palpably buzzing and crackling with animate energy pulsating through Clayoquot Sound. But the atmosphere here and around the sound would be a lot less vibrant and the colors much more subdued if Tla-o-qui-aht people and their allies hadn't risen up thirty years ago to change the course of local history. It was an uprising that ultimately reverberated around British Columbia (BC), the nation of Canada, and the world. When, in the 1980s, BC logging giant MacMillan Bloedel was preparing to clear-cut Meares Island, the Tla-o-qui-aht people and their allies took a stand against the logging industry. They didn't do it for themselves—after all, many of them worked as loggers—but on behalf of the Wah-nah-jus Hilth-hoo-is, their home. To fulfill their hereditary obligations to future generations, or "future ancestors" as they call them, they stopped the logging on the island and around the Clayoquot Sound to ensure that their traditional territory continues to sustain their people for all times.

On the opposite side of the horseshoe-shaped Meares Island, the massive Mount Colnett shelters the Cis-a-qis, or Heelboom Bay, the scene of the epic standoff between the forest industry and Tla-o-qui-aht people thirty years ago. Today, it is peaceful and quiet here. Our outboard motor is turned off, and we drift in Joe's boat with the coming tide, along the edge of the old-growth forest. Not a puff of wind blows, not a single wave slaps the side of the boat. The flotation jackets we wore on the way here are now in a heap on the bottom of the boat—the fog has finally lifted and the day is sunny and hot. A harbor seal comes up a few yards from the boat and peers at us inquisitively—nostrils flaring, whiskers fanning out. We prove neither threatening, nor very interesting, and the seal melts into the water as soundlessly as it appeared. We glide slowly past a cabin tucked into the dark cobalt shade of colossal trees at the water's edge. Further up the bank, we make out a sign propped up with a few rocks and MEARES ISLAND TRIBAL PARK cut deep into a weathered wooden board.

Industrial forestry arrived in Clayoquot Sound with a road that opened up the region for trucks and chain saws. By the early 1960s, vast swaths of old growth were being clear-cut. At the peak of industrial logging, in the 1980s, close to three and a half million cubic feet of old-growth, temperate rain forest vanished every year. Here, on the east side of Meares Island, not visible from Tofino, MacMillan Bloedel chose to set up a log boom—a barrier to collect and sort floating logs to be harvested from the island's old-growth forest. The company's plan to keep clear-cutting of Meares Island "invisible," however, failed. In November 1983, the Tla-o-qui-aht people learned that the BC government had approved logging of most of the 20,500 acres of Meares Island, their traditional home. On April 21, 1984, in defiance of the government's announcement, the hereditary chiefs declared Meares Island a tribal park to ensure that their people could continue to "harvest natural unspoiled Native foods" as well as to protect all salmon streams, herring spawning grounds, trap lines, and sacred burial sites. Working with local residents and the Friends of Clayoquot Sound, a local nonprofit originally set up in the 1970s to protect the area from logging, the Tla-o-qui-aht people organized protests at Cis-a-qis.

Resting his back against the outboard motor, Joe shares with me parts of this history as we drift. "I myself did work in forestry for twelve years before the blockade," he says. "It was a well-paying job, of course, but then it was just getting too much for me. When it was raining really hard, I'd see all the soil from the clear-cuts sliding into Kennedy Lake and the streams. Sometimes I'd look from the top of the slope down to the river below and see it running just brown, like the color of a cup of hot chocolate. I knew that's where our salmon lived. It was horrible to see. . . . Yeah, it really bothered me. I couldn't stand it anymore and quit my job! I then spent several months with my father over here at Cis-a-qis blockade.

"Our people said, 'We don't want this to happen on the island.' But the government issued logging permits anyway. Then we said, 'No, we can't have this,' and we declared the island a tribal park. We built this cabin and began carving dugout canoes right here to show our traditional ways of living and using our forest that we wanted to protect. We stood on the shore right here and welcomed the loggers when they came. But we told them that they were not allowed to bring their chain saws into our garden—our old-growth forest. They were still cutting on the other side of the channel, across from here, but we said, 'No, you can't keep doing this. Because it's going to destroy the whole forest.'"

Joe shrugs after a pause, as if trying to chase away an unpleasant memory. "Those were tough times, you know. It was dangerous for me to be in Tofino." He describes how some local residents working in the forestry industry became very upset with the protesters. During the blockade, people like Joe felt unsafe around Tofino—even walking down the street became hazardous, as the pro-logging residents would try to chase the protesters down the road with their trucks. I recall the death of Emerson on the Sápara traditional territory. A continent away, but so similar a struggle, and a danger.

The timber company representatives demanded the picketers leave the site and let the loggers get on with their job, but when the protesters ignored their demands, the loggers had no choice but to leave themselves. Immediately, MacMillan Bloedel filed a court injunction to stop the grassroots coalition from interfering with the logging operations. The two Nuu-chah-nulth nations living on Meares Island, the Tla-o-qui-aht and Ahousaht peoples, countered with an injunction of their own. The BC Supreme Court granted their request, outlawing logging on Meares until outstanding land claims were resolved. The Meares Island court injunction is still in effect today and the only activities allowed on the island are the upkeep of ecotourism trails, like the Big Tree Trail within Meares Island's Tribal Park, and the maintenance of reservoirs that supply drinking water to the municipality of Tofino across the bay—the town's sole source of freshwater.

But the struggle for the future of the Clayoquot rain forest didn't end with the court injunction and establishment of the Meares Island Tribal Park. In 1993, the BC government announced new plans to log two-thirds of the remaining old-growth forest around the sound. In response, one of the largest civil disobedience protests in the history of Canada, known as the War in the Woods, took place between June and November 1993. Blockades and arrests became a daily reality at the Kennedy River Bridge on the West Main logging road, where twelve thousand people from around the world participated in the protests. More than 850 activists in total were arrested but later released, and all charges were eventually dropped. The standoff was accompanied by a successful well-coordinated global campaign aimed at stopping clear-cutting and banning wood and paper products made out of trees from old-growth forests.

The War in the Woods didn't stop logging operations in the Clayoquot completely. It still continues today, but on a much lesser scale. Nevertheless, the protest was a watershed moment in environmental history. Not only has logging decreased 90 percent in the area since the early 1990s, but the government also established a scientific panel that developed world-class logging practices, making clear-cutting—a practice routinely favored by industry and government—a thing of the past around the sound. It was largely replaced by the single-log helicopter-based logging combined with a push for value-added wood processing, where the logs are not simply shipped out, but used locally for construction or culturally appropriate applications, like building a traditional canoe or carving a totem pole. The civil disobedience strategies and tactics used during the Clayoquot protests, like a global campaign to boycott wood and paper products made of old-growth wood, have been adopted by environmental campaigns as far afield as Amazonia and Indonesia. Finally, in part as a result of the focused global attention on the social and ecological riches of the area, the Clayoquot Sound was designated as a UNESCO Biosphere Reserve in 2003.

Back in the boat, shielding his eyes from the intense afternoon sunlight with the palm of his hand, Joe looks out toward Meares Island's shore, still covered by the ancient forest. "It was all worth it," he says. "Just look at it—our abundant garden is still here! If we didn't stop the clear-cutting, we would've ended up with the same stuff like over there." He motions toward the mountain slopes of Vancouver Island on the opposite side of the bay.

At first, it isn't obvious to me what he means. The slopes he points at are covered in a green plushy coat, not the brown or gray scabs of clear-cuts. But then I notice that most of it is younger vegetation of a lighter, almost fluorescent shade of chartreuse, unlike the darker emerald hues of the old-growth forest. The scars of old logging roads, sometimes straight and sometimes zigzagging across the slopes, cut the mountainside into segments. Even twenty years after the last clear-cut, this green veil of brush, grasses, and stunted trees cannot disguise a logged area that has yet to recover. The natural forests were replaced with artificial stands of tree seedlings of a single species of the same age, creating plantations for future wood, chip, or pulp production. While the natural forest is filled with old, middle-aged, and young trees, the post-clear-cut stands are a biological desert, with both fewer species of flora and fauna and less diverse populations of both. Millennia of rain forest evolution and adaptation—a home place of the Tla-o-qui-aht people—were erased in just a few years of industrial logging. Will it also take millennia to recover? Or can it ever recover? Especially now, as the climate is changing and wild salmon, the life-sustaining source of nutrients critical for the growth of large trees in the temperate rain forest, is unlikely to ever be as abundant as before.

<hr />

SALMON PEOPLE

The late-afternoon sun bounces off a rapeseed-yellow slide as we approach a solitary wooden dock jutting out from the shoreline of Cannery Bay, during this last stop on my tour with Joe. The spiral-shaped kiddie slide looks quite odd this far away from a playground or a water park. Some distance inland, the skeletal remains of a long-abandoned structure protrude from the thick brush. But this small cove, at the mouth of the Lower Kennedy River flowing from Kennedy Lake into

Clayoquot Sound, is such a warm, sheltered spot that there is no doubt why someone would drag the slide all the way here and nail it to the edge of the crumbling dock. It is a perfect diving spot!

"The place's called Ook Min, a calm place," says Joe, standing next to the slide. "It's always calm and beautiful here, in any weather. Doesn't matter if it's blowing southeasterly or westerly, it's always calm. In the old days, our people had fish weirs from here all the way up the Kennedy River," Joe says, pointing in the direction of Kennedy Lake. "Like, there'd be all kinds of fish jumping around right now."

Traditional Nuu-chah-nulth fish weirs were built by driving long poles into the silty bottom of the river to create a fence that would direct the migrating salmon into a trap as they pushed upstream along the shore. "The fishermen would just paddle over to the trap and take what they needed," describes Joe. "Most of the time the weirs stayed open so that the fish could pass through. But when they needed some fish, they'd close the trap and catch as much as they needed, and then they'd open the trap again for the fish to pass.

"See that big bush by the river over there?" Joe asks. "My grandparents had a house right there. I'd come and stay with them when I was a boy. We caught a lot of sockeye and would smoke it for the winter. We used every part of the fish, from head to roe," describes Joe with a smile. "Many families would move here in the summer because there was so much fish. Some would go to other places, like up the Tranquil Creek or Kennedy Lake. There was lots of fish everywhere. They'd cook, smoke, or dry it for themselves, share it with each other, and use it for their dogs." My mouth starts to water as I recall the thin, almost transparent, red strips of cold-smoked Atlantic salmon I sampled back in Jouko Moshnikoff's cabin on the Näätämö River.

In 1902, the Tofino-based Clayoquot Sound Canning Company opened a cannery here. At the time, the place was brimming with sockeye salmon heading upstream in the summer. "All they had to do was just take a boat, go out there with a net, and bring the fish in here to process and can it," explains Joe, pointing to the opposite shore, closer to the river mouth. "That's all they did, so they called this place Cannery Bay. But what a waste of fish that operation was!" Joe shakes his head in exasperation. "Just like today's fishermen. Holy, they throw a lot away! All those great big sacs of fish eggs—they'd just toss them out in the water. It's such a delicacy fried or boiled, so nourishing, it can be dried and used as a snack on a long trip. Such a waste to throw it all away . . . . Terrible!

"And when they'd fillet a fish, they'd leave about this much meat on the tail"—Joe pinches the top digit of his index finger with his thumb to indicate the thickness of wasted meat—"and just toss the rest out! Belly fat was cut off and tossed out as well. That's just crazy! But hey," he says sardonically, "the cannery was, obviously, more important than our fishery. They banned us from using our weirs around Kennedy Lake, destroying the lot of them." With the increase in canneries and more and bigger boats, the stocks of salmon and other fish dwindled.

"Then the logging came," continues Joe. "Wherever there was a clear-cut, it pretty much destroyed the spawning streams. The eroded silt washed down by rains reduced the water quality to a point where the fish could not survive. And now, there is no longer a salmon fishery here in the sound. Not like it used to be. It all kinda collapsed and the cannery was shut down and abandoned."

There are many, often interrelated, reasons for the continued decline of wild salmon in Clayoquot Sound, around Vancouver Island and mainland British Columbia. Overfishing, clear-cuts, and, more recently, climate change (warming streams and drier summers) are considered to be the most significant factors. Some efforts to arrest or reverse the decline are aimed at a holistic revival of the entire system and have shown some promise. One example is the work taking place just upstream from Ook Min, at the northwestern edge of Kennedy Lake around Kennedy Flats. This is the site of a project to restore streams where clear-cuts eroded the riverbanks and wood debris dammed up the streams. A couple of salmon hatcheries have also been operating in the area, each year releasing tens of thousands of young salmon in the streams to help rebuild the stock's numbers.

Other approaches, however, further erode the integrity of the Clayoquot Sound. Particularly worrisome is the modern "open net-pen" aquaculture, which allows free exchange between the pens containing farmed salmon and the surrounding marine environment. This approach sees the Clayoquot Sound ecosystem—the cradle of the once-abundant wild Pacific salmon—as nothing more than a "feedlot" for farmed Atlantic salmon. On our way to Ook Min, Joe took the boat past a couple of these rafts of net cages—a floating prison and a feedlot wrapped into one with barbed wire. Some of these contraptions can cover a surface as large as four football fields and contain between six hundred thousand to a million salmon at a time.

The Clayoquot Sound has been growing increasingly attractive to the ever-expanding salmon-farming industry, which arrived in British Columbia in the 1970s and, after some failed attempts by locals to raise Pacific salmon, was monopolized by Norwegian companies who are still farming Atlantic salmon here today. Most environmental organizations, First Nations, tourist companies, and the wild-salmon-fishing industry vocally oppose the expansion, calling for a ban on the open-net fish farms in BC. Still, there are more than twenty open-net salmon farms in Clayoquot Sound today, the majority of them owned by the Norwegian industry giant Cermaq, which operates in Canada, Chile, Scotland, and Vietnam, annually producing twenty-five thousand tons of salmon in BC alone. Just as they endanger the future of the Skolt Sámi traditional salmon fishery on Näätämö River, the open-net fish farms bring into the natural system of Clayoquot Sound all the problems that come with intensive livestock feedlot operations—effluent, feed, and antibiotics polluting the ecosystem that is already compromised by a legacy of clear-cut logging and overfishing.

Having a dual mandate of both looking after the wild salmon and promoting fish farming, the BC government turns a blind eye to the real threat that open-net salmon farms pose for the wild salmon stocks. Sea lice—parasites that bloom in the open-net cages—rain down on the passing wild Pacific salmon smelt, as they swim by on the way to the ocean. The salmon feedlots also are incubators for infectious diseases, such as piscine reovirus (PRV), heart and muscle inflammation (HSMI), and others that can reach epidemic proportions quickly and at any time in such a monoculture environment. This happened in Chile in 2007, when a three-year-long outbreak of infectious salmon anemia (ISA), a type of influenza, led to millions of farmed salmon being killed, thousands of jobs lost, and major financial problems for the fish-farming industry. In addition to the diseases and parasite infestation, there is also the need for predator control, with more than seven thousand seals and sea lions shot and killed between 1990 and 2010 in BC, to stop them from taking salmon from the open nets.

Still, there are more fundamental ecological issues to be considered in farming a predatory fish like salmon, because it is at the top of the food chain. It is an inefficient source of protein because it takes up to ten pounds of fish feed and fish oil to produce one pound of salmon. Converting protein and nutrients derived from fish stocks being depleted in one part of the world into supermarket-ready slabs of artificially colored pink flesh "salmon" is economically—never mind ecologically—indefensible.

"I think salmon could still come back in a healthy way," says Joe, "but the fish farms have to go. Not only do they bring diseases and sea lice, they also suck up baby salmon in their water pumps when they harvest the fish from the open-net cages. The nets cannot stop the small salmon from swimming into the holding pens and so they get sucked up together with the big fish. My friends who work there tell me, 'You should see what's happening. Every night we throw away up to four big totes of small salmon that get killed when we're harvesting.' Holy smokes! They don't report it, and don't let us see their operation either."

On the way back to Tofino, we briefly stop at Opitsaht, whose brightly colored Lego-like houses we saw that morning when we left the dock. This is a traditional winter settlement where Tla-o-qui-aht families would gather to reaffirm their bonds of kinship between different houses, or clans, after spending the preceding several months hunting, fishing, and gathering in different corners of the territory. This, too, has changed, although for the better, for today, come winter or summer, the village of Opitsaht is full of adults, elders—and kids.

Two local boys—dusty T-shirts and faded camouflage shorts flapping loose over skinny limbs—run by the brickred community hall and past a few cows of the same color meditatively grazing on a patch of greenery. Fishing rods held up at the ready in one hand like spears and tackle boxes in the other like shields, the kids clatter down the ramp to the end of the pier and, dropping their gear down on the boards, enthusiastically cast their lures. Every couple of throws they reel in a green clump of seaweed and drop to their bruised bony knees to rummage in their tackle boxes. Loudly egging each other on to catch the first fish, they sort through their shiny lures, hoping to find the one that would get them some fish instead of seaweed.

I wonder if there is anything the boys could actually catch here today. Once the backbone of the local economy, wild salmon are no longer as abundant as they used to be even when the kids' parents had fished around the Clayoquot Sound. To catch salmon nowadays, Joe travels three to five miles away from the shore, out into the open ocean, intercepting the schools migrating to the Fraser River near Vancouver, or to the Columbia River on the US side of the border. On the beach in front of the village, several thirty-foot-long wooden fishing boats are slowly decaying, half buried in the sand, a few scales of bleached-out paint still clinging to their sides. They look like the carcasses of spawned-out salmon—a reminder of abundant past and uncertain future.

TRIBAL PARKS

A couple of days after my trip with Joe, I arrange to return to Meares Island, to pay my respects to the forest elders—the ancient trees of the tribal park. I plan to visit with Cory Charlie, a tribal parks guardian, and his intrepid crew of summer assistants, as they make repairs on the Big Tree Trail. The trail was built in the 1980s, following the Meares Island forestry dispute to help the visitors and the press experience the true magnificence of the old-growth forest. From the landing at the head of the trail on the south side of the island, the elevated boardwalk meanders in a big loop among some of the most ancient living beings on earth. It wraps around the giant hemlocks, red cedars, and spruce trees, leaps over knotted tree roots, skips down some steps to a placid creek, and climbs back up again. The walk is fairly short, a half hour at a leisurely pace, but almost every tourist who travels here from Tofino by water taxi, kayak, or Tla-o-qui-aht traditional canoe spends at least twice as long, deeply touched by the encounters with the ancient woods. Every plant here has its story to tell and gifts to share. Over generations, the Tla-o-qui-aht people have learned how to listen respectfully to their voices and gratefully receive their offerings.

If the visitors come to the Big Tree Trail with a Tla-o-qui-aht guide, they might be able to steal a glimpse at a millennia-old relationship between local people and plants. They would learn that the Tla-o-qui-aht people consider the massive western red cedar—some reaching 60 feet in circumference and 180 feet in height—to be the tree of life because it bestows a multitude of gifts: canoes, totem poles, longhouses, bentwood boxes, paddles, cradles, ropes, baskets, and even clothes. The sap of Sitka spruce is the best fire starter, earning it the name of a fire tree. All kinds of berries abundant in the forest—salmonberries, huckleberries, thimbleberries, salal berries, strawberries, and blackberries—are used for food and medicine. Deer fern fiddleheads are prized as a springtime delicacy, while many of the over eight hundred species of lichens growing here are an important source of traditional medicine. For the adept, the rain forest is a shelter, a garden, a pantry, a work shed, a medicine cabinet, and a cathedral all wrapped into one.

Cory Charlie and two of his assistants—all recognizable by a green Tla-o-qui-aht Sea Serpent coiled inside a large green hoop emblazoned on the backs of their black Tribal Park uniforms—are splitting a western red cedar blowdown into planks and carrying them to the sections of the trail in need of repair. After sitting on the damp ground for three decades, the original boards and beams of the elevated boardwalk need to be replaced in many places along the trail. It is backbreaking and tedious work, especially with the inadequate tools Cory's team has at its disposal. But it has to be done, and they persevere.

"It never ends with our old trail," Cory says with a sigh. "We want to replace the whole lot, maybe three hundred meters [one thousand feet] of boardwalk or so. It's quite a job, I tell you. In the rest of the park we're opening forest floor trails, more of the bushwhacking kind. We just don't have the resources to build boardwalks everywhere we'd like to. Though that would be the best thing to do, to my mind."

When, yet again, the chain saw breaks, Cory has to call it a day. He picks up a few other tools to take back to Tofino for repairs, stuffs them into his worn and faded backpack, and sits down on the half-cut log for a smoke. In the dampness of the rain forest, the sharp and sweet aroma of red cedar sawdust reminds me of the Skolt hot sauna, roof shingles baking in the sun, and freshly grilled cedar-planked salmon—the smells evocative of the gifts of comfort, nourishment, and life that the forest bestows on people who recognize its true value.

"I was quite transient growing up," reminisces Cory. "My dad was raised here, lived here, and then moved away, taking me and my older brothers along—first to Vancouver, and then to a few other places. When I was about sixteen, he asked me to come back and live up here. I wasn't living with him at the time and was up to no good in the city. I moved home. I figured it was a great trade for me, 'cause I got the forest and the ocean, and everything. I kinda knew right away. I was like, 'Wow, this is it!' I stayed, got my wilderness certificate so that I could get jobs in the tourism industry. Then I started working as a guide on a new zip line that got going on our territory. When the tribal parks job came up, I was right there, ready. This is the best job! But, like I said, it's hard with the funding. I might have to take some time off this winter and go up to Victoria to take some courses at the university there. I want to learn about 'green design,' 'cause, when we think about the future of our tribal parks and what we need to do here, I truly believe we need to be thinking carefully about what and how we build."

The four full-time staff members at the tribal parks, Cory explains, just don't have the time to keep up with everything that needs to be done. In addition to the original Meares Island Tribal Park created by Tla-o-qui-aht in 1984, the Ha'uukmin (Kennedy Lake) Tribal Park was created in 2009, and two new parks—Tranquil Creek and Esowista—were designated in 2013. The four cover most of Tla-o-qui-aht traditional territory and more than half of Clayoquot Sound, and their upkeep is an impossible task for the few staff with almost no funds to run the office. Even getting a sense for how many visitors come to the Big Tree Trail each year is largely guesswork. But based on his experience over the last couple of years, Cory estimates that about five thousand tourists walk the Big Tree Trail board-walk between June and August—peak tourist season.

We carry the failed equipment back to the moored Tribal Parks boat—an old fiberglass dinghy with a roof and a glass bottom, now half overgrown with algae, donated to the tribal parks. Along the way, Cory reflects that it might take a couple of days to fix the chain saw, and so he has to shift his schedule and refocus his crew's attention on other activities in the parks, like finishing cutting the new trail to the top of Lone Cone mountain. Lightly built, but robust-looking, Cory emanates the poise and confidence that comes from knowing who you are, where you are from, and where you are going. He doesn't seem discouraged by the events of the day, his work in general, or the predicament of his people, instead taking it all in stride.

Patiently waiting for his assistants to load up their gear in the boat, Cory pulls on a cigarette and squints as the smoke drifts up his graying mustache stubble and melts into the long pepper-and-salt hair sticking out from under his black cadet cap. His eyes twinkle with warmth, and the way he talks to me and chats with a couple of tourists who pass us on the trail is easygoing and welcoming. He isn't just fixing an old trail, he is rebuilding a path for his people to continue looking after their land, as well as for outsiders, like me, to learn to love and care for it. As Eli Enns, the tribal parks codirector, later explains to me, these are precisely the connections the tribal parks are meant to nourish.

—∞—

A BETTER WAY

A pair of short wooden stakes protrude from the ground at the edge of a gravel pad—a new house lot on the corner of Wickaninnish Road. "Here's where the geothermal heating will get hooked up to a new house when it's built," Eli Enns says, pointing at the stakes, painted light blue and red, with GEO-SER scribbled unevenly in black Sharpie along the broad side of each. We are taking a quick tour around Eli's neighborhood in Ty-Histanis—a new community that is an expansion of Esowista, the second of two Tla-o-qui-aht reserves, just ten miles south of Tofino.

When Canada created the Pacific Rim National Park Reserve in the 1970s, the government did not consult with the Tla-o-qui-aht people and other Nuu-chah-nulth First Nations, whose traditional territories it subsumed. Among many other negative consequences for the Tla-o-qui-aht people, the park's establishment erased any future options for their community to grow, because the Esowista reserve, just a fraction of the original Tla-o-qui-aht territory, was completely surrounded by the protected area. The relationship between the park and the local Nuu-chah-nulth groups had been challenging for years. But the War in the Woods shifted the balance in favor of the First Nations' rights and the association has been gradually improving. A few years ago, a deal was brokered between the Pacific Rim National Park and the Tla-o-qui-aht people to allow for an 84-hectare expansion of the reservation. This gives Esowista some room to breathe and, more important, allows people to relocate to higher ground, up from the Esowista shoreline, which is being increasingly eroded by stronger and more frequent winter storms—another sign of changing climate.

After a few years of construction, a new Tla-o-qui-aht community, Ty-Histanis, is springing to life. More than 170 single-family houses, more than 30 duplexes, and a dozen or so elders' units are being planned, along with a school, health clinic, pharmacy, recreation center, and a bus hub. Most of it is yet to materialize, but the main infrastructure has been built, several houses raised, and some families moved in.

"As with everything the Tla-o-qui-aht people do," explains Eli, "In Ty-Histanis, we've tried to apply our traditional teachings to achieve sustainable community development. We've paid particular attention to climate change." A political scientist with expertise in constitutional law, Eli is the great-grandson of Nah-wah-suhm, a public speaker and historian for Wickaninnish, the grand chief of the Tla-o qui-aht Nation. Just as his great ancestor likely did at gift-giving potlatch ceremonies, Eli enunciates each word deliberately with the unhurried tempo of a practiced public speaker who cares a great deal about being understood and getting his points across precisely. His short black Vandyke beard frames a broad, handsome face, pulling you in like the sun crest of a totem pole.

"To imagine, and then build, Ty-Histanis in a way that takes climate change into account," Eli continues, "we managed to raise some additional funding on top of the regular government construction budget." As a result, the community was designed to reduce greenhouse gas emissions through the use of more efficient heating, electrical, and mechanical systems. A central geothermal station makes it possible for each house to have in-floor radiant heating, an important feature in the wet climate of Clayoquot Sound, especially now, when winter precipitation is expected to increase. Each household will also save money because they won't need to rely on buying electricity for heat. In addition, to deal with increasingly intense rains, more than 40 percent of the land in and around the community has been left undisturbed, several storm water retention ponds constructed, and new pavements made of porous material installed to allow water to seep through them, down into the soil, instead of letting runoff overflow the community storm sewage system. All of these architectural features are part of the Ty-Histanis climate change adaptation design.

The Tla-o-qui-aht people and their long-term partner, Vancouver-based Ecotrust Canada, also looked for different ways to reduce the community's carbon footprint, including limiting the amount of fossil fuel used in the construction and transportation of building materials. They have designed and built a model house incorporating Nuu-chah-nulth traditional longhouse designs and locally sourced wood, as part of the Standing Tree to Standing Home program. Their hope is that this more energy-efficient traditional house model will become a preferred option for the new families moving to Ty-Histanis from Esowista or Opitsaht, or even families returning to their traditional territory from other parts of British Columbia or the rest of Canada.

We walk past several new houses and empty lots to Eli's apartment, which he now shares with his uncle Joe Martin. At the apartment, Eli rolls up his sleeves and fills up the sink with hot water, tidying up the kitchen before Joe returns from a fishing trip, hopefully with some fresh salmon for dinner. Joe grew up with Eli's late father and has always been a mentor and a friend to Eli. Eli was raised by his mother's family in Brandon, Manitoba, a prairie town in interior Canada—a much more uniform landscape than Clayoquot and as far from any ocean as one can get in Canada. Growing up there, Eli looked up to the establishment and particularly its representatives, the police, as a symbol of justice and authority. But that respect was broken when, as a twelve-year-old boy, he was grabbed by the police and booked for being out on the street too late in the day. Sworn at and handcuffed by the cop, Eli cried out in disbelief to the crowd milling around, "Call the police!" Eli understood there and then that the cops hated him just for being a native kid and, following the arrest, he resolved to hate them back. But becoming a father at a young age moderated his anger against the establishment. Still, his discontent with the way the dominant Western society has been treating him and his First Nations brothers and sisters beyond the Tla-o-qui-aht Ha'huulthii has grown over the years.

He has visited his father's homeland, Clayoquot Sound, many times since his childhood. During one of these visits, Joe took him to the place where Eli's great-grandfather built a house and lived for many years. Seeing the place gave Eli an overwhelming sense of belonging and connectedness to the landscape, something that has guided his life and work ever since. His heart and mind were firmly set on changing the status quo and creating an independent Tla-o-qui-aht nation on Vancouver Island. His Tla-o-qui-aht relatives and elders recognized his passion for change but felt that he needed guidance. They introduced him to *ha-ho-pa*, Tla-o-qui-aht traditional education.

"I did traditional water ceremonies and practices for three years," says Eli after the dishes are cleaned and dried. A couple of cold bottles of local IPA in hand, we sit down on a couch in the living room to talk about tribal parks that he cofounded and their role in the Tla-o-qui-aht people's future. "Several things came out of that experience for me," Eli continues. "The first message was—'live under the heavens and up on the earth.' And what that meant to me was to be aware of the sun and the natural moon cycles that govern our lives every day and every year, and act appropriately. Simple."

Expecting a text message from a friend, Eli checks his BlackBerry. "The reception here still sucks—Ty-Histanis being a new community and all. Hang on, there is one spot that usually works." He gets up and walks back into the kitchen, past a traditional Nuu-chah-nulth wooden mask hanging by the kitchen door. Carved by a relative, the mask's mother-of-pearl eyes stare into space from under a mop of stringy cedar bark hair. A mottled feather pierces the septum connecting the blood-red nostrils with the scarlet lips. Under the mask, a canoe paddle, one of Joe's carved creations, leans against the wall. Eli places his phone on top of the kitchen cabinet against the flue of a range hood.

"There, got one bar now," he announces. "Do you want me to put yours up here too? No? Okay then, where were we?" He sinks back into the soft folds of the sofa and continues the story of tribal parks.

In the early 2000s, Eli and a couple of his Tla-o-qui-aht friends, up-and-coming leaders who had been putting their college educations to good use to advance the causes of the Tla-o-qui-aht people, realized that since the court injunction, nobody but tour operators had done much in the Meares Island Tribal Park. That became the beginning of the second stage of the tribal parks' development. In 2007, Eli and his partners launched the Tribal Parks Establishment Project. The authority to create tribal parks came from Hawiih—the Tla-o-qui-aht hereditary chiefs—supported by Section 35 of Canada's 1982 Constitution Act, which protects the rights of aboriginal peoples in Canada.

"The act doesn't go into detail as to what is an aboriginal right or what is a treaty right," expounds Eli, "it just acknowledges and affirms those things and then entrenches them in the constitution, which is the supreme law of Canada. So, we have a constitutionally recognized aboriginal right to be self-governing. And a part of our tradition of self-governance is to look after our traditional territory for the benefit of future "ancestors." Now we have to find thoughtful, creative, and innovative ways of reapplying those traditional concepts and values in a modern context of natural resource management, and this is what we are working on with the tribal parks."

By establishing Meares Island Tribal Park in 1984, the Tla-o-qui-aht people returned to managing their lands and waters according to their traditional values, rather than following the rules of the dominant Canadian society, which led to large-scale logging of their land in the first place. The Tla-o-qui-aht elders, however, were always unsatisfied with focusing solely on Meares Island without bearing in mind their entire traditional territory. They knew full well the meaning of their ancestral teachings of *hishuk ish tsa'walk*—everything is one, everything is connected.

"You can't disconnect the island from mudflats, and inlets, and rivers, and salmon," says Eli. "It's all connected. So we always knew that we need return to managing the whole of our traditional territory. But we had to do it incrementally. Since Meares Island was safe because of the court injunction, we focused on the next watershed that was threatened the most. That was the Ha'uukmin, the Kennedy Lake watershed, which became our first attempt to figure out tribal parks management based on our traditional principles."

The project team developed the Ha'uukmin Tribal Park Management and Land Use Plan, that, among other things, informs proponents of development projects about what kinds of activities are allowed in the park before the developers would even think about coming to the Tla-o-qui-aht traditional territory. Following traditional practices and laws of their people, the project team set aside the areas least disrupted by logging and other development activities as traditional *qwa siin hap*, or leave as is, areas similar to what scientists would call a conservation, or protected, area. But other parts of the tribal park that had been logged or affected in some other way, like the Kennedy Flats, are called *uuya thluk nish*, or we take care of. This is where certain types of economic development and ecosystem healing take place, like salmon habitat restoration. "Then the gold mine proposal came," continues Eli. "So we said, 'No, you can't do that,' and established the Tranquil Creek Tribal Park and the Esowista Tribal Park to protect the rest of our territory from mining. Now we have pretty much the entire traditional territory covered. But our salmon go out into the open ocean, and our responsibilities follow salmon, because what happens in international waters is going to affect what happens here. We haven't really focused on that one yet. But that is where we're trying to get Indigenous voices into discussions about international waters and the management of the Pacific Ocean."

Eli describes the Clayoquot as a true epicenter of social and economic innovation for aboriginal rights and title, which began with the Meares Island court case. In partnership with groups like the Wilderness Committee, Ecotrust Canada, and Parks Canada, the tribal parks have chosen a path toward developing a conservation economy, which is meant not to destroy, but support the natural and social systems making up Clayoquot Sound. In this, the tribal parks serve as a foundation for ensuring the Tla-o-qui-aht people's well-being. Such a model of conservation economy already existed in the past, when the resources that the lands and sea of Clayoquot Sound provided at different seasons supported thousands of people over multiple generations. Though some traditional subsistence practices, like whaling, are no longer viable, the Tla-o-qui-aht people are hoping to strengthen local traditional subsistence, trade, and exchange models with newer elements of conservation economy.

"We have access to the whole territory," says Eli, "but the issue is, the territory needs to heal. It can't bear the burden, because it's been degraded and damaged. So we need a crutch to get us through, to help out with the healing, and let the territory come back to life." Initially, he tried to come up with ways of restoring their traditional territory to the ways it was during the time of his ancestors. And quickly realized that this would not work. Climate change makes it particularly challenging now because the environmental conditions that had enabled the temperate rain forests to mature for millennia are simply no longer there. There is just not enough salmon today to bring the necessary nutrients into the system to sustain the growth of ancient trees. Moreover, the increasing air and water temperatures undermine the future of those wild salmon species, like sockeye, that depend on cold water to successfully reproduce and grow. This realization brought Eli back to another message that was revealed to him during his water healing ceremonies years ago, "Find strength in change." This kind of thinking now informs all of his work in Tla-o-qui-aht tribal parks.

"I think about it from Maslow's hierarchy of needs type perspective," Eli explains. "What are our basic needs? Water, food, shelter, and energy. The most fundamental thing is water. We need clean drinking water sources for ourselves and for the future generations, and it is one of the key resources that we have in our traditional territory in abundance. So we intend to keep it that way. At the economic level, we are planning on developing a water-bottling business that could generate revenue for our people. We'd use glass water bottles that can double as a souvenir. Something along the lines of 'Meares Island Tribal Park Water,' 'Tribal Park Water,' or 'Rain Forest Water,' or whatever. The time is right to work with the town of Tofino to ban the import of plastic water bottles so that tourists would buy our local water when they come to our territory.

"We have also initiated discussions with Creative Salmon, a local fish-farming outfit that, unlike the Norwegian-owned Atlantic salmon farms, raises Pacific salmon. There may be a good opportunity to develop an aquaponics system—a closed-containment fish farm—at Ty-Histanis. It would be an aquaculture-agriculture system, where you have some on-land closed containment fish-farming operations instead of open-water fish farming. The effluent from this would feed into the greenhouse and community garden system, and the energy for it would come from our geothermal station.

"Finally, we are working hard on ensuring our energy security. We've got our Canoe Creek run-of-the-river power project, which is environmentally friendly because it didn't require us to damn the river. It is seventy-five percent owned by us, and twenty-five percent by two people we've known for twenty-plus years. We have a twenty-five-year power purchase agreement with BC Hydro and have easy access to their transmission lines. The Canoe Creek is a 5.5-megawatt project that can provide electricity to several hundred homes. We have a couple more such hydropower projects around our territory in different stages of development.

"All in all, I personally feel that the Western economic system is fundamentally flawed and is bound to ultimately fail because it's not following the natural law. What we are doing in our climate change adaptation work now on our Ha'huulthii is, basically, preparing for the big crash, when the global markets unravel under increasing impacts of climate change. And you know what? If the crash never happens, that's fine by us. Because these're still things that need to be done—people need local jobs; they need local food security; they need access to healthier foods. So we may be just creating a better way of doing things in the long run."

At the end of my visit of Tla-o-qui-aht Ha'huulthii, Eli takes me to the top of the Wah-nah-jus, Lone Cone mountain. In the days long past, Tla-o-qui-aht whalers would spend days or weeks at the top of the mountain, fasting and seeking spiritual fortitude and guidance for their whaling expeditions. Today, an ecotourism trail, the one that Cory Charlie was working on with his crew, runs from the Opitsaht dock to the top of the mountain. After meandering through the thickets of undergrowth along the Meares Island lowlands, the marked trail begins a gradual climb up the steepening flank of Lone Cone mountain, zigzagging from a giant cedar to a towering hemlock. It is a precipitous three-hour trek, but Eli climbs Lone Cone mountain a few times every year, and his practiced gait is light, his step wide. The last quarter of the climb is almost vertical and in several places, weighed down by my heavy camera backpack, I have to scramble on all fours, dropping far behind Eli, as he easily scales large rocks and fallen trees. Earlier in the day, we had several meetings in Tofino and didn't get to catch our water-taxi ride from the dock to Opitsaht until later in the afternoon. By the time I catch up with Eli on the small rocky clearing at the top of the Wah-nah-jus, the entire landscape is infused in amber light of the setting sun.

We stand at the edge of the precipice overlooking Clayoquot Sound. There is no wind, no movement of tree branches, just the buzz of mosquitoes gaining in strength as the evening shadows gradually flood the land and sea below. We pull out water bottles to quench our thirst and pause for a few minutes before heading down the slope to make it to the Opitsaht dock by nightfall, when the water taxis stop running. Eli gazes down on the domain of his ancestors and, he hopes, many future generations of Tla-o-qui-aht people yet to come. Far below us, wakes of motorboats crisscrossing the waterway between Opitsaht and Tofino look like the golden firebird feathers floating on the surface among the small islands scattered around Clayoquot Sound.

"One of the most important teachings that every Nuu-chah-nulth person would receive," Eli says without taking his eyes off the vista, aglow in the setting sun, "was about fear. Because, as my uncle Joe reminds me over and over again, if you're afraid and you want to learn something, you might learn this much." Eli spreads his arms wide, embracing the entire Ha'huulthii in front of him. "But if you're not afraid, you can learn anything! This is part of the teachings about our roles and responsibilities in the community to each other and other living beings. For all of us are the upholders of the natural law, accountable to future ancestors."

CHAPTER EIGHT

GIFTS

LEVI THE *KAA-MUTH*

W hen we walk on this land, we do it slowly, with honor, respect, and humility, because we tread on the dust of our ancestors," says Levi Martin, a Tla-o-qui-aht elder. Towering over the table, he shakes my hand in greeting and wipes the morning dew off the wooden tabletop and bench with the sleeve of his jacket. "That's why I am a little late." He winks, sitting down across from me, his face spreading into a mischievous grin. He reminds me of his nephew Joe Martin.

"Ahhh, such a lovely day," Levi says, stretching with a sigh, straightening his gray goatee with his hand. Tofino's summer mornings are foggy, as the cool night breath of Clayoquot Sound clings to the coast, sticking to cedars, boats, beaches, and outdoor benches. But by the afternoon, the sun's rays burn openings in the mist, warming the coastal air and lifting the fog. Our damp bodies welcome the warmth, and we settle on the second-floor patio of the Common Loaf Bake Shop for lunch. Below the veranda, First Street rolls down to the Tofino docks, where water taxis whisk passengers on the short ride to Opitsaht—Levi's birthplace.

I first met Levi—a respected healer and spiritual leader—a few years ago at the International Society of Ethnobiology's congress in Tofino. His poise and wisdom—conveyed with words and actions in simple, yet profound ways—impressed me deeply. At the congress, Levi carried out several ceremonies, murmuring chants in his native Tla-o-qui-aht tongue, to welcome congress participants. Following one such ritual, he put his kelp rattle back into a satchel and pulled out several gray pebbles from the bag. They were polished smooth by the waves of Clayoquot

Sound, and had a few Tla-o-qui-aht words drawn on them in silver paint. Levi handed out the gifts, but in the hustle and bustle of the congress, I never did ask him about the inscription on mine. Now, I pull the pebble out of my pocket and place it on the table in front of him.

"What's this now?" Levi asks, brushing back his long pepper-and-salt hair before picking up the rock for a closer look. He grins in recognition, and I ask him about the inscription.

"My father shared many things with me," he responds, handing the rock back to me, "but this is the only prayer he ever taught me. It simply says, *Let all good things naturally drift toward me.* The people I meet in my life are special gifts from the Creator, so I paint the prayer on the rock amulets, and give them away as a thank-you to the Creator for his gifts. The gift doesn't have to be anything special. It could be a simple meal. An elder taught me once that sharing a meal is one of the most powerful medicines we have. So, I'm glad we're having lunch," he says with a satisfied nod, opening the Common Loaf's menu.

Born in 1945, Levi grew up immersed in Tla-o-qui-aht culture, language, and lore. The youngest of sixteen children, Levi was given a Tla-o-qui-aht name, Kaa-mitsk—a fighter and a hunter—when he was born. He spent his early days with his family, hunting, gathering, fishing, and trapping around the Wah-nah-jus Hilth-hoo-is. Like many other Indigenous children from the communities along the west coast of Vancouver Island—Ahousaht, Opitsaht, Hesquiat, Nootka, and Kyuquot—Levi was sent to the Christie Indian Residential School that was run on Meares Island by the Catholic Church between 1898 and 1983. Housing around forty Indigenous children, the residential school, also known as Kakawis, was only a couple of miles from Opitsaht, but it might have been on another continent for Indigenous children like Levi, who were taken away from their families and forced to learn a new culture, language, and set of values at the expense of their own. After leaving the school, Levi drifted around British Columbia. In his youth, he worked as a carpenter in Vancouver, a logger in Opitsaht, and finally ran a water-taxi business around Clayoquot Sound. He left his business in the mid-1970s, in search of ways to reconnect with Tla-o-qui-aht culture, traditional knowledge, and practices, and to share them with his people. He began carving, painting, and teaching the Nuu-chah-nulth language. After deciding to follow in the footsteps of his grandfather, a healer, Levi attended a holistic treatment center for First Nations in the early 1980s and began working with the Nuu-chah-nulth survivors of residential schools. He helped them learn about their own history and culture, and reclaim their ancestral ways of looking after their Ha'huulthii. That is when he got his name Kaa-muth, "the all-knowing one" in Nuu-chah-nulth.

I am at the end of my Archipelago of Hope journey, reflecting on what I have learned from the Indigenous peoples who invited me to their home-lands with open arms, generously welcoming me into their lives. What I have witnessed made it quite clear that there is no magic pill that would cure the climate change fever consuming our planet. The medicines are as diverse as the peoples and communities using them—from adjusting the seasonal migration routes of reindeer herds to avoid extreme weather events in the Arctic to burning trees to enrich the forest in Thailand, to keeping the oil in the ground in the Amazon. The circumstances of each Indigenous community are different—distinct cultures, unique histo-ries, diverse ecosystems, and multiple climate change impacts. Yet their individual predicaments are fundamentally similar—colonial history, displacement, pressure from resource extraction, and limited political power to determine their own future. To understand how Indigenous communities stay resilient in the face of all the challenges that the "civilized" world continues to throw at them, including climate change, it is essential to go beyond dissecting the specific how-to lessons, and attempt to explore the fundamental principles of how these communi-ties maintain their relationships with the living world around them. To heal the earth and rebalance our relationship with it, it is not enough to "treat" the symptoms; our medicine must penetrate to the very core of our affliction. This is why, when I meet Levi for lunch, I am seeking some guidance from the "all-knowing" Kaa-muth.

—⊗⊗⊗—

LAND IS LIFE

Everything changes over time—it's one of the great laws of nature," Levi says. "Lots of things have changed since I was a little boy—my village, my people, our forest, our climate. Some changes are for the worse, others for the better. It's what you do facing these changes that matters most. We've been working hard at slowly but surely reclaiming our relationship with our ancestors and their teachings. But we'd never go back to some of the old ways, like cannibalism, or prearranged marriages. So we change, but we have to do it right, in accordance with the laws of nature, not the laws that people invented themselves that disconnect them from life.

"I remember, once, we had a very big winter storm. It must've been the strongest one I'd ever seen and I was quite upset about it. Still, I sat there quietly. 'Listening to the silence,' I call it. I was waiting for what the Creator would choose to share with me in that moment. Then I felt a message come. It said that such storms are Mother Nature's way of cleansing herself. We pollute Mother Earth so much now that she has to work hard to clean our mess up and restore the damage we've done. All the changes we're seeing in the world are the direct result of the mess we've made. The only way we can fix it is by following our traditional teachings and staying connected—to each other, to the land, to our culture, to the Creator. We must maintain an honorable and respectful relationship with all living beings. To keep receiving the Creator's gifts, we must acknowledge that the Earth is our Mother—a living, feeling, conscious, and caring being. We must care for her in return."

It is their determination to stay connected with their Ha'huulthii and their ancestral teachings that led the Tla-o-qui-aht people to defend Meares Island from industrial logging over three decades ago. They established Tla-o-qui-aht tribal parks to protect their lands and waters from destructive practices such as deforestation, overfishing, and mining that the government has promoted, unilaterally, for decades. The old-growth coastal rain forest that is protected within tribal parks safeguards the carbon stored in the trees and the soil, protects the freshwater supply for both Tla-o-qui-aht and settler communities, supports the subsistence-based way of life of First Nations, and creates tourism opportunities that diversify their local economy. All of these are potent ingredients for a local holistic approach to climate change adaptation and mitigation.

Land is Life is the name of the nonprofit organization founded by Brian Kean to advocate the view shared by the Indigenous peoples the world over—whether they are reindeer herders in the Arctic, rice growers in Thailand, or fishermen in the Amazon. The land as a living, breathing, feeling, and thinking being. This is one of the fundamental principles that defines the relationship between Indigenous peoples and nature. It is gradually being acknowledged around the world, from the governments of Bolivia and Ecuador, who have legalized the rights of nature, to New Zealand's Whanganui River being granted the status of a legal person at the time of writing this book.

"Before we can do anything on the land, we must complete our rituals, remembering the sacredness of life," Levi says. "Our traditions teach us reciprocity. They tell us that before we receive, we must give. If we need something from the land, like a tree to make a canoe or carve a totem pole, we must perform a ceremony. Everything that we take from the land or water is a gift from our Creator. When I approach that cedar, I make a prayer. I make an offering—put down some tobacco, or some eagle down, or just a strand of hair. I explain to the tree what I'm going to do and why, and promise that I'll use her gifts with honor and respect. For salmon, for example, we return the leftovers back to the ocean, so that the spirit of salmon goes back out to sea for the fish to remain plentiful. This is what we believe in. We pay homage to the teachings of our ancestors, the *hishuk ish tsa'walk*—everything is connected. By following these teachings, we honor our salmon, we honor our Mother Earth, we honor the Creator, and we honor ourselves."

This view of Mother Earth as a loving, yet stern, sentient being deserving of our reverence and respect is very much aligned with the scientific Gaia Theory. It was first proposed by Dr. James Lovelock in the 1970s to explain how life on Earth has endured for billions of years despite significant environmental fluctuations, which included a 30 percent increase in the sun's intensity over the same period. The Gaia Theory sees the Earth as a self-regulating, interdependent, resilient, living system that, for billions of years, has maintained global temperature, ocean salinity, oxygen levels, and other environmental conditions at levels necessary for life to endure.

The principle of interdependence is fundamental to the way Indigenous communities relate to nature and is gradually gaining broader recognition around the world. "Everything is interconnected, and that genuine care for our own lives and our relationships with nature is inseparable from fraternity, justice, and faithfulness to others . . . ," Pope Francis wrote, in *Laudato Si, the Encyclical Letter on Care of Our Common Home*. "It is essential to show special care for Indigenous communities and their cultural traditions. For them, land is not a commodity but rather a gift from God and from their ancestors who rest there, a sacred space with which they need to interact if they are to maintain their identity and values."

By maintaining direct and intimate relationships with their living sacred forest, or Naku, Sápara detect, react to, and even anticipate the effects of climate change, like they did by creating medicinal gardens in response to increased instances of infectious diseases. Such tight feedbacks between the social and ecological systems, according to resilience science, boost the ability of local communities to adapt to climate change.

All the Indigenous peoples I have met along the way on The Archipelago of Hope journey are intimately aware of the web of relationships that sustains them and their traditional territories—from the mountain glaciers to the open ocean, from coastal mudflats to the rain forest, from ancestors to future generations. This interweaving of animate and inanimate, spiritual and physical, past and future, rights and responsibilities, respect and reverence, traditional knowledge and science, is fundamentally important to sustaining healthy relationships with other living beings. The interdependence of people and nature, known as biocultural diversity, is the rich nourishing soil from which the diversity of responses to climate change arises. In Altai, Russia, this interdependence has been sustained through the establishment of the Uch-Enmek Nature Park to safeguard the ancient relationship between the Altai people and their traditional territory. It preserves local livelihoods by maintaining pastures where local people can move their cattle as the seasons change, unhindered by the boundaries that would otherwise divide this vast landscape into small patches of real estate. Cultural tourism in the park brings extra income to local people, creating additional resources that could be channeled toward coping with climate change. More importantly, the park is restoring and sustaining Altai's sacred sites that, according to the local worldview, regulate the flow of energy between the cosmos and the Earth, governing weather and climate patterns, and maintaining a healthy relationship between people and the land.

KNOWLEDGE COCREATION

O ver three decades ago, we had lots of violence in our communities—drinking, fighting, even people getting killed," Levi remembers. "It felt like our culture was getting weak and we were growing more and more disconnected from the land and our ancestors. I decided then to begin my healing journey, to restore myself and help my people. We've been on that journey ever since. Along the way, I've seen a lot that gives me hope. My people are a lot stronger now. Many have set off on their own healing journeys, reconnecting with the land, our ancestors, and our traditions. An elder told me once that it may seem that many of our traditions and songs are lost, but we have nothing to worry about. They're just put away for now, stored in our collective memory, our land. It's going to be our children, he said, who'll bring them back. And, over the years, I've seen it happen. I'd take our boys and girls out to different parts of our Ha'huulthii and some of them would bring back our forgotten songs, our traditions, our knowledge—whatever gifts the Creator would choose to share with them."

Traditional knowledge bubbles up from the deep well of ancestral wisdom embedded within the Indigenous peoples' traditional territories, nourishing the long-term, intimate, and sacred relationship between Indigenous peoples and their land, water, air, and the cosmos. As Sápara people explain it, the medicinal plants from their Naku, the rain forest, keeps them healthy. Access to the traditional forest medicines helps their communities deal with skin and gastrointestinal infections, as well as parasites and snakes that are on the rise because of increased flooding. Planting traditional medicinal gardens is a much more reliable strategy in the Sápara remote communities than trying to get expensive and hard-to-access Western medications from urban centers. For the nomadic Nenets reindeer herders of Yamal, their resilience is in their traditional mobility that is impossible without an intimate knowledge of their land. Whether it is moving further north on the Yamal Peninsula to evade subjugation by the all-mighty Russian or Soviet government or avoiding winter pastures covered with ice as a result of ice-on-snow events, or altering migration routes to reach abundant summer pastures, the Nenets have relied on their traditional knowledge to move from place to place in response to anticipated and unexpected changes for centuries.

"There are four sacred, most powerful, elements that sustain life and all living things," Levi concludes. "Fire, water, air, and Mother Earth. Nothing survives without them. But as powerful as these elements are, none of them can support life on their own. Take water away, and nothing in this world could survive. The same is true for the other elements, because to sustain life, all of them must work in concert. And the way they work together is through the spirit element that connects them all. In the same way, all people—Indigenous and settlers—must work together. But we've been disconnected from the spirit for so long that we don't really know how to do it. This must change fast. We must work together and learn from each other to have any hope of dealing with all the challenges we are facing."

Environmental health and human well-being depend on how well we can detect and respond to the escalating and converging social and environmental challenges, like climate change. There is a growing body of evidence in scientific and policy-making communities showing that to maintain resilience in the face of change, we must draw on the best available knowledge, regardless of its epistemological origins—whether it is traditional knowledge rooted in millennia of meticulous on-the-land observations of seasonal animal behavior or contemporary scientific methodologies that rely on satellites to remotely capture large-scale changes. The Multiple Evidence Based (MEB) approach is an innovative framework adopted by the UN's Intergovernmental Science-Policy Platform on Biodiversity and Ecosystem Services (IPBES) that weaves together the distinct threads of Indigenous and scientific knowledge to support and enhance resilience of interlinked social and ecological systems. The MEB approach preserves the integrity of each knowledge system by recognizing that the interpretation and authentication of knowledge takes place primarily within, rather than across, knowledge systems. The process of interweaving different knowledge systems together creates opportunities for developing a deeper understanding of observed events and their consequences, facilitates joint assessment of information, and leads to new insights and innovations. The MEB approach attempts to engage Indigenous peoples in empathic, equitable, and empowering ways that support knowledge cocreation useful for decision making.

For generations, Indigenous communities the world over have been monitoring what happens on their traditional territories. When does freeze-up begin? Are there fewer animals today than a few years ago? Are there more fires in the forest? Based on these observations, they adjust their activities on the land—move their camp to a new place or stop hunting in a given area. As the climate changes and industrial development increases, the pressures on Indigenous territories are growing. To cope with such unprecedented pressures, Indigenous communities are adopting culturally appropriate monitoring approaches, methods, and tools that facilitate knowledge cocreation using traditional knowledge and conventional science. Community-Based Monitoring (CBM) is a methodology that empowers local communities to track environmental changes based on their own priorities, expertise, and traditional management practices, complimented by scientific data and methods. It is locally relevant, more acceptable than top-down monitoring programs driven by the government or industry, and can lead to positive local actions in response to observed changes.

What makes Indigenous communities uniquely valuable in the global quest for climate change solutions is that they are the "testing grounds," the "laboratories," where the traditional practices and understanding of nature meet modern technology and scientific insights, generating new knowledge critical for developing culturally appropriate and relevant climate change adaptation and mitigation responses. As I learned from the Skolts, it is the synergies between traditional knowledge and conventional science that help them maintain resilience in the face of environmental and climatic change. Traditional knowledge enables the Skolt Sámi to monitor and respond directly to the changes they observe in the status of Atlantic salmon with greater expediency and efficiency than the existing government programs. At the same time, the Skolts collaborate with the scientists on other aspects of environmental monitoring that are outside of their own areas of expertise, such as the changes in the marine portion of the salmon lifecycle. But this process of coproducing knowledge works well only when the rights of Indigenous peoples to make decisions about land use are acknowledged and respected, as required by the UN Declaration on the Rights of Indigenous Peoples (UNDRIP) that has been endorsed by 148 countries, including the United States and Canada. Recognizing the inherent rights of Indigenous peoples to be stewards of their lands and waters is key if their traditional territories are to continue to play an important role in biodiversity conservation and climate regulation.

INDIGENOUS RIGHTS

According to the Right and Resources Initiative—an NGO working on land and resource rights of Indigenous peoples and local communities—the world's 370 million Indigenous peoples make up fewer than 4 percent of the world's population, but represent close to 60 percent of the world's linguistic and cultural diversity. Their traditional territories represent more than 20 percent of the global land area, or between 30 and 50 percent of the world's collectively held and managed lands, or commons. Indigenous peoples' traditional territories support about 80 percent of the world's biological diversity and contain close to a quarter of the carbon stored aboveground in the world's tropical forests (not including the carbon stored in the soil). But despite all the benefits that Indigenous territories provide to the global community, Indigenous land rights are legally recognized on less than 20 percent of their traditional areas. The most efficient path toward enhancing climate change resilience at both local and global levels is to secure and support Indigenous peoples' rights to their lands and waters, so that they continue to support the majority of the Earth's remaining biological and cultural diversity, intact forests, undammed rivers, and ecosystem services.

As the collaboration between the Karen and scientists demonstrates, the Karen's traditional forest-management practices are good for biodiversity, local livelihoods, food security, and climate change mitigation. Molded by age-tested traditions of swidden agriculture, the Karen's territory of Hin Lad Nai is a treasure trove of biological and crop diversity that absorbs significantly more carbon than it releases each year. Shifting cultivation maintains a patchy landscape of fields, fallows, and natural areas maintaining high biodiversity; regulates local climate; and provides families with fish and game, crops and medicines, construction materials and firewood—all important for local subsistence and cash economies. For the Karen, swidden agriculture is not just a mode of production, but a spiritually rooted way of life that ensures the well-being, food security, and environmental sustainability of local communities.

UNDRIP highlights Free, Prior and Informed Consent as a fundamental principle for nurturing equitable, respectful, and just relationships between different knowledge systems. In the same way as a farmer, following ancient teachings, asks the land for permission to grow crops, the scientists and government agencies must seek consent of traditional knowledge holders to engage in a collaborative relationship. Many initiatives being developed to tackle climate change—like

UNESCO's Frozen Tombs of Altai project aimed at preserving Altai burial sites, or kurgans, from climate change—seem well meaning and even plausible. However, because most projects are developed without the full informed consent and participation of local Indigenous peoples, as required by UNDRIP, they achieve little. UNESCO's Frozen Tombs project saw the value of the kurgans only in the material objects that can be unearthed by archaeologists to be preserved and studied, but it failed to recognize the significance of Altai kurgans as sacred sites, regulating the human-environment interactions, weather, and climate, which can only be sustained if these kurgans remain intact and Altai people continue to maintain their relationship with them.

Recognizing the rights of Indigenous peoples is ultimately about advancing an alternative narrative of human relationships with the Earth. The dominant development paradigm has led to our planet's being carved up into chunks of "properties" and "states" solely based on our craving the Earth's riches while loathing sharing them with others. What a different world we would live in, if it were arranged not along the lines of fear, greed, and power, but around the intricate web of respectful and reciprocal human relationships with the Earth and all its living beings. The Indigenous peoples are the storytellers keeping this narrative alive through their actions, helping us and future generations choose a different path going forward.

HEALING JOURNEY

A bsolutely!" Tofino's mayor, Josie Osborne, responds enthusiastically when I ask her if being part of the Tla-o-qui-aht tribal park helps the town. "At a practical level, Tofino gets all of its fresh water from Meares Island. If it weren't for the Tla-o-qui-aht people, the island's rain forest would've been logged and there'd be no fresh water for us, period." Described by the independent online Canadian magazine *The Tyee* as an elected official "personifying the outgoing, clean, and green nature of the place," the fortysomething Josie Osborne became Tofino's mayor in 2013. Raised on Vancouver Island, Josie earned a degree in marine biology at the University of British Columbia and a master's in resource management at Simon Fraser University, before moving to Tofino in 1998 to work as a fisheries biologist, mostly with the Nuu-chah-nulth First Nations. Over the past two decades, before running for office, she has helped establish the Ecolodge at the Tofino Botanical Gardens, led the local Raincoast Education Society, chaired the Tourism Tofino Board of Directors, and served on many festival boards, always with the best interests of Tofinians in mind. I met Josie when she chaired the organizing committee of the International Society of Ethnobiology congress in Tofino. We have kept in touch ever since and I have talked to her about the relationship between Tofino and the Tla-o-qui-aht people.

"At a conceptual level," Josie continues, "*hishuk ish tsa'walk* teachings provide us with a framework for thinking about how we should live here and derive our livelihood from the land and sea, without depleting them. We try to use the teachings to evaluate our options. For example, it's helped us reframe the discussion about our local economy, along the lines of what Eli Enns and Ecotrust Canada call the *conservation economy*." Unlike typical industrial forestry and fisheries practices, the *conservation economy* does not diminish, but benefits, local environment and livelihoods, enhancing the resilience of local communities and ecosystems in the face of change. Just like the Karen in Thailand, the Tla-o-qui-aht people are working hard to support the elements of their traditional subsistence-based conservation economy that are still viable, like salmon fishing, and replace the old elements that are no longer feasible, like whaling, with new elements developed through culturally appropriate innovation, like tourism, renewable energy, or using local timber to build local environmentally friendly houses based on traditional Tla-o-qui-aht designs.

"Tla-o-qui-aht teachings have helped us maintain a much more holistic frame of mind, when we think about how all the little pieces fit together and affect one another," continues Josie. "It's like a spiderweb—you tug on one string and it pulls something somewhere else. Basically, we recognize Tla-o-qui-aht rights to manage their territory and are trying to do things together with them as part of the reconciliation process between Indigenous peoples and the settlers. A good practical example of the work we've done together is Monks Point, or Na-chaaks, a traditional Tla-o-qui-aht lookout point."

Born in Tofino, Captain Harold Monks Jr. sailed the world but always returned to his home in Tofino that he eventually inherited from his parents. His small house sits on two waterfront acres near Tofino Harbor, overlooking Clayoquot Sound. Hoping that one day the Monks Point Park would become a place for community to come together, Captain Monks bequeathed his property, known as Monks Point, to the Land Conservancy before he passed away in 2008. In late 2013, the Land Conservancy filed for creditor protection and the property eventually ended up with the municipality of Tofino.

"When Tofino became the owner," Josie recalls, "we felt that it was important to comanage this property with the Tla-o-qui-aht First Nation. [The] Monks family was one of the original settler families in Tofino and there's a very strong sense of European history that is important to the settler community here. But because it is their traditional territory, we went to Tla-o-qui-aht, and, after a few discussions, we all agreed to transform Na-chaaks into a reconciliation park—as a physical manifestation of our commitment to healing our relationships with First Nations. It's the first time that Tofino's ever done something like this and I think it was a real turning point for the municipality. At the moment, we only have a shared vision that we want to embark on this journey together. We don't have a specific plan yet for what the end result's going to be. We've applied for funding to get some support for the two communities to work together to determine what the future of the property's going to look like. What is important here, though, is the process itself, the very coming together to discuss and work in concert, in order to find a way forward. It is exactly the healing and reconciliation that we all need."

The Earth Charter is a globally endorsed affirmation of fundamental values and principles that "seeks to inspire in all peoples a sense of global interdependence and shared responsibility for the well-being of the human family, the greater community of life, and future generations." It describes humankind as standing at a critical juncture in Earth's history, when the future holds either great peril or tremendous promise. There is a growing recognition that we, as Albert Einstein observed, "can no longer solve problems in the same way of thinking that led to their creation." A new way of thinking, a paradigm shift, is required to sufficiently improve the nature of our relationship with the world and one another, if humankind is not to disappear into the abyss of Alan Weisman's *World Without Us*, where *Homo sapiens* are no longer part of the Earth's future.

While the scale and magnitude of various converging global crises could keep us frozen in our tracks, I hope that the stories of resilience and wisdom of Indigenous peoples described within these pages, and many similar examples from around the world, provide much needed proof and hope that a wiser way of living on Earth is still possible. According to Thomas Berry, a renowned cultural historian and ecotheologian, humankind can emerge from our current self-inflicted state of anthropocenic crisis into the light of an Ecozoic age—when our conduct will be based on the recognition of the Earth community as an integrated web of symbiotic relationships—if we are able to relearn how we, as individuals and societies, can nurture a more holistic way of relating to nature and being the world.

As Snowchange's director, Tero Mustonen, told me back in his home village of Selkie, "It's time to build new knowledge. As the land changes, we must change with it." This is not just a description of an adaptation episode, but a clarion call to all of us to embark on a healing journey, like the city of Tofino and the Tla-o-qui-aht people have. By no means will this be easy or immediately attainable for many of us. But it is undoubtedly achievable through patient perseverance, as long as we are realistic about the scope and scale of what we need to do to change the course, rather than delude ourselves with the notion that "business-as-usual" is still an option. For this to succeed, we must learn to be good allies to the Indigenous peoples.

EPILOGUE
BEING A GOOD ALLY

———

After our memorable walk through Oxford a decade ago, Dr. Nancy Turner's words stay with me. "As we search for ways to cope with converging social, environmental, and climate crises, we must find a way to be good allies to Indigenous peoples." It means, she went on to explain, committing to a long-term relationship with Indigenous communities; working together with them in respectful and ethical ways; being honest and reliable partners; keeping our promises; and finding ways to give back to the communities in culturally appropriate and respectful ways. But perhaps most importantly, it means being willing to listen to and follow their advice.

My own interest in Indigenous issues and supporting their causes has taken me in several directions. Among others, I have helped develop management approaches based on valuing Indigenous peoples' traditional knowledge and practices; supported their inherent right to have a say in whether, and how, research, conservation, and development projects unfold on their ancestral territories; backed efforts to protect their sacred sites; and cocreated initiatives to advance their responses to climate change. All of these initiatives have been developed as an attempt to help address the needs of Indigenous communities, either in direct response to their requests for assistance or through a process of community-based participatory knowledge co-production. None of them have emerged out of some naïve vision of Indigenous peoples as "noble savages" or a romantic belief that somehow we must all be magicked back into the "ancestral ways" to solve our current problems.

On the contrary, what has motivated me all these years is quite rational and pragmatic. In two decades of scholarly and direct community-based learning, observation, and participation, I have come to realize that it is the Indigenous peoples who are the true stewards of global biocultural heritage. After all, it is they who have a robust millennia-long track record of maintaining intimate relationships with the natural world, which has nourished their communities and sustained their cultures, without devouring the life-giving environment. This is the track record that they continuously strive to maintain, despite formidable odds, including fierce opposition from the "developed" world. The "accomplishments" of our own "modern" society, however, are a lot more recent, paltry, and have had much more destructive consequences for life on Earth.

This is why, like any eager student, I have been compelled to follow mentors who demonstrate a deeper understanding of their field. I choose to learn from the teachers with a holistic understanding of both secular and sacred dimensions of the human-environment relationship, because this understanding has produced positive and tangible results for both humans and the world around them. There are no better instructors on this journey than Indigenous peoples. Following them, as Dr. Turner stressed, means learning to be a good ally.

In an opinion piece for the CBC website, Clayton Thomas-Müller—a Pukatawagan campaigner with 350.org, a public speaker, and writer on the issues of Indigenous rights and environmental and economic justice—wrote that "in order to be truly effective, Indigenous allies must not take up space meant for our own front-line voices . . . when it comes to collective Indigenous resilience, let us speak for ourselves."* I respect and fully support this message. Yet I also feel it is important for non-Indigenous allies, like myself, to share our own stories, in order to try to articulate the reasons for choosing the road we follow, and, in this way, share our journey with others who are contemplating, or already following, a similar path. It seems to be particularly relevant now, as our postcolonial societies are grappling with the issues of inter-racial and intergenerational justice, Indigenous rights, decolonization, equity, and reconciliation.

In addition to creating a platform for Indigenous peoples to share their stories, concerns, and ideas, this book is my attempt to share the lessons I have learned along the way about being a good ally to Indigenous peoples. As I continue on my journey, I would like to promise that I will continue to practice what I have learned from my Indigenous friends over the years. I pledge to be a good ally to them, to other Indigenous peoples, and to continue to:

- Acknowledge the folly of nontolerant worldviews rooted in the idea that people are separate from, and dominant over, nature.

- Celebrate Indigenous wisdom that has nourished people and their relationship with the natural world for millennia, and the fundamental role of the wisdom keepers, both men and women, who have maintained it since time immemorial.

---

* http://www.cbc.ca/news/indigenous/gord-downie-let-us-speak-for-ourselves-1.4179478

- Continue to learn from Indigenous Knowledge holders and to affirm their knowledge, rights and relationships wherever and whenever possible.

- Advance approaches that value multiple ways of knowing in decision-making, in particular based on traditional knowledge, for the benefit of all living beings.

- Acknowledge that human beings are an integral part of an indivisible, self-regulating, living community of inextricably linked and interdependent beings—our Earth Community, or Gaia, or Mother Earth, as she is known to many Indigenous peoples of the Americas.

- Honor Mother Earth and act responsibly to ensure that the pursuit of personal and humankind's goals contributes to, and not subtracts from, the well-being of the future generations of all beings in living, nonliving and spirit realms, that form our Earth Community.

- While accepting change as an essential and natural part of life—representing not only loss but also an opportunity for growth, reorganization, and positive transformation—remember that our intentions and actions affect the trajectory of that change.

- Practice fundamental principles of resilience—restraint, respect, reciprocity, and reverence—when facing challenges and other beings whom we might, or might not, fully understand.

- Avoid perpetuating past injustices and commit to building respectful, beneficial, long-term relationships that support genuine partnerships and collaborations with Indigenous peoples around the globe.

My hope is that *The Archipelago of Hope* becomes more than just words on paper. That it turns into the flagstones on a road to healing, reconciliation, and positive transformation. As I put the finishing touches on the manuscript, I am working with my long-term partners to create "The Archipelago of Hope" outreach program and a community-focused traveling exhibition program that would enable Indigenous community members to share their own stories with one another, their neighbors, decision-makers, and the broader global community.

We are also establishing "The Archipelago of Hope Indigenous Resilience Fund," so that any profits earned from the book sales, as well as any donations to the projects profiled in the book, can go directly to the relevant communities, their representative organizations, or their partners. So that eventually, in the words of my friend and teacher Tero Mustonen, the "complete rebirth on the land" becomes a real option for all communities facing climate change.

SOURCES

—⚬⚬⚬—

General References

Alexander, C. et al., 2011. Linking Indigenous and Scientific Knowledge of Climate Change. *BioScience* 61 (6): 477–484.

Berkes, F., et al. 2003. *Navigating Social-Ecological Systems: Building Resilience for Complexity and Change*. Cambridge, UK: Cambridge University Press.

—— 1999. *Sacred Ecology: Traditional Ecological Knowledge and Resource Management*. Philadelphia: Taylor and Francis.

Bohensky E, and Y. Maru. 2011. Indigenous Knowledge, Science, and Resilience: What Have We Learned From a Decade of International Literature on "Integration"? *Ecology and Society* 16 (6).

Chianese, F. 2016. *The Traditional Knowledge Advantage: Indigenous Peoples' Knowledge in Climate Change Adaptation And Mitigation Strategies*. IFAD. Available online: http://www.uncclearn.org/learning-resources/library/14809 and https://www.ifad.org/documents/10180/2a1e3eb4-51a3-4746-8558-2fc1e6d3e645.

Climate and Traditional Knowledge Workgroup (CTKW). 2014. *Guidelines for Considering Traditional Knowledge in Climate Change Initiatives*. Available online: www.climatetkw.wordpress.com.

Cochran, P., et al. 2013. Indigenous Frameworks for Observing and Responding to Climate Change in Alaska. Climatic Change. Available online: www.ihrfg.org/sites/default/files/Indigenous_Frameworks.pdf.

Comberti, C., T. Thornton, and M. Korodimou. 2016. "Addressing Indigenous Peoples Marginalization at International Climate Negotiations: Adaptation and Resilience at the Margins." Working paper, Environmental Change Institute, University of Oxford, UK.

Davis, W. 2009. *The Wayfinders: Why Ancient Wisdom Matters in the Modern World*. House of Anansi Press.

—— 2002. *Light at the Edge of the World: A Journey Through the Realm of Vanishing Cultures. National Geographic*.

——, et al. 2008. *Book of Peoples of the World: A Guide to Cultures*. National Geographic.

Galloway McLean, K. 2010. *Advance Guard: Climate Change Impacts, Adaptation, Mitigation and Indigenous Peoples: A Compendium of Case Studies*. Darwin, Australia, United Nations University—Traditional Knowledge Initiative. Available online: http://i.unu.edu/media/ourworld.unu.edu-en/article/1148/Advance_Copy-Advance_Guard_Compendium.pdf.

Harding, S. 2009. *Animate Earth: Science, Intuition and Gaia*, 2nd edition. Green Books.

—— 2015. Towards an Animistic Science of the Earth. In Harvey G., ed. *The Handbook of Contemporary Animism*. Acumen Handbooks. Available online: http://wildethics.org/essay/towards-an-animistic-science-of-the-earth/.

Harmon, D. 2002. *In Light of Our Differences: How Diversity in Nature and Culture Makes Us Human*. Washington, DC: Smithsonian Institution Press.

Huntington, H. 2000. Using Traditional Ecological Knowledge in Science: Methods and Applications. *Ecological Applications* 10: 1270–1274.

International Labor Organization (ILO), 2017. Indigenous Peoples and Climate Change: From Victims to Change Agents through Decent Work. International Labor Office, Gender, Equality and Diversity Branch. Available online: http://www.ilo.org/wcmsp5/groups/public/---dgreports/---gender/documents/publication/wcms_551189.pdf.

IPCC, 2014. Climate Change 2014: Impacts, Adaptation, and Vulnerability. Contribution of Working Group II to the Fifth Assessment Report of the Intergovernmental Panel on Climate Change. Cambridge University Press.

Hansen, K., K. Jepsen, and P. Jacquelin, eds. IWGIA. Copenhagen, 2017. The Indigenous World. Available online: http://www.iwgia.org/iwgia_files_publications_files/0760_THE_INDIGENOUS_ORLD_2017_eb.pdf.

Forest Peoples Program. 2015. Status and Trends in Traditional Occupations: Outcomes of a Rapid Assessment. Available online: http://www.forestpeoples.org/sites/fpp/files/publication/2016/05/fpp-status-trends-trad-occupations-english-web-16.pdf.

Lovelock, J. 2005. *Gaia: Medicine for an Ailing Planet.* Gaia Books.

———— 2000. *Gaia: A New Look at Life on Earth* 3rd ed. Oxford University Press.

Maffi, L., and E. Woodley, eds. 2010. *Biocultural Diversity Conservation: A Global Sourcebook.* London: Earthscan.

————, ed. 2001. *On Biocultural Diversity: Linking Language, Knowledge, and the Environment.* Smithsonian Institution Press.

Meltofte, H. ed. 2013. Arctic Biodiversity Assessment. Status and Trends in Arctic Biodiversity. Conservation of Arctic Flora and Fauna, Akureyri, Iceland. Available online: http://arcticlcc.org/assets/resources/ABA2013Science.pdf.

Menzies, C., ed. 2006. *Traditional Ecological Knowledge and Natural Resource Management.* Lincoln, NE: University of Nebraska Press.

Muller, S. 2012. "Two Ways": Bringing Indigenous and Non-Indigenous Knowledge Together. Pages 59–80 in Weir, J., ed. *Country, Native Title and Ecology.* Australian National University Press.

Nakashima, D., et al. 2012. *Weathering Uncertainty: Traditional Knowledge for Climate Change Assessment and Adaptation.* UNESCO and UNU.

Ostrom, E., et al., eds. 2002. *The Drama of the Commons.* National Academy Press.

Oviedo, G., et al. 2000. *Indigenous and Traditional Peoples of the World and Ecoregion Conservation: An Integrated Approach to Conserving the World's Biological and Cultural Diversity.* Indigenous and Traditional Peoples and the Global 200 Ecoregions. Gland, Switzerland: WWF-International and Terralingua.

Reid, W. et al., eds. 2006. *Bridging Scales and Knowledge Systems: Concepts and Applications in Ecosystem Assessment.* Island Press.

Ricketts, T. 2010. Indigenous Lands, Protected Areas, and Slowing Climate Change. *PLoS Biology* 8 (3). Available online: http://journals.plos.org/plosbiology/article?id=10.1371/journal.pbio.1000331.

Rights and Resources Initiative. 2015. Who Owns the World's Land? A Global Baseline of Formally Recognized Indigenous and Community Land Rights. Washington, DC: RRI. Available online: http://www.rightsandresources.org/wp-content/uploads/GlobalBaseline_web.pdf.

Roosvalt, A., and M. Tegelberg. 2015. Media and the geographies of climate justice: indigenous peoples, nature, and geopolitics of climate change. tripleC 13 (1): 39–54. Available online: http://www.triple-c.at/index.php/tripleC/article/viewFile/654/687.

Salick, J., and A. Byg. 2007. *Indigenous Peoples and Climate Change. A Tyndall Center Publication.* Available online: http://www.ecdgroup.com/docs/lib_004630823.pdf

Sobrevila, C. 2008. *The Role Of Indigenous Peoples in Biodiversity Conservation: The Natural but Often Forgotten Partners.* World Bank, Washington, DC. Available online: https://siteresources.worldbank.org/INTBIODIVERSITY/Resources/RoleofIndigenousPeoplesinBiodiversityConservation.pdf.

Stevens, C. et al. 2014. Securing Rights, Combating Climate Change: How Strengthening Community Forest Rights Mitigates Climate Change. World Resources Institute. Available online: http://www.wri.org/publication/securing-rights-combating-climate-change.

Tebtebba Foundation. 2013. Developing and Implementing Community-Based Monitoring and Information Systems: The Global Workshop and the Philippine Workshop Reports. Available online: http://www.tebtebba.org/index.php/content/271-developing-and-implementing-cbmis-the-global-workshop-and-the-philippine-workshop-reports.

Tengo, M., et al. 2014. Connecting diverse knowledge systems for enhanced ecosystem governance: the multiple evidence base approach. Ambio. 43: 579–591.

Veit, P., and K. Reytar. 2017. By the Numbers: Indigenous and Community Land Rights. http://www.wri.org/blog/2017/03/numbers-indigenous-and-community-land-rights.

Walker, B., and D. Salt. 2012. *Resilience Practice: Building Capacity to Absorb Disturbance and Maintain Function*. Island Press.

——— 2006. *Resilience Thinking. Sustaining Ecosystems and People in a Changing World*. Island Press.

Wilder, B., et al. 2016. The Importance of Indigenous Knowledge in Curbing the Loss of Language and Biodiversity. *BioScience* 66 (6): 499–509.

Skolt

Gertz, E. 2016. Indigenous People Are Fighting Finland's Plan to Log Ancient Forests. TakePart. March 24, 2016. Available online: http://barentsobserver.com/en/society/2015/10/500-year-old-skolt-sami-document-joins-memory-world-13-10.

——— 2015. The Fatal Thaw: The Sámi Fight to Preserve an Ancient Culture as the Arctic Warms. TakePart. November 11, 2015. Available online: http://www.takepart.com/feature/2015/11/30/arctic-people-fight-back-against-climate-change.

——— 2015. 500-Year-Old Skolt Sami Document Joins "Memory of the World". Barents Observer. October 13, 2015. Available online: http://barentsobserver.com/en/society/2015/10/500-year-old-skolt-sami-document-joins-memory-world-13-10.

Greenpeace. 2005. Lapland: State of Conflict—How the Finnish Government is Abusing the Forest Rights of Sámi Reindeer Herders. Available online: http://www.greenpeace.org/international/en/publications/reports/lapland-state-of-conflict/.

Helander, E., and T. Mustonen., eds. 2004. *Snowscapes, Dreamscapes: Snowchange Book on Community Voices of Change*. Tampere Polytechnic Publications.

Ingold, T. 1976. *The Skolt Lapps Today*. Cambridge University Press.

Jepsen, J., et al. 2008. Climate Change and Outbreaks of the Geometrids *Operophtera Brumata* and *Epirrita Autumnata* in Subarctic Birch Forest: Evidence of a Recent Outbreak Range Expansion. *Journal of Animal Ecology* 77 (2): 257–64. Available online: https://www.ncbi.nlm.nih.gov/pubmed/18070041.

Kuokkanen, R. 2008. Sami Rights Policy in Finland: Delay Tactics Until the Problem Disappears? Available online: https://rauna.wordpress.com/?s=sami+rights+policy.

Lawrence, R., and K. Raitio. 2011. Forestry Conflicts in Finnish Sápmi: Local, National and Global Links. IWGIA. Available online: http://www.iwgia.org/iwgia_files_publications_files/IA_4-06_Finland.pdf.

Mustonen, T. 2017. Endemic Time-Spaces of Finland: From Wilderness Lands to "Vacant Production Spaces." *Fennia* 195: 1–20. Available online: file:///Users/gleb%201/Downloads/58971-121-70744-4-10-20170615.pdf.

Mustonen, T. 2015. Communal Visual Histories to Detect Environmental Change in Northern Areas: Examples of Emerging North American and Eurasian Practices. *Ambio*. 2015 Dec; 44 (8): 766-77. Available online: https://www.ncbi.nlm.nih.gov/pubmed/26008615.

—— 2013. Re-birth of Indigenous Arctic Nations and Polar Resource Management: Critical Perspectives from Siberia and Sámi Areas of Finland. *Journal Biodiversity* 14 (1). Available online: http://www.tandfonline.com/doi/abs/10.1080/14888386.2012.725652.

Mustonen, T., and P. Feodoroff. 2013. Ponoi and Näätämö River Collaborative Management Plan. Snowchange Cooperative. Available online: http://www.snowchange.org/pages/wp-content/uploads/2014/05/Naatamo_sisus_1205_p.pdf.

Mustonen, T., and A. Lehtinen. 2013. Arctic Earthviews: Cyclic Passing of Knowledge among the Indigenous Communities of the Eurasian North. *Sibirica* 12 (1): 39–55.

Mustonen, T., and K. Mustonen. 2011. *Eastern Sámi Atlas*. Vaasa, Finland: Snowchange Cooperative.

Pelto, P. 1973. *The Snowmobile Revolution: Technology and Social Change in the Arctic.* Cummings Pub. Co.

Vepsalainen, V. 2003. The Sami people in Finland, Land Rights, Linguistic Rights and Right to Self Government. Available online: http://www.tolerance.cz/courses/papers/papers2003/virpi.doc.

Nenets

Bourne, J. 2016. In the Arctic's Cold Rush, There Are No Easy Profits. *National Geographic*. March. Available online: http://www.nationalgeographic.com/magazine/2016/03/new-arctic-thawing-rapidly-circle-work-oil/.

Degteva, A. 2013. Nantes Migration in the Landscape: Impacts of Industrial Development in Yamal Peninsula, Russia. Pastoralism: Research,

Policy and Practice. Available online: https://link.springer.com/ article/10.1186/2041-7136-3-15.

Evladov, V. 1998. *The Land of Yamal: Album of Yamal Expeditions.* Moscow: Novosti Press.

Forbes, B. 2008. Equity, Vulnerability and Resilience in Social-Ecological Systems: A Contemporary Example from the Russian Arctic. *Equity and the Environment.* Volume 15, 203–236. Available online: http://library.arcticportal. org/418/1/B._Forbes_-_Equity%2C_Vulnerability_and_Resilience_in_ Social_Ecological_Systems._A_Contemporary_Example_from_the_Russian_ Arctic.pdf.

———, et al. 2016. Sea Ice, Rain-on-Snow and Tundra Reindeer Nomadism in Arctic Russia. *Biology Letter* 12. Available online: http://rsbl. royalsocietypublishing.org/content/12/11/20160466.

———, et al. 2013. Cultural Resilience of Social-Ecological Systems in the Nenets and Yamal-Nenets Autonomous Okrug, Russia: A Focus on Reindeer Nomads of the Tundra. *Ecology and Society.* Available online: https://www .ecologyandsociety.org/vol18/iss4/art36/.

———, et al. 2010. High Resilience in the Yamal-Nenets Social-Ecological System, West Siberian Arctic, Russia. *Proceedings of the National Academy of Sciences of the United States of America* Early Edition. Available online: http://www.pnas. org/content/106/52/22041.full.pdf.

Golovnev, A. and G. Osherenko. 1999. *Siberian Survival: The Nenets and Their Story.* Cornell University Press.

Hunt, E. 2016. Nightmare Before Christmas: Siberia Plans to Cull 250,000 Reindeer Amid Anthrax Fears. *The Guardian.* September 30. Available online: https:// www.theguardian.com/world/2016/sep/30/nightmare-before-christmas -siberia-plans-to-cull-250000-reindeer-amid-anthrax-fears.

Krupnik, I., and N. Narinskaya. 1998. *Living Yamal.* Soviet Sport.

Kryazhimskiy, F., et al. 2012. Simulation Modelling of the System "Vegetation Cover—Domestic Reindeer" in the Yamal Peninsula: Could Global Warming Help to Save the Traditional Way of Land Use? *Procedia Environmental Sciences* 13, 598–605. Available online: https://www.researchgate.net/ publication/257728529_Simulation_Modelling_of_the_System_Vegetation_ Cover_-_Domestic_Reindeer_in_the_Yamal_Peninsula_Could_Global_ Warming_Help_to_Save_the_Traditional_Way_of_Land_Use.

Kumpula, T., et al. 2011. Land Use and Land Cover Change in Arctic Russia: Ecological and Social Implications of Industrial Development. *Global Environmental Change* 21: 550–562. Available online: https://www2 .uef.fi/documents/1336630/1336643/Kumpula_etal_GEC_2011. pdf/7fbf71a4-ff30-48a6-8c71-71b1cb326089.

Luhn, A. 2016. Anthrax Outbreak Triggered by Climate Change
Kills Boy in Arctic Circle. *The Guardian.* August 1. Available
online: https://www.theguardian.com/world/2016/aug/01/
anthrax-outbreak-climate-change-arctic-circle-russia.

Montaine, F. 1998. Nenets: Surviving on the Siberian Tundra. *National Geographic.*
March.

Rytkheu, Y. 1983. People of the Long Spring. *National Geographic.* February.

Shedchenko, A. 2014. *Yamal Energy—to Russia: Traditions, Innovation, Collaboration.*
Penta Press.

Trenin, D., and P. Baev, 2010. The Arctic: A View from Moscow. Carnegie
Endowment for International Peace. Available online: http://
carnegieendowment.org/files/arctic_cooperation.pdf.

Turaev, V., et al. 2011. *Encyclopedia of Indigenous Peoples of the North, Siberia and
the Far East of the Russian Federation. Centre for Support of Indigenous Peoples
of the North (CSIPN).* Moscow.

Altai

Almashev, C. 2007. *Notes from the Expeditions to the Sacred Mountains of The World.
Gorno-Altaisk. Fund of Sustainable Development of Altai (FSDA).* [In Russian].

——— 2010. Sacred Places of Altai: Methodological Guidelines for Data Collection,
Mapping and Cataloguing of Sacred Places for Their Protection. FSDA. [In
Russian].

Beniston, M. 2003. Climatic Change in Mountain Regions: A Review of Possible
Impacts. *Climatic Change* 59: 5–31.

Bourgeois, J., et al. 2007. Saving the frozen Scythian tombs of the Altai Mountains
(Central Asia). *World Archaeology* 39 (3): 458–474. Available online: http://
www.tandfonline.com/doi/abs/10.1080/00438240701504585.

Bryce, J. 1921. Western Siberia and Altai Mountains: With Some Speculations on the
Future of Siberia. *National Geographic.* May.

Bukker, I. 201. Tattoos of Princess of Altai Conceal Mankind's Biggest
Mysteries. Pravda. Available online: http://www.pravdareport.com/science/
mysteries/05-04-2011/117452-Princess_of_Altai-0/.

Butorin, A. 2009. Golden Mountains of Altai World Heritage Property. UNDP.
Available online: http://www.nhpfund.org/files/golden-mountains-of-altai
-world-heritage-property.pdf.

Debonnet, G., and H. Lethier. 2012. Reactive Monitoring Mission Golden Mountains of Altai World Heritage Property. Russian Federation 10–15 May 2012.
UNESCO World Heritage Centre—IUCN Mission Report.

Halemba, A. 2006. *The Telengits of Southern Siberia: Landscape, Religion and
Knowledge in Motion.* Routledge.

Junhi, H. 2007. Impact of the Climate Change on the Frozen Tombs in the Altai Mountains. Heritage at Risk 2006/2007. UNESCO World Heritage Centre.

Kaltenborn, B., et al., eds. 2010. High Mountain Glaciers and Climate Change—Challenges to Human Livelihoods and Adaptation. United Nations Environment Program. Available online: https://www.zaragoza.es/contenidos/medioambiente/onu/343-eng.pdf.

Kokorin, A., ed. 2011. Assessment Report: Climate Change and its Impact on Ecosystems, Population and Economy of the Russian Portion of the Altai-Sayan Ecoregion. WWF-Russia. Available online: https://www.wwf.ru/data/publ/climate/assessment_climate_altai_eng_.pdf.

Lukonina. 2008. The Golden Mountains at the Center of Eurasia. WWF-Russia.

McCannon, J. 2002. By the Shores of White Waters: The Altai and its Place in the Spiritual Geopolitics of Nicholas Roerich. *Sibirica* 2 (2): 166–189.

Ministry of Natural Resources of Altai Republic. 2007. The UNESCO World Heritage Site. The Altai Golden Mountains.

Polosmak, N., and C. O'Rear. 1994. A Mummy Unearthed from the Pastures of Heaven. *National Geographic*, October.

Roerich, N. 1983. *Altai-Himalaya: A Travel Diary*. Arun press.

Rubik, B. Measurement of the Human Biofield and Other Energetic Instruments. Chapter 20. In Freeman, L. ed. In *Energetics and Spirituality*. Foundation for Alternative and Integrative Medicine.

Shahgedanova, M. 2010. Glacier Shrinkage and Climatic Change in the Russian Altai from the Mid-20th Century: An Assessment Using Remote Sensing and PRECIS Regional Climate Model. *Journal of Geophysical Research* 115. Available online: http://onlinelibrary.wiley.com/doi/10.1029/2009JD012976/abstract.

Shodoev, N. 2012. *Spiritual Wisdom from the Altai Mountains: Altai Bilik*. Moon Books.

Stenger, V. 1999. Bioenergetic Fields. *The Scientific Review of Alternative Medicine* 3 (1). Spring/Summer. Available online: http://greenmedicine.ie/school/images/Library/The-Physics-of-%27Alternative-Medicine%27.pdf.

Tarunov, A. 2004. *Altai: Cultural Treasures*. Heritage of Russian Federation. Ivan Feodorof Press. [In Russian]

Zhernosenko, I. 2009. World of Altai Culture. Study Guide for 8–9 Grades. FSDA. [In Russian]

Znamenski. A. 2005. Power of Myth: Popular Ethnonationalism and Nationality Building in Mountain Altai, 1904–1922. Acta Salvica Iaponica. *Tomus* 22: 25–52. Available online: http://src-h.slav.hokudai.ac.jp/publictn/acta/22/znamenski.pdf.

UNESCO. 2008. Preservation of the Frozen Tombs of the Altai Mountains. Available online: http://unesdoc.unesco.org/images/0018/001853/185364e.pdf.

Sápara

Acosta, A. 2009. Leaving the Oil in the Ground: A Political, Economic and Ecological Initiative in the Ecuadorian Amazon. Americas Program Special Report. Available online: http://www.academia.edu/4241727/Leaving_the_Oil_in_the_Ground_A_Political_Economic_and_Ecological_Initiative_in_the_Ecuadorian_Amazon.

Bass M., et al. 2010. Global Conservation Significance of Ecuador's Yasuní National Park. *PLoS ONE* 5 (1). Available online: http://journals.plos.org/plosone/article?id=10.1371/journal.pone.0008767.

Bilhaut, A. 2003. The Zápara Indians: The Consecration of an Endangered People. *Museum International.* Vol. 55 (2): 25–31. Available online: http://onlinelibrary.wiley.com/doi/10.1046/j.1350-0775.2003.00422.x/abstract.

Binder, C. *Case Study: Burlington Resources Inc. v Ecuador/Kichwa Indigenous People of Sarayaku v Ecuador. Committee on the Implementation of the Rights of Indigenous Peoples of the International Law Association (ILA).* Available online: https://papers.ssrn.com/sol3/papers.cfm?abstract_id=2810062.

Case, M. 2006. Climate Change Impacts in the Amazon: Review of Scientific Literature. WWF. Available online: https://wwf.fi/mediabank/1064.pdf.

Castillo, M., et al. 2016. *La Cultura Sápara en Peligro ¿El Sueño es Posible? La lucha de un pueblo por su supervivencia frente a la explotación petrolera.* Quito: Terra Mater, la Nación Sa-para del Ecuador y NAKU. Available online: http://terramater.ec/wp-content/uploads/2017/01/libro-sapara.pdf.

Clark, K., and M. Becker. 2007. *Indigenous Peoples and State Formation in Modern Ecuador.* University of Pittsburgh Press. Available online: https://upress.pitt.edu/htmlSourceFiles/pdfs/9780822961468exr.pdf.

Clynes, T. 2016. As Oil Companies Dig into Yasuní National Park, Ecuadorians Are Fighting Back. *Audubon.* Winter. Available online: http://www.audubon.org/magazine/winter-2016/as-oil-companies-dig-yasuni-national-park.

Coates, K. 2016. The Myth of the Virgin Rainforest. *Discover Magazine.* May 6. Available online: http://blogs.discovermagazine.com/crux/2016/05/06/the-myth-of-the-virgin-rainforest/#.WXyJh9MrLNA.

Cultural Survival. 2016. Observations on the State of Indigenous Human Rights in Ecuador. Prepared for The United Nations Human Rights Council Universal Periodic Review, 27th Session, Third Cycle. *Cultural Survival Quarterly.* Available online: https://www.culturalsurvival.org/sites/default/files/ECUADOR%20UPR2016%20final.pdf.

de Koning, F., et al. 2011. Bridging the Gap between Forest Conservation and Poverty Alleviation: The Ecuadorian Socio Bosque Program *Environmental Science & Policy* 14: 531–542. Available online: http://www.sciencedirect.com/science/article/pii/S1462901111000657.

EDF. 2015. Tropical Forest Carbon in Indigenous Territories: A Global Analysis. Available online: https://www.edf.org/sites/default/files/tropical-forest-carbon-in-indigenous-territories-a-global-analysis.pdf.

Finer, M. Oil and Gas Projects in the Western Amazon: Threats to Wilderness, Biodiversity, and Indigenous Peoples. *PLoS ONE* 3 (8). Available online: http://journals.plos.org/plosone/article?id=10.1371/journal.pone.0002932.

Fernandez, M. 2015. Assessing Local Vulnerability to Climate Change in Ecuador. *Springer Plus* 4: 738. Available online: https://www.ncbi.nlm.nih.gov/pubmed/26640750.

Gaechter, D. 2007. Recolonizing Ecuador's Oriente: Oil, Agriculture, and the Myth of Empty Lands. MA Thesis. The University of British Columbia.

Gari, J. 2001. Biodiversity and Indigenous Agroecology in Amazonia: The Indigenous Peoples of Pastaza. *Etnoecológica* 5 (7): 21–37. Available online: https://www.researchgate.net/publication/284034435_Biodiversity_and_Indigenous_Agroecology_in_Amazonia_The_Indigenous_Peoples_of_Pastaza.

Hill, D. 2014. Ecuador Pursued China Oil Deal while Pledging to Protect Yasuní, Papers Show. *The Guardian*. February 19. Available online: https://www.theguardian.com/environment/2014/feb/19/ecuador-oil-china-yasuni.

——— 2013. Why Ecuador's President is Misleading the World on Yasuni-ITT. *The Guardian*. October 15. Available online: https://www.theguardian.com/environment/andes-to-the-amazon/2013/oct/15/ecuador-president-misleading-yasuni.

IPCCA Secretariat. 2011. Sápara Knowledge and Climate Change in the Amazon. Workshop Report. Sápara Territory-Ecuador. Available online: http://ipcca.info/ipcca-meeting-2011-02-17-sapara-knowledge-and-climate-change-in-the-amazon.

Kauffman, C., and P. Martin. 2016. Testing Ecuador's Rights of Nature: Why Some Lawsuits Succeed and Others Fail. Paper Presented at the International Studies Association Annual Convention. Atlanta, GA, March 18, 2016. Available online: http://static1.squarespace.com/static/55914fd1e4b01fb0b851a814/t/5748568c8259b5e5a34ae6bf/1464358541319/Kauffman++Martin+16+Testing+Ecuadors+RoN+Laws.pdf.

Koenig, K. 2016. Ecuador's Next Amazon Oil Battle: Indigenous Peoples on the Front Line. *The Ecologist*. April 4. Available online: http://www.theecologist.org/News/news_analysis/2987497/ecuadors_next_amazon_oil_battle_indigenous_peoples_on_the_front_line.html.

Krause, T., et al. 2013. Evaluating Safeguards in a Conservation Incentive Program: Participation, Consent, and Benefit Sharing in Indigenous Communities the Ecuadorian Amazon. *Ecology and Society* 18 (4): Available online: http://dx.doi.org/10.5751/ES-05733-180401.

Larre, C. 2009. Yasuní-ITT Initiative: A Big Idea from a Small Country. UNDP-Ecuador. Available online: http://www.eldis.org/document/A61550.

Moreno Tejada, J. 2016. Rhythms of Everyday Trade: Local Mobilities at the Peruvian-Ecuadorian Contact Zone During the Rubber Boom (c. 1890–1912). *Asian Journal of Latin American Studies* 29 (1): 57–82. Available online: https://www.researchgate.net/publication/296112705_Rhythms_of_Everyday_Trade_Local_Mobilities_at_the_Peruvian-Ecuadorian_Contact_Zone_during_the_Rubber_Boom_c_1890–1912.

Moya, A. 2007. Sápara: The Aritiakus—Sons and Daughters of the Red Monkey. UNESCO. Available online: http://unesdoc.unesco.org/images/0016/001604/160494m.pdf.

Nobrea, C., et al. 2016. Land-Use and Climate Change Risks in the Amazon and the Need of a Novel Sustainable Development Paradigm. *PNAS* 113 (39): 10759–10768. Available online: http://www.pnas.org/content/113/39/10759.full.

Pappalardo, S., et al. 2013. Uncontacted Waorani in the Yasuní Biosphere Reserve: Geographical Validation of the Zona Intangible Tagaeri Taromenane (ZITT). *PLoS ONE* 8 (6). Available online: http://journals.plos.org/plosone/article?id=10.1371/journal.pone.0066293.

Reider, R. 2005. Oil and Chicha: Indigenous Movements and Survival in the Ecuadoran Amazon. *Tropical Resources* 24, Spring.

Swing, K. 2012. Science in Yasuní Sheds Light on Impacts of Oil Development in Amazon. *National Geographic*. Available online: https://voices.nationalgeographic.org/2012/12/26/science-in-yasuni-sheds-light-on-impacts-of-of-oil-development-in-amazon/.

——— 2011. Day of Reckoning for Ecuador's Biodiversity. *Nature* 469. Available online: http://www.nature.com/news/2011/110119/full/469267a.html.

———, et al. 2012. Oil Development on Traditional Lands of Indigenous Peoples Coinciding Perceptions on Two Continents. *Journal of Developing Societies* 28, 2: 257–280. Available online: http://journals.sagepub.com/doi/abs/10.1177/0169796X12448760?journalCode=jdsb.

Viatori, M., and G. Ushigua. 2007. Speaking Sovereignty: Indigenous Languages and Self-Determination. *Wicazo Sa Review* 22 (2): 7–21. Available online: https://muse.jhu.edu/article/219796.

——— 2007. Zápara Leaders and Identity Construction in Ecuador: The Complexities of Indigenous Self-Representation. *Journal of Latin American and Caribbean Anthropology* 12 (1): 104–133. Available online: http://onlinelibrary.wiley.com/doi/10.1525/jlca.2007.12.1.104/abstract.

——— 2005. New Bodies, Ancient Blood: "Purity" and the Construction of Zápara Identity in the Ecuadorian Amazon. *Tipití: Journal of the Society for the*

Anthropology of Lowland South America 3 (2) Article 5. Available online: http://
digitalcommons.trinity.edu/tipiti/vol3/iss2/5.

Wasserstrom, R. and S. Reider. 2009. Oil Development, Deforestation, and
Indigenous Populations in the Ecuadorian Amazon. Paper presented at
the 2009 Meeting of the Latin American Studies Association. Available
online: http://s3.amazonaws.com/academia.edu.documents/44885053/Oil_
Development_Deforestation_and_Indige20160419-18420-1n6h4so.pdf?AWS
AccessKeyId=AKIAIWOWYYGZ2Y53UL3A&Expires=1501344418&Signa
ture=EpGvZdcofPVSzCzfkXHyBoxYId4%3D&response-content
-disposition=inline%3B%20filename%3DOil_Development_Deforestation_
and_Indige.pdf.

Warmikuna, S. 2016. Sapara Nation: Its History and Genocide in the
Making. Working Paper. Acción Ecológica. Available online: http://
indigenouswomenrising.org/docs/Sapara-Report-English-FINAL.pdf.

Zuckerman, A. and K. Koenig. 2016. From Well to Wheel: The
Social, Environmental and Climate Costs of Amazon Crude.
Amazon Watch. Available online: http://amazonwatch.org/
news/2016/0928-from-well-to-wheel.

Karen

Agrawal, A. 2004. Governing Agriculture-Forest Landscapes to Achieve Climate
Change Mitigation. *Global Environmental Change* 28: 270–280. Available
online: https://www.inogov.eu/wp-content/uploads/2015/04/1-s2.0-
S095937801400168X-main.pdf.

Baker, C. 2000. Thailand's Assembly of the Poor: Background, Drama, Reaction.
South East Asia Research 8 (1): 5–29. Available online: http://www.redd-
monitor.org/wp-content/uploads/2014/07/ae13.pdf.

Bradbear, N. 2009. Bees and their Role in Forest Livelihoods: A Guide to the
Services Provided by Bees and the Sustainable Harvesting, Processing and
Marketing of their Products. FAO. Available online: http://www.fao.org/3/
a-i0842e.pdf.

Brookfield, H., et al., eds. 2002. *Cultivating Biodiversity*. ITDG Publishing.

Cairns, M., ed. 2015. *Shifting Cultivation and Environmental Change: Indigenous
People, Agriculture and Forest Conservation*. Earthscan from Routledge.

Carling, J. 2015. Asia Report on Climate Change and Indigenous Peoples. Available
online: http://www.eldis.org/document/A100574.

Celli, G. 2003. Honey Bees as Bioindicators of Environmental Pollution. *Bulletin
of Insectology* 56 (1): 137–139. Available online: https://www.researchgate.net/
publication/242202509_Honey_bees_as_bioindicators_of_environmental_
pollution.

Chotiboriboon, S., et al. 200 Thailand: Food System and Nutritional Status of Indigenous Children in a Karen Community. Available online: http://www.fao.org/3/a-i0370e/i0370e09.pdf.

Chouvy, P. 2013. An Atlas of Trafficking in Southeast Asia: The Illegal Trade in Arms, Drugs, People, Counterfeit Goods and Natural Resources in Mainland Southeast Asia. I.B. Tauris. Available online: http://citeseerx.ist.psu.edu/viewdoc/download?doi=10.1.1.635.9057&rep=rep1&type=pdf.

Delang, C. 2010. *Living at the Edge of Thai Society: The Karen in the Highlands of Northern Thailand*. Routledge.

——— 2002. Deforestation in Northern Thailand: The Result of Hmong Farming Practices or Thai Development Strategies? *Society and Natural Resources* 15: 483–501. Available online: https://www.sciencebase.gov/catalog/item/50578b0ce4b01ad7e02820eb.

Dresslera, W. 2015. Examining How Long Fallow Swidden Systems Impact Upon Livelihood and Ecosystem Services Outcomes Compared with Alternative Land-Uses in the Uplands of Southeast Asia. *Journal of Development Effectiveness* 7 (2): 210–229. Available online: http://www.cifor.org/publications/pdf_files/WPapers/WP174Clendenning.pdf.

Erni, C. 2015. Shifting Cultivation, Livelihood and Food Security. New and Old Challenges for Indigenous Peoples in Asia. Food and Agriculture Organization of the United Nations. Available online: http://www.fao.org/3/a-i4580e.pdf.

——— 2009. Shifting the Blame? Southeast Asia's Indigenous Peoples and Shifting Cultivation in the Age of Climate Change. *Indigenous Affairs* 1/09: 38–49. Available online: http://www.iwgia.org/iwgia_files_publications_files/IA_1-2009_Shifting_Blame_SE_Asia.pdf.

Fox, J. 2000. Shifting Cultivation: A New Old Paradigm for Managing Tropical Forests. *BioScience* 50 (6): 521–528. Available online: https://academic.oup.com/bioscience/article/50/6/521/261059/Shifting-Cultivation-A-New-Old-Paradigm-for.

——— 2000. How Blaming "Slash and Burn" Farmers is Deforesting Mainland Southeast Asia. Analysis from the East-West Center. No. 47. Available online: https://scholarspace.manoa.hawaii.edu/bitstream/10125/3832/1/api047.pdf.

Greenpeace. 2006. Crisis of Opportunity: Climate Change in Thailand. Available online: http://www.greenpeace.org/international/en/publications/reports/crisis-or-opportunity-climate/.

Hett, C. 2012. A Landscape Mosaics Approach for Characterizing Swidden Systems from a Redd Perspective. *Applied Geography* 32: 608–618. Available online: http://www.cifor.org/library/3692/a-landscape-mosaics-approach-for-characterizing-swidden-systems-from-a-redd-perspective/.

IWGIA. 2012. Drivers of Deforestation? Facts to Be Considered Regarding the
    Impact of Shifting Cultivationin Asia. Submission to the SBSTA on the Drivers
    of Deforestation by Asia Indigenous Peoples Pact (AIPP) and International
    Work Group for Indigenous Affairs (IWGIA). Available online: http://unfccc.
    int/resource/docs/2012/smsn/ngo/235.pdf.

Kunstadter, P. 1972. Spirits of Change Capture the Karens. *National Geographic*.
    February: 266–285.

Lietaer, C. Impact of Beekeeping on Forest Conservation, Preservation of Forest
    Ecosystems and Poverty Reduction. Available online: http://docplayer.
    net/21622856-Impact-of-beekeeping-on-forest-conservation-preservation-of
    -forest-ecosystems-and-poverty-reduction-charlotte-lietaer-1.html.

Marks, D. 2011. Climate Change and Thailand: Impact and
    Response. *Contemporary Southeast Asia* 33 (2): 229–58.
    Available online: http://www.transre.org/files/3114/6522/5151/
    Climate_Change_in_Thailand_TransRe_Fact_Sheet_No.2.pdf.

Norther Development Foundation (NDF). 2011. Climate Change, Trees and Livelihood:
    A Case Study on the Carbon Footprint of a Karen Community in Northern
    Thailand. AIPP, IWGIA, and Oxfam. Available online: http://www.iwgia.org/
    publications/search-pubs?publication_id=510.

Padoch, C., and M. Pinedo. 2010. Saving Slash-and-Burn to Save Biodiversity.
    Biotropica 42 (5): 550–552. Available online: http://onlinelibrary.wiley.com/
    doi/10.1111/j.1744-7429.2010.00681.x/full.

Padoch, C., and W. Denevan. 1988. *Swidden–Fallow Agroforestry in the Peruvian
    Amazon (Advances in Economic Botany, vol 5)*. The New York Botanical
    Garden.

Popkin, G. 2015. Indigenous People Could be Key to Storing Carbon in Tropical
    Forests, New Report Concludes. *Science*. Available online: http://www
    .sciencemag.org/news/2015/12/indigenous-people-could-be-key-storing
    -carbon-tropical-forests-new-report-concludes.

Rattanawannee, A., and C. Chanchao. 2011. Bee Diversity in Thailand and the
    Applications of Bee Products. In Grillo, O., and G. Venora, eds. *Changing
    Diversity in Changing Environment*. Available online: http://library.umac.mo/
    ebooks/b2811310x.pdf.

Rerkasem, K. 2001. Shifting Cultivation in Thailand: Land Use Changes in the
    Context of National Development. Available online: http://m.mekonginfo.org/
    assets/midocs/0002587-farming-shifting-cultivation-in-thailand-land-use
    -changes-in-the-context-of-national-development.pdf.

Roshetko, J. 2005. Smallholder Agroforestry Systems for Carbon Storage. *Mitigation
    and Adaptation Strategies for Global Change* 12: 219–242. Available online:
    https://link.springer.com/article/10.1007/s11027-005-9010-9.

Southeast Asia START Regional Center. 2010. Preparation of Climate Change
	Scenarios for Climate Change Impact Assessment in Thailand. Available online:
	http://startcc.iwlearn.org/project/copy4_of_hydro-agronomic-economic-model
	-for-mekong-river-basin-and-local-adaptation-in-thailand-model-development.
Trakasuphakon, P. 2007. Space of Resistance and Place of Local Knowledge in Northern
	Thailand Ecological Movement. Doctoral Thesis. Chiang Mai University.
Tangjitman, K. 2015. Potential Impact of Climatic Change on Medicinal
	Plants Used in the Karen Women's Health Care in Northern Thailand.
	Songklanakarin J. Sci. Technol. 37 (3): 369–379. Available online: http://rdo.psu.
	ac.th/sjstweb/journal/37-3/37-3-15.pdf.

Tla-o-qui-aht

Barlee, G. 2012. The Results Are In: Wild Salmon Need Action Now. *Huffington
	Post.* Available online: http://www.huffingtonpost.ca/gwen-barlee/bc-wild
	-sockeye-salmon-cohen-report-fraser-river_b_2060769.html.
Bartlett, M. 1973. The Communist Insurgency in Thailand. *The Marine
	Gazette.* Available online: https://www.mca-marines.org/gazette/
	communist-insurgency-thailand.
Brown, F. and Y. Brown, eds. 2009. Staying the Course, Staying Alive—Coastal First
	Nations. Fundamental Truths: Biodiversity, Stewardship and Sustainability.
	Biodiversity BC. Victoria, BC. Available Online: www.biodiversitybc.org.
Bunsha, D. 2013. What Clayoquot Sound Faces Now: A Historic Opportunity to
	Protect BC Old Growth Forest, Through New Partnerships. August 19, *The Tyee.*
	Available online: https://thetyee.ca/Opinion/2013/08/19/Clayoquot-Faces-Now/.
Chadwick. D. 2003. Pacific Suite. *National Geographic.* February.
Clayoquot Sound Scientific Panel. 1995. First Nations' Perspectives Relating to
	Forest Practices Standards in Clayoquot Sound.
Clayoquot Climate Change Adaptation Capacity Building Initiative. 2010. Volume
	I: Report. Francis, G. 2010. Clayoquot Sounds Biosphere Reserve. Periodic
	Review, August 2010.
Coste, T. 2013. Clayoquot Sound: On the Edge. *Wilderness Committee* 32 (2). Available
	online: https://www.wildernesscommittee.org/sites/all/files/publications/2013_
	clayoquot-sound_web.pdf.
D'Auria, G. 2013. The Summer BC's Woods Roared Back: When Trees Fell in
	the Forest, the World Heard Clayoquot Sound—A Look Back, 20 Years On.
	The Tyee. August 10. Available online: https://thetyee.ca/Life/2013/08/10/
	BC-Woods-Roar-Back/.
Furness, E. 2012. Climate Change: Assessing the Adaptive Capacity of Community
	Forests. MS Thesis. University of British Columbia. Available online: https://
	open.library.ubc.ca/cIRcle/collections/ubctheses/24/items/1.0072914.

George, E. 2003. *Living on the Edge: Nuu-Chah-Nulth History from an Ahousaht Chief's Perspective*. Sonois Press.

Goetze, T. 2005. Empowered Co-Management: Towards Power-Sharing and Indigenous Rights in Clayoquot Sound. *Anthropologica* 47 (2): 247–265.

Griffiths, D. 2007. *Tonquin: The Ghost Ship of Clayoquot Sound*. Tonquin Foundation.

———, et. al. 2004. *Echachist: A Preliminary Archaeological Survey and Analysis with Ethnographic Notes*. Tonquin Foundation.

Guppy, W. 1997. *Clayoquot Soundings: A History of Clayoquot Sounds, 1800s to 1980s*. Grassroots Publications.

Hutchinson, J. 2011. Monitoring Riparian Restoration: Lessons Learned in Clayoquot Sound. MS Thesis. Royal Roads University.

Karpiak, M. 1998. Modelling Nuu-chah-nulth Land Use: The Cultural Landscape of Clayoquot Sound. MS Thesis. The Department of Archaeology. Simon Fraser University.

Lavoie, J. 2012. Clayoquot Sound Fish Farm Approval Sparks Lawsuit Threat: Proposed Clayoquot Sound Site Divides Neighbouring First Nations. *Times Colonist*. October 18.

Lerner, J, Editor. 2011. Climate Change Adaptation in Clayoquot Sound: Ahousaht, Hesquiaht, and Tla-o-qui-aht Community-based Climate Change Adaptation Plan, Phase II Report. Prepared by Equilibrio and Ecotrust Canada.

Loucks L. and A. Day. "Socio-economic Resilience Assessment: Developing a Socio-economic Resilience Assessment Framework for the West Coast Vancouver Island Communities and Marine-use Sectors," in T. Okey and L. Loucks, eds. "Social-Ecological Assessment for the Marine and Coastal Areas of the West Coast of Vancouver Island," The Tsawalk Partnership, West Coast Aquatic, Port Alberni, BC (2011).

Mabee, H., and G. Hoberg. 2004. Protecting Culturally Significant Areas through Watershed Planning in Clayoquot Sound. *The Forestry Chronicle* 80 (2): 229–240.

Masso, M. 2005. Tla-o-qui-aht Nation Building Strategy: Ha'wiih and Ma'uas (Chiefs and Houses). MA. A Community Governance Project Report. University of Victoria. September 2005.

Mychajlowycz, M. 2009. Overview of Logging in Clayoquot Sound: 2000–2009. Friends of Clayoquot Sound.

Nielsen, A. 2005. Weirs: Report and Annotated Bibliography. Submitted in partial fulfillment of ES481A: Community-based Research in Clayoquot Sound (Summer Session 2005). School of Environmental Studies, University of Victoria Available online: http://www.clayoquotalliance.uvic.ca/es481a/_pdf/ES%20481A%20Student%20practicals/ES481A_ANielsen_Weirs.pdf.

Parai, B., and T. Esakin. Beyond Conflict in Clayoquot Sound: The Future of Sustainable Forestry. Canadian Foreign Service and Clayoquot Biosphere Trust (CBT).

Parker, A., et al. 2006. Climate Change and Pacific Rim Indigenous Nations. Northwest Indian Applied Research Institute (NIARI), The Evergreen State College, Olympia, Washington, USA. Available online: http://academic. evergreen.edu/g/grossmaz/IndigClimate.pdf.

Pynn, L. 2013. Bones from Aboriginal Whaling Site Near Tofino Give Insight into Ancient Coastal Cultures. *Times Colonist.* August 9. Available online: http:// www.timescolonist.com/news/local/bones-from-aboriginal-whaling-site-near -tofino-give-insight-into-ancient-coastal-cultures-1.574337.

Reimchen, P. 2001. Salmon Nutrients, Nitrogen Isotopes, and Coastal Forests. *Ecoforestry* (Fall).

Sharon, K. 2013. Diseases and Wild Salmon Don't Mix. *Ecojustice.* Available online: https://www.ecojustice.ca/wp-content/uploads/2012/08/Ecojustice_news_ Summer_2013_V3_Print.pdf.

Slattery, J. 2005. Lessons for Community-based Research from the Corporate Appropriation of an Aboriginal World View. Paper prepared in partial fulfillment of course requirements for ES 481A: Community-Based Research in Clayoquot Sound. School of Environmental Studies. University of Victoria.

Temple, N., ed. 2005. *Salmon in the Great Bear Rainforest.* Raincoast Conservation Society, Victoria, BC.

Tla-o-qui-aht First Nations. 2009. Esowista New Community District Geoexchange Energy System. Report.

Tla-o-qui-aht Tribal Park. 2013. *Tla-o-qui-aht Tribal Parks!* Vol 32. (6). Available online: https://www.wildernesscommittee.org/sites/all/files/publications/2013_ tla-o-qui-aht_Paper-Web-2.pdf.

Tla-o-qui-aht Tribal Park. 2008. Haa'uukmin (Kennedy Lake Watershed) Land Use Plan. Drat, May 2008.

Turner, N. and H. Kuhnlein. 1982. Two Important "Root" Foods of the Northwest Coast Indians: Springbank Clover (*Trifolium wormskioldii*) and Pacific Silverweed (*Potentilla anserina ssp. pacifica*). *Economic Botany* 36 (4): 411–432.

Turner, N. and K. Turner. 2008. "Where our Women Used to Get the Food": Cumulative Effects and Loss of Ethnobotanical Knowledge and Practice; Case Study from Coastal British Columbia. *Botany* 86 (2): 103–115. Available online: http://firstnationshealing.com/resources/Turner.pdf.

Vodden, K. and B. Kuecks. 2003. *The Clayoquot Green Economic Opportunities Project Taking Steps Towards a Conservation Economy. Volume One: Findings and Recommendations.* Available online: http://focs.ca/wp-content/ uploads/2014/02/Green-Economic-Study-Vol-1.pdf.

NGOS THAT SUPPORT
INDIGENOUS COMMUNITIES
FEATURED IN THE BOOK

ASHIÑWAKA—ASSOCIATION OF SAPARA WOMEN OF ECUADOR
Gloria Ushigua, President
T: 099 986 2480
E: gloriaushigua@yahoo.es
W: https://ashinwaka.wordpress.com

The Association of Sápara Women of Ecuador, ASHIÑWAKA, was created in 2009 to respond to the fundamental need to protect the human rights of Sápara women who have historically suffered from violence and discrimination, both within their communities and in the urban centers of the country. ASHIWAKA defends the rights of women, and promotes equal participation of Sapara women in political, cultural, and social spaces.

CONVERSATIONS DU MONDE
Nicolas Villaume, Director
465 Calle Ramon Ribeyro, Miraflores, Lima, Peru
T: +511 999 009 076
E: n.villaume@gmail.com
W: www.conversationsdumonde.org

Founded in Paris in 2004 by French photographer Nicolas Villaume, the association CONVERSATIONS DU MONDE (CDM) primary focuses on promoting oral tradition and cultural awareness using the emotional power of combined arts (photography, videos, Internet and new media) to create quality multimedia exhibitions from grass roots communities to leading international museums and education organisations. CDM has been involved in more than 50 multimedia venues worldwide, from the most remote places like Tambobamba, a small community of the Andes in Peru, to the most popular museums like the Smithsonian in Washington DC.

INSIGHTSHARE
Nick Lunch, Director
106 Cowley Road, Oxford, UK
C: +44 (0)7766 178533
E: nlunch@insightshare.org
W: http://www.insightshare.org

Founded in 1999, InsightShare uses Participatory Video as a powerful community engagement tool to build a grassroots movement of practice. IsnghtShare envisions a world where healthy and resilient communities draw upon local knowledge, experience, skills, generational wisdom and intuition to exert influence over the critical issues they face.

LAND IS LIFE
Casey Box, Executive Director
C: +1 (646) 812-6255
E: casey@landislife.org
W: http://www.landislife.org/

Since its founding in 1992, Land is Life has supported a broad, trusted network of Indigenous leaders, communities and organizations defined by solidarity, transparency and a shared vision of the future. Drawing from the collective strength of its global network, Land is Life addresses local challenges and opportunities while upholding Indigenous Peoples right to self-determination.

PGAKENYAW ASSOCIATION FOR SUSTAINABLE DEVELOPMENT (PASD)
Prasert Trakansuphakon, Director
146 Moo 2, T. Sansainoi, A.Sansai P.Chiang Mai 50210 Thailand
T: +66 81 9934641
E: ptrakan@gmail.com
W: www.pasdthailand.org

The Pgakenyaw Association for Sustainable Development (PASD) is a local indigenous organization with legal status from the Thai government, granted in 2009. PASD aims to support the community-based sustainable development of the Karen by building on their traditional knowledge and natural resource management systems for human wellbeing and biodiversity.

SÁMI NUE'TT
Pauliina Feodoroff, co-Director
C/O Tiina Sanila-Aikio, Sanilantie 36, 99800 Ivalo, Finland
T: +358 40 7364475
E: pauliinafeodoroff@gmail.com
W: http://www.saaminuett.fi/

Saa'mi Nue'tt is a cultural association working to safeguard and transfer the biocultural heritage of the Skolt Sámi for the future generations by revitalizing and strengthening the Skolt Sámi language and culture.

SNOWCHANGE COOPERATIVE
Dr. Tero Mustonen, Director
Havukkavaarantie 29, FIN81235 Lehtoi, Finland
T: +358 40 7372424
E: tero@snowchange.org
W. http.//www.snowchange.org/

Founded in 2000, Snowchange is an organisation devoted to the advancement of Finnish traditions and culture. It is also a global network of local and Indigenous communities around the world, as well as a strong scientific organisation working with the Arctic Council, Intergovernmental Panel on Climate Change, Indigenous Peoples Climate Change Assessment, National Science Foundation in the USA, and others

TENGRI (SCHOOL OF SOUL ECOLOGY) & UCH ENMEK ETHNOCULTURAL NATURE PARK
Danil Mamyev, Director
st. Sovetskay, 78, vil. Onqudai, Altai Republic, 649440, Russia
T: +7(38845)26426
E: danil-mamyev@yandex.ru
W: www.uchenmek.ru

Founded in 1995, Tengri (the School of Soul Ecology) works on reviving traditional knowledge of Altai by implementing a holistic system of activities that help preserve, strengthen and re-create the relationship between the people and the Sacred Earth. In 2001, Tengri established Uch Enmek Nature Park to protect the natural and cultural space of the sacred Karakol Valley.

ACKNOWLEDGMENTS

—⚉—

T*he Archipelago of Hope* is a labour of love, an important stepping-stone on a winding road of discovery, and a chance to reflect on the lessons learned. The quest might be personal, but the pursuit is by no means a solitary one. The journey would not have been possible without the generosity, kindness, and support of countless human and non-human beings that I have been fortunate to meet and travel alongside. Along the way, the love of my wife and son has nourished my body and soul, and their support made my long absences from home possible.

I am indebted to the Indigenous communities who have welcomed me into their lives, endured my ignorance, patiently shared their wisdom, while steering me toward a deeper understanding of our changing world. I am thankful to the Indigenous communities, organizations, and individuals profiled in the book for allowing me to take photographs, record interviews, and share these materials in a book, and related print and web-based publications and exhibits, to help raise awareness about climate change. I can only hope that the important stories I have tried to capture visually and write about, do some justice to the wisdom and resilience of the Indigenous cultures; the beauty of their ancestral territories; and the significance of their traditional knowledge, wisdom, and governance, for the well-being of us all.

I am grateful to Michael Sanders, Jessica Abbe, and Chez Lily who have encouraged me along the way and provided honest feedback on the book's early drafts. Their faith in the project during its lengthy gestation and incubation phases, kept me going.

Many experts in the fields of Indigenous rights, biocultural diversity, resilience, and climate change adaptation and mitigation have generously shared their valuable time and expertise to help inform my thinking and patiently correct my mistakes. My deepest thanks go to Janis Alcorn (Center for Humans and Nature), Marina Apgar (Institute of Development Studies), Alejandro Argumedo (Asociación ANDES), Patricia Cochran (Alaska Native Science Commission), Antonella Cordone (International Fund for Agricultural Development—IFAD), Nigel Crawhall (Indigenous Peoples of Africa Co-ordinating Committee—IPACC), Taghi Farvar (Centre for Sustainable Development and Environment—CENESTA), Stephan Harding (Schumacher College), Terence Hay-Edie (United Nations Development Program—UNDP), Henry Huntington (The Pew Charitable Trusts), Mike Jones (Swedish Biodiversity Center), Sam Johnston (United Nations University), Marie Kvanstrom (Swedish Biodiversity Center), Stephen Leahy (Society of Environmental Journalists), Luisa Maffi (Terralingua), Gary Martin (Global Diversity Foundation), Aroha Mead (Kāhui Māori), Gonzalo Oviedo (International Union for Conservation of Nature – IUCN), Jules Pretty (University of Essex), Rajindra Puri (University of Kent), Nonnet Rayo (Rights + Resources Initiative), Phrang Roy (North East Slow Food Agrobiodiversity Society—NESFAS), John Scott (Convention on Biological Diversity—CBD), and Peggy (Margaret) Smith (Lakehead University).

The expertise and *joie de vivre* of my agent, Jacqueline Flynn, of Joelle Delbourgo Associates, have been precious gifts in transforming my ideas into publishable material. The enthusiasm and gentle, but firm, guidance of my publisher, Jessica Case, of Pegasus Books, have helped transform this material into a book.

However great are the intentions, or grandiose the ideas, they rarely translate into reality without financial support. I am grateful to The Christensen Fund, Swift Foundation, Ontario Arts Council, and many individual supporters through *The Archipelago of Hope* Indiegogo crowd funding campaign, notably Artem Ponomarev, Natasha Akhmetgalieva, and John Swift, whose generosity made the last field trip to the Amazon possible.

My thanks go to the accomplished storytellers, namely Paul Hawken, Bill McKibben, David Suzuki, Scott Wallace, and Sheila Watt-Cloutier, for their advance praise of the project and the book. I hope *The Archipelago of Hope* lives up to their generous endorsements.